THE VER~

𝕿𝖍𝖊 𝕯𝖆𝖎𝖑𝖞 𝕿𝖊𝖑𝖊𝖌𝖗𝖆𝖕𝖍

BOOKS OF OBITUARIES

"The wondrous Hugh Massingberd ... As obituaries editor of *The Daily Telegraph* from 1986 to 1994 he did two important things: he encouraged vivid, sometimes outrageous pen-portraits rather than pious lists of achievements, and included delightful oddities who would never have found a place in the stuffy columns of former years." *The Spectator*

"Hugh Massingberd single-handedly transformed the slightly stuffy formula of the newspaper 'obit' into a high comic form. *The Daily Telegraph* obituaries which he commissioned, although penned by diverse hands, all bear his stamp – his novelistic delight in human oddity, his capacity, where due, for hero-worship (particularly of sporting, military or theatrical luminaries) and his delicately anarchic sense of fun ... Among the hundreds of us newspaper hacks today there is a tiny handful of true artists at work. Of this select band, Massingberd is king." *Country Life*

"Nothing funnier or more stirring than these volumes has arrived in print for some time." *New Yorker*

THE VERY BEST OF
The Daily Telegraph
BOOKS OF OBITUARIES

HUGH MASSINGBERD has written or edited some 40 books, including works of genealogical reference, studies of royalty and social history and series of illustrated volumes on palaces, grand hotels and country houses, great and small. His five collections of obituaries, *The Daily Telegraph Book of Obituaries: A Celebration of Eccentric Lives*, *The Daily Telegraph Second Book of Obituaries: Heroes and Adventurers*, *The Daily Telegraph Third Book of Obituaries: Entertainers*, *The Daily Telegraph Fourth Book of Obituaries: Rogues* and *The Daily Telegraph Fifth Book of Obituaries: Twentieth-Century Lives*, were all best-sellers and are available as Pan paperbacks. The fifth volume was short-listed for the inaugural Bollinger Everyman Wodehouse Prize for Comic Writing in 2000.

Also in this series

The Daily Telegraph
BOOK OF OBITUARIES
A Celebration of Eccentric Lives

The Daily Telegraph
SECOND BOOK OF OBITUARIES
Heroes and Adventurers

The Daily Telegraph
THIRD BOOK OF OBITUARIES
Entertainers

The Daily Telegraph
FOURTH BOOK OF OBITUARIES
Rogues

The Daily Telegraph
FIFTH BOOK OF OBITUARIES
Twentieth-Century Lives

THE VERY BEST OF
The Daily Telegraph
BOOKS OF
OBITUARIES

Edited by

HUGH MASSINGBERD

PAN BOOKS

First published 2001 by Pan Books
an imprint of Pan Macmillan Ltd
20 New Wharf Road, London, N1 9RR
Basingstoke and Oxford
Associated companies throughout the world
www.panmacmillan.com

A selection of material taken from
The Daily Telegraph BOOK OF OBITUARIES: A Celebration of Eccentric Lives (1995)
The Daily Telegraph SECOND BOOK OF OBITUARIES: Heroes and Adventurers (1996)
The Daily Telegraph THIRD BOOK OF OBITUARIES: Entertainers (1997)
The Daily Telegraph FOURTH BOOK OF OBITUARIES: Rogues (1998)
The Daily Telegraph FIFTH BOOK OF OBITUARIES: Twentieth-Century Lives (1999)

ISBN 0 330 48470 2

5 7 9 8 6 4

A CIP catalogue record for this book is available from
the British Library.

Typeset by SetSystems Ltd, Saffron Walden, Essex
Printed and bound in Great Britain by
Mackays of Chatham plc, Chatham, Kent

For Andrew McKie

INTRODUCTION

WITH THE publication of *The Daily Telegraph Fifth Book of Obituaries: Twentieth-Century Lives*, I called it a day and slipped off the stage. Now, to my surprise, as I exit from the stage door, I find myself being accosted by the producer and told to return to the boards for a brief reprise of some of the favourite numbers in the show. I feel rather like Bertie Wooster coming on once more at the end of the musical *By Jeeves* for the positively final medley "Wizard Rainbow Banjo Mix".

The "surprise" factor in the saga of the *Books of Obituaries* has, though, always been a key element. Back in the late 1980s – when I was actually working at the coalface of obits, as it were – various kind readers would write in from time to time with the suggestion that some of the colourful biographical short stories that we were publishing might be worth collecting together between hard covers. One Wodehousian scholar cheered us on by saying that he was filing away all the eccentric peers and dotty dowagers whose lives we were celebrating in a box devoted to the proposition that the Master had been dealing in reality not fantasy all along. Eventually, and with the enthusiastic encouragement of Marilyn Warnick, then the *Telegraph*'s publishing director, I came round to the idea that some sort of anthology might be worthwhile. Our then assistant obits editor, Claudia FitzHerbert, by way of an occupation to subsidise maternity leave, was given the task of assembling a vast pile of photocopied paste-ups of a few hundred of the most diverting obits that seemed worth preserving between hard covers. Claudia also ingeniously devised a giant, rather spooky collage of the faces that had adorned the obits column which we hoped might serve as a cover illustration. Unfortunately this work of art, which used to flutter above the obits desk at the *Telegraph* offices, mysteriously vanished. So, for a long time, did the book project.

At my insistence, the bulky mountain of material was despatched to a discerning one-man-band publisher I admired in the depths of the country. There it remained for a year or so. Finally, the sage delivered his verdict to Marilyn: "It would not sell in any significant quantities." Obits, the general feeling seemed to run, were an esoteric taste. The limelight was never likely to fall on our obscure backwater. Generally content with this state of affairs, we proceeded with the daily grind and rather forgot about the idea of a book, even though readers continued to call for one.

Then, in 1994, my own active career in the field of obits ended after I collapsed with a heart attack. "Got the obit ready?" was the impeccably professional first reaction of one seasoned hack, so I learnt, when the news came through from Casualty. After quadruple bypass surgery, I reluctantly gave up the obits chair and took on supposedly light duties on the *chaise-longue* as the paper's television critic. Overwhelmed with nostalgia for obits, I was suddenly enraptured by the thought of an anthology commemorating the eight exciting and exhilarating years I had spent on "the morgue". Fortunately, Marilyn Warnick had never wavered in her support for the project and soon we had a deal with Macmillan Reference Books for a single-volume anthology.

The publishing editor, Judith Hannam, turned out

to be a fan of the obits column and, to my delight, told me that she was not seeking a dry-as-dust gathering of worthies but rather "a celebration of eccentric lives". This was to become the book's subtitle. A plan was worked out whereby I chose a hundred of the fruitiest characters we had celebrated during my eight years on the desk. Although officially billed as a work of reference, there was just the squeak of potential there for it to be taken up, perhaps, as a "bedside book".

To assemble my favourite obits, in strict chronological sequence (the bizarre juxtapositions that ensue are, of course, part of the deadpan humour), was like a dream come true. All my life I had seen history and biography as a marvellous excuse to tell funny stories, strange anecdotes, about people. Before joining the *Telegraph* I had spent 15 years trying to inject some amusement and colour into genealogical works of reference, to make such heavy tomes a treasure-house of tales. Now, at last, everything seemed as if it might be coming together.

Under Judith's wise guidance, the book took shape along classically simple lines. She began the blurb with the introduction (the "hook" of any obit) from one of her own favourite figures from the column:

DENISA LADY NEWBOROUGH, who has died aged 79, was many things: wire-walker, nightclub girl, nude dancer, airpilot. She only refused to be two things – a whore and a spy – "and there were attempts to make me both," she once wrote.

Quietly, without any great fuss and with a very modest print-order, *The Daily Telegraph Book of Obituaries: A Celebration of Eccentric Lives* was published by Macmillan

Reference Books in the autumn of 1995. A few encouraging reviews began to hint at something I had long suspected, but never quite dared to believe, that there were far more "obit-fanciers" out there than the newspapers' marketing wallahs had ever realised. Then, as the buzz went round, a remarkable number of shrewd judges, Jeffrey Bernard and A.N. Wilson among them, chose the title as their "Book of the Year". To general amazement, it began to feature on Bestseller Lists. Reprints simply could not keep pace with demand. Indeed, at a crucial moment in the Christmas rush, when a "Number One" hit even seemed on the cards, stocks were exhausted.

Sales picked up again in the New Year and the book took an unusual journey from being a Reference Book hardback to a Pan paperback. At a celebratory lunch (always a barometer for a hungry author), Judith commissioned me to edit two further volumes, this time for the General List, covering *Heroes and Adventurers* and *Entertainers*. These duly appeared in hardback in 1996 and 1997 respectively, with the paperbacks following a year later in each case. Well as these did, I rather imagined that *Entertainers* would bring down the curtain on the series, but when Georgina Morley of Macmillan, egged on by Susannah Charlton of Telegraph Books, pointed out the possibilities of a fourth volume on *Rogues*, I naturally found myself unable to resist. And a millennial collection of *Twentieth-Century Lives* struck us as the right way to finish off. The ultimate thrill, when things seemed to come full circle, was when this fifth volume was shortlisted for the inaugural Bollinger Everyman Wodehouse Prize for Comic Writing in 2000.

For Wodehouse, with his life-enhancing humour, had

always been the guiding star for my approach to obituary writing. The first question I asked of any aspiring obituarist was: "Are you familiar with the work of the Master?" It will therefore come as no surprise that this fond farewell medley includes a generous sprinkling of eccentrics who might well have strayed from the pages of P.G.W.

Thus in Mayfair we meet our old friend Denisa Lady Newborough ("convicted . . . of permitting her maisonette . . . to be used for the purpose of habitual prostitution, though her conviction was quashed on appeal"). Down at Land's End we find the 4th Earl Russell (who called for "universal leisure for all") crocheting his own trouserings "out of string". Out in Africa, the late Duke of Montrose, a Rhodesian politician, considers that "the African is a bright and promising little fellow up to the age of puberty" whereupon he becomes totally obsessed with "matters of sex". Further afield, in the Philippines, the 3rd Lord Moynihan (who "provided, through his character and career, ample ammunition for critics of the hereditary principle") is pursuing his various occupations:

> bongo-drummer, brothel-keeper, drug smuggler and police informer, but "Tony" Moynihan also claimed other areas of expertise – as "professional negotiator", "international diplomatic courier", "currency manipulator" and "authority on rock and roll".

Those mourning the disappearance of the hereditary element in the House of Lords may well look back with nostalgia at such Wodehousian ornaments of the Peerage as the 13th Viscount Massereene and 6th Viscount Ferrard (who pointed out during a debate on the Brixton Riots of the early 1980s that he was "the only member who has spoken today who has had agricultural estates in Jamaica"); the foxhunting 2nd Lord Daresbury; and the 2nd Lord Milford, a Communist whose telephone in the Cotswolds was bugged during the Second World War. "Oh, come on, Constable," he would remonstrate. "Get off the line!" A voice would reply: "Sorry, Sir." We leave the Peerage with another *femme fatale* in the Denisa Lady Newborough mould – Bapsy Marchioness of Winchester, who wrote to her husband: "May a viper's fangs be forever around your throat and may you stew in the pit of your own juice." (Talking of fangs, the brothel-keeper Marie-la-Jolie, Marseille's most infamous madam, also featured in these pages, could only run, we are told, to "one rotting fang".)

Descending to the Baronetage, we pay our respects to the champion wrestler Sir Atholl Oakeley, 7th Bt, author of *Blue Blood on the Mat*; to Dr Sir Ewan Forbes of Craigievar, Bt (registered as a girl at birth – due to "a ghastly mistake"); and to Sir Hugh Rankin, 3rd Bt, variously riveter's mate, Cavalry trooper, sheep-shearer, Muslim, Buddhist, dwarf-fir forest crawler and self-styled "blood-red militant Communist in every possible way – *absolutely blood-red*". Sashaying out from the ranks of the Landed Gentry comes "Bunny" Roger, the bachelor dandy who claimed to have advanced through enemy lines during the Second World War with his chiffon scarf flying as he brandished a copy of *Vogue*.

Among the mixed bag of Royalty represented in this selection are Empress Zita of Austria, "the last surviving consort of the "Big Four" belligerent monarchs in the First World War; Helle Cristina Habsburg Windsor, who claimed to have been "born on the steps of the throne" ("So awkward for her mother", as one Lisbon wag observed); the Wali of Swat, with his fondness for Brown Windsor soup; and Princess Brown Thrush, a leader of the Matinnecock Indian nation, otherwise a New York school-luncheon server called Lila Harding. We are also reminded of how the idiosyncratic herald James Frere planned to sustain himself during the Queen's Coronation in 1953 in Westminster Abbey.

Men and women of the cloth include the Reverends Michael Bland ("Get the violence off the streets and into the Church where it belongs") and Peter Gamble ("who admitted . . . that his homosexuality had been the mainspring of his personal life . . . and was obliged to spend the last years of his teaching career at Harrow School"). The dubious prophet Bhagwan Shree Rajneesh finds a place, as does the infinitely worthier Bertha Lindsay, last Eldress of the Shakers and author of the cookbook *Seasoned with Grace*.

Although we may have joked about "the Moustaches" (a sobriquet for the never-ending military candidates in the queue for the column, based on Delia Lady Rumpers' observation in Alan Bennett's farce *Habeas Corpus* that her husband, "Tiger", only went into the Army "in order to put his moustache to good purpose"), it was an affectionate mockery, born of bemused repect. We all knew that the Moustaches – that pantheon of paladins, knights errant, heroes of the Western Front, the Battles of Britain and the Atlantic, bristling brigadiers and bastions of the Raj who had tangled with the wily Fakir of Ipi, burnt-up "Guinea Pigs", whose spirit had not been extinguished, wizard prangers and undercover agents for Special Operations Executive in occupied Europe – were the pride and joy of the obits page.

Among the *"Boy's Own* Heroes" saluted once more

are George Ives, the last surviving soldier of the Boer War (who complained that "youngsters in their eighties or nineties were apt to let themselves go"); Tom Baker, the Suffolks' demon sniper on the Somme; and Brigadier "Mad Mike" Calvert of the Chindits ("one of the finest fighting soldiers produced by the British Army in the Second World War"). We celebrate such legends of aviation history as Sir Thomas Sopwith and Sir Frank Whittle; as well as one of the first "Guinea Pigs", Group Captain Tom Gleave; Colonel Maurice Buckmaster and Harry Rée of SOE; and a possible model for James Bond, Commander "Biffy" Dunderdale. Sergeant Fred Kite, who won the Military Medal three times in the Second World War, is an excellent example of the principle that obits are not reserved for officers only.

Recalling the days of Empire and the Raj are Brigadier Ted Hughes (present at the farcical Siege of Spin Baldak, the last occasion when a British Army unit used scaling ladders, when it was observed that "the enemy should have been chloroformed before the operation took place"); Lieutenant-Colonel Geoffrey Knowles (who as a subaltern in Srinigar was bitten in the buttocks by a bear – he survived but the bear expired); and Brigadier "Speedy" Bredin, who would step briskly into his crisp shorts which stood erect in the corner of his office, having been starched by the faithful *dhobi wallah*. Lieutenant-Colonel "Titus" Oatts commanded a levy of naked head-hunting Nagas in the jungle who, he recalled, "regarded throwing hand-grenades as effeminate". Commander "Braces" Bracegirdle of the Australian Navy was asked by one of his sailors for compassionate leave on the grounds that his home town was under flood water 6ft deep, and his wife was only 5ft 3ins high.

Braces silently handed over an orange box and stamps to post it.

How inspiring it is to recall the enduring image of an English officer, Digby Tatham-Warter, strolling nonchalantly about "the Bridge Too Far" at Arnhem sporting an old bowler hat and a tattered umbrella. "That thing won't do you much good", comments a comrade-in-arms, to which Tatham-Warter replies: "But what if it rains?"

Nor are the heroines neglected. On parade again are the aviatrices Peggy Salaman (with her lion cubs doused in *Eau de cologne*) and "Aggie" Agazarian of the Air Transport Auxiliary; the indomitable Australian nurse Nell Allgrove ("If you couldn't laugh at the Japs, you'd had it") and Odette Hallowes, who was barbarously tortured by the Gestapo as an SOE agent but survived to be awarded the George Cross.

Of the learned professions, James Watts, who popularised the pre-frontal lobotomy, is a macabre representative of medicine, whereas the trenchant Sir Melford Stevenson of Truncheons ("A lot of my colleagues are just constipated Methodists") and Judge Michael Argyle ("You are far too attractive to be a policewoman – you should be a film star") uphold the judicial traditions of Beachcomber's Mr Justice Cocklecarrot. Few lawyers could merit the forensic skills of the serial escaper Alfie Hinds. Also coming under the legal umbrella are the hangman Albert Pierrepoint (landlord of Help the Poor Struggler public house) and "Big Bambino" Rizzo ("I'm gonna be so tough as Mayor [of Philadelphia], I gonna make Attila the Hun look like a faggot"). The villains include "Big Vinnie" Teresa, *capo* of the New England Mafia.

Moving on naturally to the world of politics, we are

re-acquainted with President Carter's "beer-drinking good ol' boy" brother, Billy; the flamboyant Sir Nicholas Fairbairn (who described his recreations as "making love, ends meet and people laugh"); the Communist dockland agitator Jack ("All out!") Dash; and the Fascist Norfolk squire Andrew Fountaine (who described the Attlee administration as "a group of conscientious objectors, national traitors, semi-alien mongrels and hermaphrodite Communists"). Down under, "Big Russ" Hinze of Queensland described himself as "the roughest, toughest bloody politician you could come across".

Continuing the descent into depravity, the Street of Shame is represented by the columnists Sir John ("Only poofs drink white wine") Junor and Jean Rook, alias "Glenda Slag". Journalists from further afield include the genial Jack de Manio, presenter of the *Today* programme before it became so insufferably priggish, and the *Oldham Chronicle*'s own "Fellwalker", Len Chadwick ("As he strode along, Chadwick would regale the young boys who were his most frequent companions – he was homosexually inclined – with interminable but inspired monologues, often in Esperanto").

The eccentric artist Lawrence Isherwood also hailed from the North-West: he was driven by his muse to abandon a career as a cobbler and eventually concentrated on imaginary nude studies of such figures as Barbara Castle (adorned with traffic signs), Mary Whitehouse (given five breasts), Field Marshal Viscount Montgomery of Alamein (medals retained) and Dusty Springfield (sold to a Hampshire pig farmer for 75 guineas). Among the authors are the unavoidable poets Laura Riding and Charles Horace Jones (complete with knuckleduster); the literary *femme fatale* Barbara Skelton; and the Soho novelist Robin Cook, who observed that "an Eton background is a terrific help if you are into vice at all".

Still in Soho, Ian Board is behind the bar of the Colony Room shaping and nourishing his magnificent nose. Across London, the erratic *restaurateur* Peter Langan is biting unwary customers' ankles. Up in Cambridge no less idiosyncratic hospitality is being offered by Kim de la Taste Tickell of the Tickell Arms ("I'm not having South London garage proprietors and their tarts in here! . . . *Out, out, out!*") and by the snobbish Sadie Barnett on King's Parade ("He was such a gent," she remarked of one of her residents, "when he was sick he was always sick out of the window"). And across the Atlantic the gluttonous Walter Hudson attributes his 85 stones to "food, *food*, FOOD!"

In choosing my favourite obits for this final selection I had no particular categories in mind but, now I come to tot up a rough and ready set of classifications, it is only to be expected that Showbiz scores the most heavily. One more time, then, for such *monstres sacrés* of high and low camp as Liberace (who once, "perhaps to lend himself an air of ruggedness with which nature had not chosen to endow him", adopted the stage-name of "Walter Busterkeys"), Hermione Gingold ("But, my dear, you simply *must* come – it's Corset Week at Swan & Edgar"), "Duggie" Byng, Divine (once voted "filthiest person alive"), Charles Hawtrey, Tiny Tim, Dorothy Squires and Fanny Cradock. Hollywood adds its own tinsel to the proceedings in the sagas of such Silent sirens as the humourless Pola Negri ("I was the greatest film actress in the world") and the hypochondriacal Edwina Booth, "White Goddess" in *Trader Horn*. There is room, too, for "the Sweater Girl", Lana Turner (discovered in Schwab's drug-store on Sunset Boulevard) and the Gabor matriarch Jolie.

From the gallery of much-loved British character actors come Wilfrid Hyde White and the ubiquitous "other rank" Victor Maddern – never to be forgotten for fluffing his lines in *Dixon of Dock Green*. Given the words, "It's down at Dock Green Nick", the redoubtable supporting player came out with: "It's down at Dick Green Dock." Trying to correct himself he then said: "It's down at Dock Green Dick." Finally, the exasperated Maddern cried out: "Who writes these bloody scripts? Can't I just say 'down at the nick'. F*** Dock Green!"

Other once-familiar television faces include Doris Speed, otherwise "Annie Walker" in *Coronation Street*; Ronald Allen and Ann George from *Crossroads*; Jess ("The Bishop") Yates from the excruciating *Stars on Sunday*; the medium Doris Stokes; and the exhibitionist "Stunnagran" Anne Cumming – though in her case it tended to be other parts of the anatomy that demanded attention. Upholding the great comic tradition are Les Dawson (of whom, as Arthur Marshall said, "we could do with more like him"), Kenny Everett, Ronnie Scott and Vivian Stanshall. From the world of Pop we find Larry Parnes, Serge Gainsbourg (who used a 1928 Rolls-Royce, occasionally, "as an ashtray") and Nico, of the Velvet Underground, who, it is noted, "gave up heroin for bicycling, which was to turn out the more dangerous amusement – she died when she fell off a bicycle when on holiday".

Under the Big Top we spot Anton LaVey, founder of the Church of Satan, who began his career in the circus, putting his head into the jaws of a lion – "when the beast removed a chunk of his neck, however, he decided to look for alternative employment". And up in the ring for eternity is "Big Daddy", the 28-stone wrestler (real name, Shirley Crabtree) whose leotard was made from the chintz covers of his wife's sofa.

Fade to black, and the closing credits. Like showbiz, the obits game is very much a collaborative process and I feel sure that my successors in the obits chair – David (Lewis) Jones, Kate Summerscale, Christopher Howse and now Andrew McKie – would agree that we should acknowledge the vital contributions made over the years by all our deputy and assistant editors, editorial assistants, secretaries, specialist experts and contributors. These have included (in alphabetical order) Nicholas Bagnall, the late Tom Baistow, Andrew Barrow, Trevor Beeson, Mark and Gillian Bence-Jones, the late Chaim Bermant, Edward Bishop, David Bowman, Craig Brown, Aurea Carpenter, Robert Chalmers, Will Cohu, Simon Courtauld, James Delingpole, Philip Eade, Hugh Fearnley-Whittingstall, Claudia FitzHerbert, the late Stan Gebler Davies, Dave Gelly, Jim Godbolt, Dean Godson, Derek Granger, Robert Gray, Tim Heald, Diana Heffer, James Hogg, the late David Holloway, Graham Hutchings, George Ireland, Julian Keeling, Charles Kidd, Gerard Kiley, John Lanchester, Cynthia Lewis, Imogen Lycett Green, Adam McEwen, John McEwen, J.R.H. McEwen, Martine Onoh, James Owen, the late Anthony Powell, Georgia Powell, Katherine Ramsey, Martha Read, Stanley Reynolds, John Martin Robinson, Eric Shorter, Don Stacy, Gavin Stamp, Alan Stanbrook, the late E.W. Swanton, Damian Thompson, David Twiston Davies, Nicholas Usherwood, Martin Van Der Weyer, Hugo Vickers, Ian Waller, the late Philip Warner, the late Auberon Waugh, Geoffrey Wheatcroft, David

Williamson, the late John Winton and Sir Peregrine Worsthorne. Finally, in a spotlight all of her own, a curtain call for the enchanting princess of the obits page, Teresa Moore, stalwart secretary of the desk through every incarnation.

HUGH MASSINGBERD
London, May 2001

SIR ATHOLL OAKELEY, BT

SIR ATHOLL OAKELEY, 7th Bt, who has died aged 86, was a champion wrestler, an impresario of giants, master of a former Bristol pilot cutter offering rugged holiday cruises and an authority on *Lorna Doone*.

A veteran of nearly 2,000 bouts, he described his career as a wrestler in an engaging autobiography, *Blue Blood on the Mat* (1971). He was heavyweight champion of Great Britain from 1930 to 1935, of Europe in 1932 and remained unbeaten on a 17-bout tour of America, helping to offset the traditional picture of horizontal British heavyweights.

Although only 5 feet 9 inches tall, Oakeley was broad in the beam. He started wrestling seriously after being beaten up by a gang of louts and built up his body by drinking eleven pints of milk a day for three years. This regimen had been recommended by the giant wrestler Hackenschmidt, who later told Oakeley that the quantity of milk prescribed had been a misprint.

Giants always held a particular fascination for Oakeley. He liked to recall how he had bent a man of 9 feet with a half-nelson which it took several other wrestlers sitting on his opponent to untangle.

He received his distinctive cauliflower ear in a bout in Chicago when, as he recalled, Bill Bartuch "got me in a scissors grip between his knees".

His active career came to an end in 1935 when he broke his shoulder. He then acted as manager to Jack Sherry, the world heavyweight champion, for four years, and later promoted championship wrestling at the Harringay Arena.

Among the wrestlers he staged was Gargantua, a 50-stone German with a 90-inch chest measurement, for whom special travelling arrangements had to be made with British Railways.

Edward Atholl Oakeley was born in 1900, the grandson of Sir Charles Oakeley, 4th Bt, a Bengal Cavalryman who was also an amateur heavyweight prize fighter. The baronetcy was created in 1790 for an ancestor who was Governor of Madras.

Oakeley was educated at Clifton and Sandhurst and commissioned in the Oxfordshire and Buckinghamshire Light Infantry. He was Army marathon and 10-mile track champion shortly after the First World War.

His interest in wrestling had first been aroused by reading *Lorna Doone* as a boy. The novel and its background remained a lifetime interest and in 1969 he published *The Facts on which R. D. Blackmore based Lorna Doone*. He mounted a lengthy and ultimately successful campaign to persuade the Ordnance Survey to change the map of Exmoor, showing that the Doone Valley was sited at Lank Combe rather than Hoccombe.

At the time he succeeded to the baronetcy on the death of his cousin Sir Charles Oakeley, 6th Bt, in 1959, Sir Atholl was making his living by taking people on cruises aboard his cutter *Seabreeze* from Hamble.

His first three marriages ended in divorce. He is survived by his fourth wife, the former Shirley Church; by a son of the second marriage; and by a daughter of the fourth. He also adopted a son.

The son of the second marriage, John Digby Atholl Oakeley, the well-known yachtsman, former America's

Cup skipper and Olympic helmsman, now becomes the 8th Baronet.

January 8 1987

LIBERACE

LIBERACE, the flamboyant American popular pianist who has died aged 67, was the world's single highest paid performer throughout the 1960s and 1970s.

He appeared in concert halls, theatres, ballrooms, nightclubs and also in several films, notably as the deaf pianist in the spectacular flop *Sincerely Yours* (1955) and as an unctuous "casket" salesman in an otherwise unmemorable film of Evelyn Waugh's *The Loved One* (1965).

Liberace's extraordinary success as an entertainer can be credited to his peculiarly American synthesis of sentimentality, bravado and showmanship.

For one devoted to extravagance in an age of puritanical austerity, there was bound to be a backlash. It came in peculiarly venomous form from the journalist William Connor writing as "Cassandra" in the *Daily Mirror* in 1956 when Liberace appeared at the London Palladium.

"He reeks with emetic language that can only make grown men long for a quiet corner, an aspidistra, a handkerchief and the old heave-ho" was one of the milder passages from this celebrated tirade. Cassandra also described the performer as "this deadly, winking, sniggering, snuggling, chromium-plated, scent-impregnated, luminous, quivering, giggling, fruit-flavoured, mincing, ice-covered heap of mother-love."

3

However, the passage that caused most offence to both the star and his mother read: "He is the summit of sex, the pinnacle of masculine, feminine and neuter, everything that he, she and it can ever want."

After denying his homosexuality in the High Court in London in 1959, Liberace won libel damages of £8,000 and an apology.

Wladizu Valentine Liberace (known to his besotted public as "Lee") was born in Milwaukee on May 16 1919. His Italian father had enjoyed some small success as a French horn player, and as a bit-part actor in silent movies before concentrating on his career as a grocer.

His Polish mother, Frances, had been a concert pianist before her marriage, and throughout her life maintained her interest in showbusiness, calling Liberace's younger brother Rudolph Valentino Liberace after the screen idol of the time.

A child prodigy, Liberace performed before Paderewski at the age of seven and a half. "Some day that boy may take my place," commented the celebrated pianist.

His career began on more formal lines than those along which it would progress. After one tour as a soloist with the Chicago Symphony Orchestra, Liberace found himself attracted to a less-restrained form of music and dress, much to the chagrin of his father, a musical purist.

He found much sympathy though, from his mother, to whom he always remained devoted, later exhibiting many of her personal effects, including her knitting basket, in his own Liberace museum in Las Vegas.

This attachment to his mother was to form an important part of his stage persona: invariably in attendance at his concerts, she would happily wear furs and jewellery identical to her performing son's, and the audience would applaud both of them for their pride in their mutual devotion.

Perhaps to lend himself an air of ruggedness with which nature had not chosen to endow him, he adopted the stage name "Walter Busterkeys" when he embarked on his early career in a dance band, but swiftly changed hats, calling himself simply "Liberace" and playing up his already bizarre character.

"I began to disarm my audience and say what people were thinking before they could say it. I heckled myself," he once said.

The first sign that Liberace had embarked upon a road along which reticence would never ride came when he placed a candelabra on his piano when playing for the dance band. At this, the dam of discretion appeared to burst: first came a white tail suit, followed by stage patter about his mother and his philosophy of life, then a gold lamé jacket and a diamond-studded tailcoat.

His piano playing, though unfaltering, was never rigid in its adherence to tradition: of the 153 pages of Tchaikovsky's First Piano Concerto, he would perform only the first twelve and the last four, adding four bars in the middle of his own creation.

As success grew, so too did flamboyance: in 1984, he was spotted wearing a $300,000 (£200,000) rhinestone-studded Norwegian blue fox cape with a 16-foot train; and last year (1986), stepping on stage out of a Rolls-Royce painted with Stars and Stripes, he was witnessed in red, white and blue hotpants.

Liberace's private tastes were similarly steeped in an absence of sobriety. His master bedroom was painted with a re-creation of the Sistine Chapel ceiling, his lawn was centrally heated, his swimming pool was piano-shaped and among his possessions – or "happy-happies" as he liked to call them – was a piano made out of 10,000 toothpicks.

He is also credited with having invented a lavatory that could disappear into a bathroom floor at the flick of a switch. "There's no reason why you should walk into a bathroom and see a toilet. It's unglamorous," he explained.

His adoring audience – he averaged 27,000 Valentine cards and 150 marriage proposals a year – admired him for converting the sophistication of classical music into something a little more catchy and plush, for his love of luxury, his self-deprecating sense of humour and his seemingly innocuous flirtatiousness.

In 1982 his formerly resident secretary-cum-chauffeur, Scott Thorson, brought a "palimony" suit against Liberace. The case was eventually settled out of court last year whereby, in return for $95,000 in cash, a Rolls-Royce, two other motor cars and a couple of dogs, Thorson agreed to drop the action.

"Nobody loves me but the public," he said time and time again.

He was unmarried.

February 5 1987

DENISA LADY NEWBOROUGH

DENISA LADY NEWBOROUGH, who has died aged 73, was many things: wire-walker, nightclub girl, nude dancer, airpilot. She only refused to be two things – a whore and a spy – "and there were attempts to make me both," she once wrote.

She was also a milliner, a perfumier and an antiques dealer; but her real metier, in early life at least, was what she called "profitable romance". Her opinions on the subject of presents from gentlemen would have done credit to the pen of Anita Loos: "I have never believed that jewels, any more than motors cars, can be called vulgar just because they are gigantic."

Her admirers included the Kings of Spain and Bulgaria, Adolf Hitler (whose virility she doubted), Benito Mussolini (whom she described as "a gigolo") and Sheikh ben Ghana (who gave her 500 sheep). When she lived in Paris, she had no fewer than five protectors – all "shareholders" as she termed them – and persuaded each, who was ignorant of his fellows, to part with a flat or a house.

She was earlier married to Jean Malpuech, the Governor of Laos, who had died. But the climax of this stage of her career came in 1939 with her marriage to the 61-year-old 5th Lord Newborough as his second wife. They were divorced in 1947.

Denisa Josephine Braun was born on April Fool's Day, 1913, in Subotica, Serbia. In her early teens she ran away to Budapest, where for a time she slept under bridges with tramps. Then, styling herself "Baronne de Brans", she became a nude dancer and mistress of boyars, including a pair of twins. A decade of adventures followed, in Sofia, Bucharest, Paris, St Moritz and Berlin.

She spoke 14 languages. She served as a transport officer with the Red Cross at the beginning of the Second World War but was dismissed in 1941 because she was not of British birth.

In 1946, shortly before her divorce from "Tommy"

Newborough, a receiving order was made against her for debts of £951, which she attributed to losses at bridge when her skill had been impaired by unhappiness. She recovered her finances by designing outrageous hats – "The Nicotine Hat", for example, which was covered with cigarettes, with half-smoked imitations hanging over the bridge.

In 1958, she published an autobiography, *The Fire in My Blood*, the flavour of which may be surmised from such chapter headings as "Gipsy Love", "Elegant Sin in Bucharest" and "On the Trail of the White Slavers".

She was convicted in 1964 of permitting her maisonette in Davies Street to be used for the purpose of habitual prostitution, though her conviction was quashed on appeal.

Lady Newborough was a great beauty and she was charming and funny. By conventional standards, her morality matched her flaming red hair but she remained as proud of the one as of the other.

She is survived by her daughter Juno, who is married to a dentist.

March 28 1987

BRIGADIER TED HUGHES

BRIGADIER TED HUGHES, who has died aged 89, took part in the Siege of Spin Baldak in 1919 – the last occasion when a British Army unit used scaling ladders.

Then a subaltern of 22 in the 1st Gurkhas, Hughes was serving in the third Afghan War. The Amir Abdullah had declared war and begun to invade India which he imagined was too war-weary and denuded of troops to resist the Afghan attack. But the Indian Army had 10,000 men encamped on the Afghan border in May 1919 and it was decided that the first retaliatory action must be to capture the key fort of Spin Baldak.

In his subsequent account of his experiences – a richly sarcastic memoir that was enjoyed more by his contemporaries than by his senior officers – Hughes wrote: "The Higher Command – acting doubtless on the excellent principle that if you can't surprise the enemy it is better to surprise your own side than no one at all – supplied little or no information about the fort and its garrison."

It was, however, known that the fort was enclosed in a 200-yard-long, 15-foot-high outer wall and within this was an even higher wall. Hughes's regiment was ordered to take the south side with scaling ladders.

The plan was first to place the scaling ladders in the ditch, so that the regiment could climb down one side and then up the other. Then the men were meant to climb the wall, haul up the ladders, climb down, go through the ditch, and then climb the next wall.

Hughes observed that the Gurkhas were "greatly diverted by this simple plan and declared that nothing like it had been seen since the siege of Jerusalem". The observation was made, though, that the enemy should have been chloroformed before the operation took place.

Hughes continued: "0300 hours saw that mighty army move forward to the storming of the fortress. Everything was to be done in deathly silence – not a whisper was to rouse the unsuspecting Afghans. Indeed, the only sounds were the crashing of ammunition boxes and entrenching tools as the mules threw their loads –

and the thudding of hooves as they bolted into the night: every few seconds the air was split by the yells of some officer urging the men to greater silence or the despairing call of some NCO who had lost his section.

"A sound as of corrugated iron being dropped from a great height denoted that the scaling ladders were being loaded on the carts: with these two exceptions, no one would have had an inkling that several thousand armed men were pressing forward to the fray."

In the event the scaling ladders were too short even for descending into the ditches but fortunately the Afghan garrison commander had no stomach for a fight in the fort and retreated with his army to the hills. The British occupied the fort for a month, strengthened the defences, and improved the water supply; then they handed it back to the Afghans.

Hughes's story of the siege of Spin Baldak, which differed considerably from the official version, made him an obvious choice for a posting to Iraq whence he proceeded in 1920 with a draft from his own battalion to join the 3/5th Gurkhas who were engaged in suppressing an Arab rebellion.

Francis Edmund Charles Hughes was born in 1897 and commissioned from Sandhurst into the 1st Battalion of the 1st Gurkhas in 1916. He served in Waziristan the following year and again in the 1920s.

In 1924 Hughes was awarded the silver medal of the Royal Humane Society for a brave attempt to save a life on the Beas river.

In the 1930s he attended the Staff College and served on the general staff of Meerut District. During the Second World War he served in the Western Desert and Burma.

April 17 1987

DORIS STOKES

DORIS STOKES, who has passed over aged 67, was an internationally celebrated medium, known as "The Gracie Fields of the psychic world".

She made much of her ordinariness, eschewing the mystery and glamour of Mme Arcati for a more cosy approach. In her highly successful roadshow, *An Audience with Doris Stokes*, she appeared on stage in a chintz armchair with a simple flower display beside it, she wore studiedly dowdy frocks and a permanently waved hair-do, and invariably addressed her audiences (for the most part female and inclined to tears) as "lovey" and "dear".

Having warmed them up with a few jokes about sexual practices in the afterlife, she regaled them with a flood of "messages" – usually on domestic subjects (dining suites, garage doors) – from such dead relations as "Uncle Wilf" and "Auntie Dot". In recent years, when she had been raised by American television to the status of a "spiritualist superstar", she had much contact with dead celebrities (particularly John Lennon and Elvis Presley), and made extensive use of the medium of tabloid newspapers. Her followers included Ronnie Kray and Derek Jameson.

She claimed in her various books (*Voices in My Ear*, *More Voices in My Ear*, *Innocent Voices in My Ear*, *A Host of Voices*, etc.) to have helped the police with a number of murder inquiries – though all the police forces she mentions have denied receiving any such assistance.

Doris Stokes was born in 1920 at Grantham, Lincolnshire – a street away from the birthplace of Margaret Thatcher. She described her childhood as "unhappy and confused", plagued as it was by inexplicable voices.

She first visited a medium at the age of thirteen, when her dead father announced himself to her. But she did not become a medium herself until she was twenty-four when she was invited to a spiritualist church after the death of her son.

She claimed to have visited "the Other Side", and said that its denizens "were not floating around in white sheets or sitting on clouds strumming a golden harp".

She said that the "voices . . . just spill out of my mouth and I don't know what I'm saying *half* the time. I suppose I'm a bit like a telephone exchange."

Some of her spillages gave rise to sceptical jokes about crossed lines. "He went very quickly," she told one member of her audience.

"He was ill for six months," came the reply. "Well, he went very quickly at the end, lovey."

Mrs Stokes lived in a bungalow in South London and a mobile home in Kent. She is survived by her husband John, a faith healer, and her adopted son Terry, a bus driver and part-time psychic.

May 12 1987

HERMIONE GINGOLD

HERMIONE GINGOLD, the British character actress who has died in New York aged 89, was a theatrical legend, celebrated for her "high camp" mannerisms, flamboyant eccentricity and outrageously funny remarks, delivered in her extraordinary gurgling tones.

To modern cinema and television audiences Miss Gingold was best known for her comparatively restrained performances in *Gigi* (in which she sang "I remember it well" with Maurice Chevalier) and as Mme Armfeldt in *A Little Night Music*, which she also played on stage on Broadway and in London in the 1970s. But an older generation of theatregoers will principally recall the Gingold genius in "intimate revue", where she projected an immensely forceful stage presence.

The kind of satirical revue in which she made her special reputation has long since ceased to exist; and as the late W. A. Darlington, the dramatic critic of *The Daily Telegraph*, wrote: "For those who never had the experience of watching her at work, she must remain beyond imagination."

In Miss Gingold's heyday the prohibitive power of the Lord Chamberlain was still absolute and the limits within which he could be persuaded to permit any personal satire of public figures were narrow. Consequently, the theatre took the way of safety and confined its more barbed attacks to its own world; Miss Gingold's intimate revues were full of wicked "in-jokes".

Thus, when it was said that a performance by Larry Olivier had been a *tour de force*, Miss Gingold observed in her most lugubrious tones that Donald Wolfit in the same role had been "forced to tour".

Hermione Gingold was one of those rare performers who are capable of spontaneous witty repartee off the stage as well as on. At a Foyles' literary luncheon a fellow guest explained that she was engaged in public relations. Miss Gingold looked startled, murmuring, "I prefer to keep mine private."

A playwright who had asked the actress's opinion of his script was told, "My dear boy, in future I advise you never to write anything more ambitious than a grocery list."

Attempting to persuade a friend to visit London from the depths of the country, she said, "But, my dear, you simply *must* come. It's Corset Week at Swan & Edgar."

Miss Gingold had an endearingly individual approach to life. In New York she was regularly seen rummaging through other people's dustbins. On one occasion she found a complete set of *Encyclopædia Britannica*, on another an antique table. Characteristically she was quite unrepentant: "A lot of millionaires started in the junk business."

Hermione Ferdinanda Gingold was born in London on "December 9" (as she wrote in her *Who's Who* entry – the omitted year was 1897) and trained for the stage with Rosina Filippi. She made her first appearance on the stage at His Majesty's Theatre shortly after her 11th birthday in 1908, as the herald in *Pinkie and the Fairies* with Sir Herbert Tree.

It was not, however, until 1932 that she made any real mark. That season she played a series of parts at the old Gate Theatre. In 1936 her peculiar talent for revue was recognised when she appeared in *Spread it Abroad* at the old Saville, and two years later she scored a notable success in *The Gate Revue*.

This show transferred in 1939 to the Ambassadors, where she enjoyed a phenomenal series of personal triumphs in intimate revue during the war years. *Sweet and Low*, *Sweeter and Lower* and *Sweetest and Lowest* firmly established Miss Gingold as a star.

Her name was frequently linked with that of another revue star, the late Hermione Baddeley; inevitably they were known as "The Two Hermiones", even if they were not always on the most harmonious terms. In 1949 the Hermiones appeared together in a spectacularly undisciplined revival of Noël Coward's drunken farce *Fallen Angels* at the Ambassadors. While Miss Baddeley spat bread pellets at the audience, Miss Gingold did suggestive things with a table napkin.

The two actresses' behaviour incurred the Master's severe displeasure, but the nightly outrages packed in the audiences. By the end of the hugely successful run, the two leading ladies (or "Gorgeous Gargoyles" as Frank Marcus described them) were reputedly no longer on speaking terms.

In 1951 Miss Gingold made her first appearance on the American stage in the revue *It's About Time*. From then on she spent most of her career in the United States, appearing in films, television and "legitimate" plays as well as revue. Her films included *Around the World in 80 Days*, *Bell, Book and Candle* and *The Music Man*.

In 1965 she was back in London playing the part of Mrs Roepettle in *Oh Dad, Poor Dad, Mama's Hung You in the Closet, and I'm Feelin' So Sad*, which she had earlier taken over on Broadway. In 1969 she was Agnes Derrindo in *Highly Confidential* at the Cambridge.

When Harold Prince was holding auditions for Stephen Sondheim's *A Little Night Music* in 1972, Miss Gingold turned up uninvited. The director told her that she should not bother to play a woman of seventy-four. "But, Mr Prince," she replied, "I *am* seventy-four."

Later she enjoyed another success in *Side by Side by Sondheim*. Her versatility was reflected in her touring one-woman show and her recordings of *Façade* and *Lysistrata* even if her character parts on American television tended to the grotesque.

She was the author of an hilarious autobiography, *The World is Square: My Own Unaided Work* and *Sirens Should Be Seen Not Heard*.

Miss Gingold also had a remarkable flair for interior decoration, and collected china as well as objects from dustbins.

Both her marriages, to Michael Joseph and the lyric writer Eric Maschwitz, ended in divorce. She had two sons by the first marriage, one of whom survives.

May 25 1987

POLA NEGRI

POLA NEGRI, who has died at San Antonio, Texas, aged 92, was the legendary silent-screen siren whose career ranged from the 1914 Polish film *Love and Passion* to Walt Disney's *The Moonspinners*, made in England in 1964.

Essentially an actress of strong personality, she exuded an aura of slink and mink, of vamping heroes that stayed vamped. Although her three husbands were styled baron, count and prince, she was more famous for her liaisons with Rudolph Valentino and Charlie Chaplin as well as a bitter row with her rival Gloria Swanson.

As an actress she had distinct limitations, being almost devoid of humour and incapable of suggesting light and shade. After being smitten with her blonde hair, smouldering eyes and usually black clothes, American audiences began to go off her offbeat pseudo-culture and, with the advent of sound, found her thick Polish accent almost incomprehensible.

Yet she was Queen of Hollywood in the transition period between the decline of the earlier vamps such as Theda Bara and the great stars of the 1930s, Greta Garbo and Marlene Dietrich.

Born Barbara Apollonia Chalupiec in 1894 at Janowa, Poland, she was supposedly the child of a gypsy violinist who died in exile in Siberia. His daughter, who abbreviated her second forename to Pola and took a surname from the Italian poet Ada Negri, worked as a dancer and violinist before making her stage debut in Warsaw in 1913.

Negri made three films with Aleksandr Hertz before being brought to Berlin for a play by Max Reinhardt. She rapidly became a star of the German cinema, but it was the series of costume films she made with the young director Ernst Lubitsch, particularly *Carmen* (1918) and *Madame du Barry* (1919), which became an immense success in America under the title *Passion*, that led Paramount to invite her to the United States in 1922.

Her first American films fell far short of her German

17

work until she made *Forbidden Passion* with Lubitsch in 1924. Raoul Walsh's *East of Suez* (1925) and Malcolm St Clair's *Good and Naughty* were among her other films, but while her star began to dim Negri started to attract widespread attention with her private life.

She had married first Baron Popper, a Polish Army officer; then, in Berlin, the Polish Count Eugene Domski after a tempestuous affair which involved an escape from his castle. He was granted a divorce, but when she told the world of her devotion to Charlie Chaplin the Count turned up to challenge the comedian to a duel. Later, there were several well-publicised engagements until she met Rudolph Valentino. "Our souls", she proclaimed, "met upon our lips, and we were one. Two aching hearts, tired of the battle."

A year later Valentino died, and Negri made a dramatic appearance at his funeral, clad all in black, with a doctor and a nurse, dressed entirely in white, supporting her on either side. "All joy has fled from my life for ever," she cried, fainting over his coffin.

Six months afterwards, she married the *soi-disant* Prince Serge Mdivani, a Georgian. "I did love my husband; I adored Valentino; and I grew very fond of Charlie Chaplin," she said. "But Serge means more to me than them all."

"I have no doubt that at the time she was sincere," observed Campbell Dixon, *The Daily Telegraph* film critic, in the advance obituary he wrote on her in 1931. "But her temperament was something she could not control if she would, and soon she was announcing that yet another romance was broken. 'Pola', she said, 'is cursed with an unlucky star of love' – one of the many pronouncements which revealed both her habit of dramatising herself and her complete lack of humour."

Negri left Hollywood to make a film in England, *The Woman He Scorned*, which was not a success, and began to make another in Paris – only to tear up her contract and pay £4,000 compensation because there was no bathroom in the studio. It was later claimed that she sacrificed the £1,000 a week contract because the script required her to strip to the waist and undergo ordeal by fire.

Her name continued to be linked with supposed fiancés, including an unnamed former British MP and Adolf Hitler. Hitler was said to have considered her his favourite actress, and she made a supposedly brilliant comeback in the 1935 German film, *Mazurka*, directed by Willi Forst, though its real sensation was a 16-year-old Garbo-lookalike. There were even stories that the dictator had sent special agents to Poland to check her Aryan blood.

But she settled in Nice, and shortly before the Second World War successfully sued a French newspaper which had described her as one of the three great rivals for the dictator's love, winning £56 damages.

By the time Miss Negri returned to America in 1941, she wanted to forget her romantic past. "Ah no, ah no. I've had no romances," she told reporters who met her at the New York dockside. "I now think only of my work. I belong to the public." Immigration officers were less sure about this: she had arrived without an entry permit.

Another film, *Hi Diddle Diddle*, followed in 1943. For her last 30 years she settled in Texas, attracting brief attention in London when she appeared, dressed in black as always, with a cheetah which went with her cameo part in *The Moonspinners*.

Only an autobiography, *Memoirs of a Star*, describing her love affairs with Chaplin and Valentino, brought her to any public notice again in America. But she never forgot her past glory. Even when in hospital during her last illness she continued to put on her false eyelashes, and she rose in her bed to tell a young doctor who did not know who she was: "I was the greatest film actress in the world."

August 4 1987

DOUGLAS BYNG

DOUGLAS BYNG, who has died aged 94, was one of the most redoubtable entertainers of the 20th century, celebrated especially for his outrageous comedy songs and risqué female "characters", most of which he wrote himself.

His achievements as an *artiste* in revue, variety, cabaret and indeed as a pantomime dame were legendary. He was accorded the sobriquet of "High Priest of Camp" long before the theatrical word "camp" became part of common usage.

"Duggie" Byng's skill in performance vanquished prudery. His material – a trifle rude but never crude – was to range from such numbers as "Sex Appeal Sarah", "Milly the Messy Old Mermaid" and "The Lass who Leaned against the Tower of Pisa" to "The Girl Who Made Them Pay in Peyton Place" and "Playboy Club Bunny".

Without sacrificing style and subtlety – Byng's "class" was never in doubt – he was able at times to make his allusions explicit without causing offence. Before his day, if the borderline was reached and suggestion became no longer implicit, then the performer courted disaster, but no member of Duggie Byng's audience felt any worse for being presented with fact properly told – better that than fancy improperly told or bluntly hinted at.

He held the floor during the Blitz at the old Café de Paris in London's West End, where his billing was "Byng: Bawdy but British". After the place was bombed he continued to render his own favourite romantic ballad (as he called it), "Blackout Bella", to the troops throughout Britain and in the Far East.

Douglas Byng was born at Nottingham in 1893. His mother's maiden name was Coy.

Educated at Waverley School, Nottingham, Stanley House, Cliftonville, and in Germany, he worked initially as a designer of theatrical costumes and was never to lose his love of dressing up.

He made his professional debut as a performer in concert party at Hastings on the eve of the First World War. After a spell on tour in such shows as *The Girl in the Taxi* and *The Cinema Star*, he arrived in the West End as an understudy in *Theodore and Co* in 1916, eventually getting on to the stage the following year.

A crop of comedies and farces followed before he tasted twice-nightly variety on tour with Harry Day's revue *Crystal* from 1922 to 1924. He scored a signal success as Eliza the Cook in *Dick Whittington* with his own number "Oriental Emma of the Harem".

After that there was no going back. Byng's singular talent for observing and creating characters on the distaff side soon proved to be his greatest asset as a comedian.

His unmistakable presence was a feature in most of the Cochran revues at the London Pavilion in the 1920s, including *On with the Dance* – in which he portrayed a *passé* spinster preparing for bed in the sketch *Oranges and Lemons* – *One Damn Thing after Another* and *This Year of Grace*.

It was also in the hectic 1920s that Byng found his feet in cabaret. After the shows at the Pavilion he would go on to the Chez Henri Club where together with Laurier Lister he would send up the sister acts of the period like the Trix Sisters, Bettie and Babs and Lorna and Toots Pounds. "The Cabaret Boys", as they were known, pioneered this sort of transvestite comedy turn. Recalling this period of his career, Byng said it was "the first slightly *queer* number of the lot".

When he made his cabaret debut in New York in 1931 Byng was billed as "London's most important cabaret star". In Monte Carlo shortly afterwards he was announced as "*l'acteur extraordinaire anglais*".

Although appearing in his heyday in some of the most outstanding revues between the two world wars, Byng's appeal transcended typecasting. Thus at the Alhambra in the 1930s he presented a one-man pantomime, *Hop O' My Thumb*, when he made his first appearance on a trapeze bar, warbling, as he descended just above the footlights: "I'm Doris, the Goddess of Wind".

He followed this burlesque with others in the same mould: offbeat monologues which were gems of their kind. His arboraceous interpretation of "I'm a Tree" vied with such curiosities as "Whistler's Mother's Mum" and

"The Girl Who Went and Found It at the Astor". Then there was that never to be forgotten policewoman, a well-known "sight" of Piccadilly, whom Byng wickedly impersonated to the life in *Hi Diddle-Diddle* at the Comedy in 1934.

During the Second World War Byng was busy in musicals and variety, as well as cabaret and entertaining the troops. Afterwards he appeared in some more comedies and farces, the best remembered being Feydeau's *Hotel Paradiso* with Alec Guinness. He also turned up spasmodically on television, notably in the series *Before the Fringe* in the 1960s when he sang, or rather recited, some of the old revue songs.

It is thought that faint echoes of Douglas Byng may have contributed to the character of Max Pilgrim, the cabaret performer in Anthony Powell's great novel sequence *A Dance to the Music of Time*.

Even in semi-retirement, during the last years, Byng could not resist "getting back into harness" when he would occasionally team up with another veteran, Billy Milton, in a double act that delighted their old fans. Until finally moving to Denville Hall, the Actors' Charitable Trust Home, he lived at Brighton, a town he found "both breezy and salty".

Characteristically he composed his own epitaph:

So here you are, old Douglas, a derelict at last.
Before your eyes what visions rise of your vermilion
*   past.*
Mad revelry beneath the stars, hot clasping by the lake.
You need not sigh, you can't deny, you've had your bit
*   of cake.*

August 26 1987

LIEUTENANT-COLONEL GEOFFREY KNOWLES

LIEUTENANT-COLONEL GEOFFREY KNOWLES, who has died aged 87, survived a mauling by a black bear in Kashmir in 1922, and soldiered on to command Prince Albert Victor's Own Cavalry, 11th Frontier Force, against Rommel's Afrika Korps in North Africa and the Japanese in Burma.

One of the last British officers to join the old Indian Army from Cheltenham College through the Officer Cadet Battalion, Newmarket, in the final weeks of the First World War, Knowles completed his training at Madras before joining Prince Albert Victor's Own Cavalry on the North-West Frontier in 1920 in the aftermath of the third Afghan War.

Obtaining privilege leave in the summer of 1922, Knowles decided to try his luck with black bear and set off from Srinigar with a friend and two shikaris who were reputed to know the best areas for finding this species. Living up to their reputation the shikaris produced a large black bear, walking towards Knowles and his companion. When the bear was eight yards away Knowles fired and hit the bear in the shoulder, sending it rolling down the hillside.

Restraining his shikari from rushing down after it, Knowles cautiously followed the bloodstains. Then, as he described it in *The Piffer*, journal of the Punjab Frontier Force: "With a loud 'Woof Woof' the bear came out of some undergrowth ahead of us and walked towards us on all fours."

At this point the edge of the narrow path gave way causing Knowles to fall head first and knock himself out on a rock. The last he could remember was the bear coming through the bushes, about to land on his backside.

After biting Knowles through the thigh and implanting his pawmarks on his posterior, the bear made off and the next Knowles knew was a shikari nursing his head in his lap with tears falling on his brow. Back at camp his friend doused the wounds with iodine, and later that day Knowles heard that the bear had died. Returning to the regiment he was advised to stick to duck shooting.

The early part of the Second World War found Knowles serving as second-in-command of the regiment in the Middle East before returning to India to command the 3rd Gwalior Lancers. But following the loss, as a prisoner, of Colonel "Bolshie" Tatham, Knowles was posted back to the desert to command Prince Albert Victor's Own.

Knowles took the regiment back to India to retrain in armoured cars before participating in a number of vital actions in Burma. Assisting the relief of Kohima in March 1944, his squadrons kept the Dimapur–Kohima road open until June when they headed a breakthrough to the south, meeting Colonel Cyril Morrison's tanks of the 7th Cavalry, coming up from Imphal.

Although Knowles handed over command to Morrison at the Chindwin river at Christmas 1944, his part in the later successes of the Prince Albert Victor's Own was reflected in his appointment as OBE.

After staff appointments in Burma and India, serving as Military Secretary from 1948 to 1952 to Governors-General of Pakistan, and further staff appointments at the War Office and in Jamaica, Knowles retired in 1957 to Suffolk where he served as a county councillor.

He is survived by his wife, Sally.

December 3 1987

THE WALI OF SWAT

THE LAST WALI OF SWAT, MIANGUL ABDUL JAHANZEB, who has died in his 70s, was a veritable Poo-bah, holding sway over that remote North-West Frontier principality for 20 years before handing over his ruling powers to Pakistan in 1969.

When the Queen dropped in on the Wali in 1961, many echoed the couplet of Edward Lear about his forbear: "*Who or what/Is the Akhund of Swat?*" It emerged that the Wali was a hard-working administrator of a state variously described as an "Islamic Ruritania" or a "Himalayan Switzerland".

He spent long hours at his desk in his modest rose-bowered bungalow palace overlooking the long green valley where orange trees contrast vividly with a breath-taking backdrop of the snow-capped Hindu Kush. A neatly turned-out figure very much in the English manner, the Wali favoured traditional English fare and had a fondness for Brown Windsor soup.

26

Sporting recreation was plentiful for this Frontier Highland laird and his guests, as Prince Philip found in his first visit of 1959, and then when accompanying the Queen in 1961. The palace had its own golf course and Swat is renowned for its hill partridges, wild duck and trout.

The Wali was a descendant of the mystery man in the Lear couplet who was in fact born Abdul Gaffur into a cowherding family of Upper Swat, in the early part of Queen Victoria's reign, and revealed mystic powers – eventually being recognised as a "Messenger of God", or Akhund.

The Akhund's ascendancy and accumulation of wealth owed much to the belief among the Swat Pukhtun that their success in 1863 in fighting the British to a standstill was due to his *baraka*, or charismatic power. The Akhund's death in 1877 left a power vacuum which was eventually filled by the Akhund's only living descendant, Miangul Abdul Wadud. Styling himself the Badshah and assuming the powers of a total dictator, he created the state of Swat.

In 1926, the British, deciding to go along with the Badshah, sanctioned his rule, bestowing on him the title of Wali, and granted him a subsidy. In 1949, two years after Swat joined the newly created Pakistan, retaining local autonomy, the Wali abdicated and was succeeded by his son Miangul Abdul Jahanzeb.

The second Wali exchanged his father's despotic rule for a reign of firm benevolence, more in keeping with the 1950s, though continuing to control all aspects of life in Swat.

No argument was brooked; indeed lawyers were

barred. The Wali *was* the law. The non-interference by Pakistan was assured by the marriage of two of the Wali's sons to daughters of President Ayub Khan.

Such was the Wali's prestige in Islamabad that, in 1966, President Ayub insisted he be addressed as "Highness" and received a 15-gun salute on all official occasions. Unfortunately, Ayub's patronage eventually backfired with popular reaction against him in Pakistan. His fall combined with unrest in Swat which led to Pakistan's takeover and the conclusion of the dynasty in 1969.

In his later years, the Wali was pained by Swat's declining status as an increasingly lawless district in the Malakand division of the North-West Frontier province of Pakistan.

November 7 1987

EARL RUSSELL

THE 4TH EARL RUSSELL, who has died aged 66, was the eccentric elder son of the philosopher Bertrand Russell and caused the occasional sensation in the House of Lords with his outrageous speeches.

In 1978, during a debate on aid for victims of crime, Lord Russell had to be called to order after a singularly rambling and incoherent discourse. As he was advocating total abolition of law and order, and saying that police should be prevented from raping youngsters in cells, he was interrupted by Lord Wells-Pestell, from the Labour Government's Front Bench, and reminded of the length of time he had been speaking. Without any further comment the Earl left the Chamber.

In his speech from the cross benches Russell referred to modern society and the effects of automation in factories. Then he said: "There should be universal leisure for all, and a standing wage sufficient to provide life without working ought to be supplied ... so that everybody becomes a leisured aristocrat – aristocrats are Marxists. . . . Police ought to be totally prevented from ever molesting young people at all, from ever putting them into jails and raping them and putting them into brothels or sending them out to serve other people sexually against their wills."

Peers seemed startled as he continued: "In a completely reorganised modern society, women's lib would be realised by girls being given a house of their own by the age of 12 and three-quarters of the wealth of the State being given to the girls so that marriage would be abolished and the girl could have as many husbands as she liked . . ."

Finally Russell told the House of Lords: "Mr Brezhnev and Mr Carter are really the same person . . ."

The full text of this extraordinary outburst was published subsequently by Lord Russell's mother, Dora, and the Old Etonian anarchist and playwright Heathcote Williams, who described Russell as "the first man since Guy Fawkes to enter the House of Parliament with an honest intention". The pamphlet, illustrated by Ralph Steadman, quickly became a collectors' item and essential reading for the "psychedelic Left".

In 1985 Russell received a less courteous hearing from Their Lordships when he read out a carefully prepared question on the leadership of the IRA and suggested that the organisation might have a legitimate role in resolving Ireland's problems.

John Conrad Russell was born in 1921 and received his early education at his parents' experimental co-education school in Hampshire where there were no compulsory lessons and the children were permitted to call their teachers rude names. At the age of 13 he proceeded to the progressive Dartington Hall in Devon and after his parents' divorce he joined his mother in America, attending the University of California at Los Angeles, and Harvard.

From 1943 to 1946 he served with the RNVR and subsequently worked briefly for the Food and Agriculture Organisation of the United Nations in Washington and as an administrative assistant with the Treasury.

Following the dissolution of his own marriage to Susan Lindsay (daughter of the American poet Nicholas Vachel Lindsay) in the mid 1950s, Russell – or Viscount Amberley as he was styled by courtesy – became something of a recluse, spending his time writing and crocheting. His published works included a slim volume entitled *Abandon Spa, Hot Springs*.

To one visitor in the early 1960s he said: "I like to sit and think and write my thoughts. The few people who have seen my work find it too deep for them." He then pointed proudly to a pair of trousers hanging on the wall by a nail. "I crocheted these out of string," he said. "It took me a long while because I didn't have a pattern. I had to keep trying them on."

Although he succeeded to the earldom (created for the Victorian Prime Minister, Lord John Russell) in 1970, the new Earl received only an annuity of £300 from his father's £69,000 estate. The following year he issued a Chancery Division summons against Bertrand Russell's fourth wife and the executors.

He and his mother, who died in 1986, lived in a dilapidated Cornish cottage near Land's End. He died aboard a train to Penzance. A post-mortem was being held but police say there are no suspicious circumstances surrounding his death.

Lord Russell had two daughters, one of whom survives. The heir to the title is his half-brother, Conrad Sebastian Robert Russell, Astor Professor of British History, University College, London, born in 1937, who now becomes the 5th Earl Russell.

December 18 1987

SIR MELFORD STEVENSON

SIR MELFORD STEVENSON, who has died aged 85, was celebrated as a no-nonsense judge – perhaps the sternest since Lord Chief Justice Goddard – whose handing down of stiff sentences led to occasional calls for his removal by the liberal establishment.

Regarded as one of the legal profession's most robust characters, the name of his house in Sussex, Truncheons, symbolised his singular blend of judicial toughness and humour. Upon his retirement after 22 years on the bench in 1979 at No 1 Court, Old Bailey, he was likened to a lion.

Stevenson's caustic court-room comments frequently stirred up controversy. Bookmakers were disgusted by his description of them as "a bunch of crooks" – as were Mancunians when he said of a husband in a divorce case: "He chose to live in Manchester, a wholly incomprehensible choice for any free man to make."

He once told a man acquitted of rape: "I see you come from Slough. It is a terrible place. You can go back there." Passing sentence after a bribes case, Stevenson said to another: "You have tried, and to some extent succeeded, in converting Birmingham into a municipal Gomorrah."

Sir Melford was both subject and source of numerous anecdotes, many of them emanating from his beloved Garrick Club. He was overheard to observe that the Kray twins had only told the truth twice in the course of their trial for murder, over which he presided: first when one brother referred to a barrister as "a fat slob", and secondly when the other brother claimed that the judge was biased.

Another story concerned Stevenson's unsuccessful attempt to enter Parliament as a Conservative at Maldon, Essex, in the 1945 General Election. He opened his campaign by announcing that he wanted a clean fight and would therefore not be alluding to "the alleged homosexuality" of his Labour opponent, Tom Driberg.

Stevenson's subsequent reference to the 1967 legislation reforming the homosexual laws as a "buggers' charter" led to a reprimand from the Lord Chancellor. One day in 1976, three of his decisions were changed by the Court of Appeal, driving him to criticism for which he later apologised. A Commons motion calling for his removal was then withdrawn.

Sentencing six Cambridge students in 1970 for a demonstration against the Greek regime which caused extensive damage at the Garden House Hotel, he caused a sensation by his remark that the sentences would have been more severe had the students not been "exposed to the evil influence of some senior members of the university".

Although staunchly in favour of the death penalty – soon after his retirement he called for its return for all murders – Stevenson's career at the Bar included a notable defence brief: that of Ruth Ellis, who murdered her lover and became the last woman to be hanged in Britain. He also represented the Crown in Jomo Kenyatta's appeal against his conviction in the Mau Mau trial in Nairobi and was a member of the prosecution team in the famous murder trial of Dr Bodkin Adams, the Eastbourne physician.

When asked if he was hurt by criticisms during his career, Sir Melford commented: "A lot of my colleagues are just constipated Methodists."

The son of a minister at Beckenham Congregational Church, Aubrey Melford Steed Stevenson was born in 1902, educated at Dulwich and was called to the Bar by the Inner Temple in 1925, practising in common law. He took Silk in 1943 while serving in the Army, and as a major and deputy judge-advocate had plenty of experience of courts martial during the Second World War.

In 1945 he was judge-advocate at the Hamburg war-crime trial of German U-boat men who were sentenced to death for machine-gunning survivors of torpedoed ships.

Stevenson was Recorder of Rye from 1944 to 1951; chairman of West Kent Quarter Sessions from 1949 to 1955; and Recorder of Cambridge from 1952 to 1957 when he was made a High Court Judge and received a knighthood.

After four years in the Probate, Divorce and Admiralty Division, he was appointed to the Queen's Bench Division. He was presiding judge on the South-Eastern Circuit from 1970 to 1975. Sir Melford was sworn of the Privy Council in 1973.

In retirement, Sir Melford enjoyed something of an Indian summer on television where his trenchant views, laced with dry wit, earned him a wide circle of admirers.

Twice married, Stevenson had a daughter by the first marriage and a son and a daughter by the second (to Rosalind Wagner, sister of Sir Anthony Wagner, the herald and genealogist).

December 29 1987

LEN CHADWICK

LEN CHADWICK, who has died aged 72, was perhaps the most gifted representative of that peculiarly northern institution, the outdoor columnist.

His weekly article for the *Oldham Evening Chronicle*, written throughout the 1950s and 1960s under the *nom de plume* of "Fellwalker", was a model of the columnist's craft and an inspiration to all ramblers and mountain walkers west of the Pennines.

Chadwick was an extraordinary character. Slight of frame, with streaming white hair, a lantern jaw and hooded eyes, he was dirty, unkempt and poor, dressed in disreputable cast-offs and always without a permanent home. He smoked incessantly, talked in a quick jabber through toothless gums and wrote – in prose or verse – with a boundless energy for the physical horizon.

His hardihood and appetite for miles defied belief: he would cover thirty or forty each day of every weekend or holiday, at a spring-heeled step which most would term a run; and over any terrain, even among the peat-hags and mires of the Pennine moors which were his favourite haunt.

A classic autodidact, as he strode along Chadwick would regale the young boys who were his most frequent companions (he was homosexually inclined) with interminable but inspired monologues – often in Esperanto – on subjects ranging from the history of socialism or his prisoner-of-war experiences to the poetry of Ebenezer Elliott. The boys were often driven to the limits of their endurance, but if they lasted the course the experience was profoundly educative.

Aside from his writing Chadwick supported himself by a series of menial jobs – as a typist in a pool of 16-year-old girls, as an ice-cream salesman and as a clerk in a clothing factory. In the late 1970s his tenuous balance and careering pace of life were cruelly affected by a stroke; and when he recovered he was lamed by a broken ankle. Quite destitute, he spent his declining years in an old people's home at Oldham.

January 7 1988

DIVINE

DIVINE, who has died at Los Angeles aged 42, was an obese female impersonator who achieved cult status for his outrageous performances in such "underground" films as *Lust in the Dust*.

At the time of his death he was about to break into mainstream cinema with *Hairspray*, a nostalgic look at Baltimore, *circa* 1962, in which he has two starring roles – as a housewife and as a racist television station owner. The film was released recently in America where it received generally excellent reviews and is likely to be an international hit.

Divine also made some records – "You May Think You're a Man" and "Walk Like a Man" among them – and so helped pioneer a style of pop music known as "hi-energy", which has a wide following among homosexuals.

Though he was once voted "filthiest person alive" Divine was a shy and pleasant character when he took off his female costume and make-up. He said recently that his sluttish persona was just a mask. "I hate that, when they call me a transvestite," he said of his cha-cha heels and thigh-splitting spandex dresses. "Those are my work clothes. That's how I make people laugh."

Harris Glen Milstead, to give him his real name, was born in 1945 and began his career as a hairdresser in Baltimore, Maryland. He was renamed by the film director John Waters, who made a series of films about Divine and his seedy cronies. Waters' black and white productions, made in the 1960s and 1970s, are essentially a suburban, and rather wilder version of Andy Warhol's New York films of that period.

Waters, who had been at school with Divine, filmed the hideous brown streets of downtown Baltimore, strewn with rubbish and lined with junk shops, in a style which borrowed the bad taste of B-grade horror movies in much the same way as Warhol borrowed his style from "porn flicks".

Among the freakish cast of such films as *Pink Flamin-*

gos, *Female Trouble* and *Desperate Living*, Divine stole the show with the amusing flair of an amateur actor, as he engaged in such grotesque activities as eating dog excrement (apparently to make a satirical point about America's gross consumerism). And as the star grew ever fatter, so his husky voice and gigantic *embonpoint* became underground trademarks. Nightclub acts, disco records and ubiquitous "public appearances" added to his *louche* glamour.

Divine made a great splash at the Cannes Festival three years ago in the film *Polyester*, in which he played a housewife victimised by a swindling Casanova. After his previous film, *Lust in the Dust*, he had become an acknowledged character-actor star, with a New York apartment and a Florida home to show for it.

At the time of his death Divine was in Hollywood to film an episode of the television show *Married . . . With Children* in which he was to play the role of Uncle Otto.

He was unmarried.

March 9 1988

Sir Hugh Rankin, Bt

Sir Hugh Rankin, 3rd Bt, an eccentric remarkable even by the rarefied standards of the baronetage, who has died aged 88, was variously a riveter's mate in a Belfast shipyard; a trooper in the cavalry; a sheep shearer in Western Australia and runner-up in the All-Britain Sheep Judging Competition; president of the British Muslim Society and vice-president of the World's

Buddhist Association; and a campaigner for "an independent Red Republic of all Scotland, excluding Orkneys and Shetland".

His death deprives *Who's Who* of possibly its most entertaining entry. He listed his recreations as "golf (holds an amateur record amongst golfers of Gt Britain in having played on 382 separate courses of UK and Eire), shooting, coarse fishing, hunting, motoring, cycling on mountain tracks to tops of British mountains (Pres. Rough Stuff Cycling Assoc. 1956), the study of ancient track ways; bowls, tennis, archaeology (wife and himself are only persons who have crawled under dwarf fir forest for last ½ mile of most northerly known section of any Roman road in Europe, terminating opposite end of Kirriemuir Golf Course) . . ."

Born in 1899 in the middle of the Tunisian desert, the elder son of the traveller and big game hunter Sir Reginald Rankin (who survived being frozen to sleep in the Andes, shot the largest snow leopard on record in India and searched for the extinct giant sloth in Chile), he was christened Hubert Charles Rhys Rankin but later changed his first name to Hugh. At one stage he adopted the surname of Stewart-Rankin and during his Muslim period also briefly assumed the forename of Omar.

He was educated at Harrow but ran away to work in a Belfast shipyard before joining the 1st Royal Dragoon Guards as a trooper. In 1921 he was broad-sword champion of the cavalry, but the following year, while serving in Ireland during the Troubles ("on the wrong side, I'm afraid"), he was shot by a sniper and invalided out of the Army.

Rankin, who wrote articles on agricultural stock, then devoted himself to the study of sheep, being elected president of the Clun Forest Sheep Breeders' Association in 1928. Ten years later he represented British sheep breeders in petitioning the Government on the problems of the industry. At the time he succeeded to the baronetcy in 1931 he was a "piece-work" shearer in Western Australia, covering the area between Bunbury and Broome.

During travels in the Middle East, Rankin came under the influence of the Muslim peer, the 5th Lord Headley, whom he succeeded in 1935 as president of the British Muslim Society. But a few weeks later he resigned after a rowdy meeting: "They were very rude . . . and knew nothing of law and order or methods of procedure. I was disgusted with the whole lot of them."

He then formed a new society along orthodox and non-sectarian lines and in 1937 was the British representative to the first all-European Muslim Congress in Geneva.

During the Second World War he served as a captain in the Royal Army Service Corps in India but on being demobilised, "realised what an awful fool I had been to fight for Britain. If a revolution comes – and come it must after the next world war – I'll do my damnedest to see it succeeds."

He said that he had "always hated and loathed the Christian religion. The Muslim religion is a fighting one, so I dropped it and became a Buddhist." From 1944 he was a practising non-theistic Theravda Buddhist and claimed to be the second "Britisher" to perform the Holy Buddhist Pilgrimage.

In 1959 he declared it was "no news" that Abominable Snowmen existed: "It is part of our known belief that five Bodhisattvas ('Perfected Men') control the destiny of this world. They meet together once a year in a cave in the Himalayas to make their decisions. One of them lives permanently on the higher Himalayas. One of them lives in the Scottish Cairngorms." Sir Hugh said that he and his wife had clearly seen the latter Bodhisattva in the Larig Ghru Pass.

Rankin's political affiliations were equally varied: he joined the Labour party in 1939 and was subsequently a Dominion Home Ruler for Scotland, a Scottish Nationalist, a Scottish Communist and a Welsh Republican Nationalist. In *Who's Who* he stated that he held "extreme political views" and was "now left-side Labour".

In 1950 he was elected to Perth County Council and declared, "I am a blood-red militant Communist in every possible way. *Absolutely blood-red.*" He was a virulent critic of the Forestry Commission's alleged policies of depasturisation and turning out crofters and tenants.

In 1965 he claimed to be "the only baronet in the United Kingdom who is living on national assistance" and added that his title had always been a hindrance. Asked what job he might like, he replied: "Anything. Anything except being a butler. I hate snobbishness."

Among Sir Hugh's myriad distinctions were being Hereditary Piper of the Clan Maclaine and a *"News of the World* Knight of the Road (for courtesy in motor driving)".

His first wife Helen, widow of Captain Colin Campbell and eldest daughter of Sir Charles Stewart, the Public Trustee, died in 1945; he married secondly, in 1946, Robina Kelly, a nurse, who survives him.

There were no children of either marriage and the baronetcy passes to Sir Hugh's nephew, Ian Niall Rankin, born 1932, whose mother, Lady Jean Rankin, is a long-standing Woman of the Bedchamber to Queen Elizabeth the Queen Mother.

May 2 1988

THE REVEREND MICHAEL BLAND

THE REVEREND MICHAEL BLAND, who has died aged 67, had an unhappy tenure as Rector of Buckland and Stanton with Snowshill, Gloucestershire, which combined the Church politics of a Trollope novel with the social comedy of one by Mrs Gaskell.

A former intelligence officer in the RAF, the bachelor Bland had the physical presence of a heavyweight boxer and what he himself described as "a latter Ciceronian haircut". He was appointed to the living in 1958 and remained there until shortly before his death: but his effective ministry ended in 1969 when he was charged in a Consistory Court at Gloucester for neglect of duties and conduct unbecoming a clergyman.

Wearing full convocation dress of cassock, gown, scarf and hood with white band, he made Anglican history as the first person to be tried under the Ecclesiastical Jurisdiction Measure of 1963. He was tried on four charges of neglecting his duties: by leaving church before Divine Service ended; refusing to baptise a baby; preventing a parishioner from entering the church to declare publicly his dissent to the marriage of his son at the time the banns were published; and repelling another parishioner from Holy Communion without lawful cause.

41

Furthermore he was alleged to have written rude letters to six people; made offensive and hurtful remarks to parishioners; indulged four times in fits of temper in church; and to have been generally short-tempered in the course of his dealings. Under the charge of making offensive remarks, Bland was alleged at a parochial church council meeting to have said in effect that he hated his parishioners.

He was also said to have called one parishioner a liar and to have told him he should be ashamed of himself for taking part in Holy Communion when his purpose in attending church was to hear his daughter's marriage banns read. Finally, Bland was alleged to have told the council that on the day he found no one in the church when he arrived to conduct a service, he would have achieved what he wanted to do: he could then run the church the way he wanted without the local squire's paid servants and tenants.

Bland, defended in court by Geoffrey Howe, was sentenced to be deprived of his living. But the verdict was overturned on appeal to the Court of Arches, which simply administered a formal rebuke and allowed him to return to his parish. The legal fees incurred by the diocese of Gloucester amounted to some £30,000.

Michael Bland was born in 1921 and read history and theology at St Peter's College, Oxford, before preparing for ordination at Wycliffe Hall.

Curacies at Southampton, Milford-on-Sea and Newbury from 1952 to 1958 were followed by his appointment to Buckland and Stanton with Snowshill, where it was soon apparent that his ministry was not going to be a success.

Any hope that once the court case was ended there

would be a recovery of pastoral relations between the Rector and his parishioners quickly was dashed, for Bland seemed incapable of carrying out his work in a way that was appropriate and acceptable. Asked about the angry emotions felt by some of his congregation, he said: "Quite right. Get the violence off the streets and into the Church where it belongs."

For many years Sunday services in Buckland were attended only by the Rector's housekeeper. All attempts by bishops, archdeacons and others failed and the sad situation came to an end only recently when Bland was persuaded to accept retirement.

July 2 1988

NICO

NICO, who has died in Ibiza aged 49, was the Dietrich of the 1960s: an exquisite blonde, melancholy and amused, she sang about the mysteries of sorrow and sin, and radiated sex and angst in roughly equal measures. She obviously knew too much about men and took too many drugs.

Nico's style was throwaway, cool, essentially urban. Her allure owed much to Berlin, where she passed her infancy in the post-war rubble; and her apotheosis occurred in New York, as one of Andy Warhol's "superstars", a product of his Factory of the Arts.

Between Berlin and New York came Rome, where she caught the eye of Federico Fellini, the film director; Paris (Alain Delon, the actor, by whom she later had a child); and London (Brian Jones of the Rolling Stones).

She pursued careers as underwear salesgirl, model, actress and singer.

Nico was born Christa Pavloski, at Cologne in 1938. Her father died in a concentration camp when she was two, and her mother took her to live with her grandfather, a railwayman, near Berlin.

In 1950 she and her mother moved to Ibiza. After a protracted idyll on that island and a brief period in Rome, appearing in Fellini's *La Dolce Vita*, Nico moved to Paris, where she entered the Bohemian world she was later to reign over. Five years later she moved, via London, to New York, where she studied at the Lee Strasberg school of acting – in the same class as Marilyn Monroe.

Nico was soon taken up by Warhol, and adopted her definitive role of *femme fatale*.

When Warhol was introduced to her by Bob Dylan in 1965 she was singing "intimate songs" at the Blue Angel Lounge on East 55th Street.

Warhol had recently taken control of the Velvet Underground – a rock group which opposed the prevailing cult of Californian "peace and love" with raucous songs about sado-masochism, homosexuality and heroin – and decided that Nico should become a member.

The Velvets bowed to their patron, but were unenthusiastic about the new recruit, particularly as she expected to take over the singing from Lou Reed. They played tricks on her, sabotaging her microphone and so on, and the songs Reed wrote for Nico tended to mock their singer.

None the less, the Velvet Underground and Nico were for a time a potent combination: her deadpan, eerie voice contrasted well with their amphetamine-fuelled guitar playing and street-gang choruses.

The two styles are at their most pointed in "Femme Fatale", in which Nico sings mournfully about a character not unlike her own, and the band delivers the one-line chorus in a bored, sneering tone:

> *Everybody sees*
>   *(She's a femme fatale)*
> *The things she does to please*
>   *(She's a femme fatale)*
> *She's just a little tease . . .*
>   *She's going to smile to*
>   *make you frown*
> *What a clown . . .*

It was her finest hour. Towards the end of 1967 Reed took full control of the band and dispensed with the services of Nico, Warhol and Cale.

Nico resumed her solo career, recording a collection of cover versions on an LP called *Chelsea Girl* (she had starred in Warhol's film of the same name). She made a new friend in the singer Jim Morrison, who urged her to write and perform her own material. Borrowing an idea from the poet Allen Ginsberg, Nico acquired an Indian pump organ to accompany her depraved Germanic lullabies.

Cale proved an abiding influence, and she produced four LPs in collaboration with him: *Marble Index*, *Desert Shore*, *The End* and *Camera Obscura*.

She also appeared in ten avant-garde films directed by her lover, the French film director Philippe Carelle.

In recent years Nico dyed her hair jet black, moved to Manchester and became a pillar of the "punk" movement, of which the Velvets had been the forerunners. She also gave up heroin for bicycling, which was to turn out the more dangerous amusement – she died when she fell off a bicycle while on holiday.

July 25 1988

MARIE-LA-JOLIE

MARIE-LA-JOLIE, who has died at Marseille aged 82, was a celebrated brothel-keeper in that city's criminal heyday, when the *vieux port* was a world centre for white-slaving and drug-trafficking.

Marie Paoleschi was born at Marseille in 1906 and became a prostitute aged 17, at the suggestion of a petty gangster with whom she had fallen in love at a dance.

Her career took her to the Pigalle district of Paris, and to such outposts of her trade as Saigon and Buenos Aires. But Marseille was always her home, and after many vicissitudes she set up her own establishment there.

A few years ago Marie-la-Jolie published her memoirs in two volumes, which gave a hair-raising account of film stars and gangsters – notably the Guerini brothers, notorious for the "French Connection"; of a life of smuggling, corruption, prison, vendettas and champagne.

When she was warned that her revelations might endanger her safety she was unworried: "At my age, who cares?"

Marseille's most infamous madam ended her days in a small flat near the waterfront: alone, toothless save for one rotting fang, but content to have outlived nearly all her old associates.

August 18 1988

BILLY CARTER

BILLY CARTER, who has died aged 51, was President Jimmy Carter's hard-drinking roly-poly brother whose bibulous verandah-chair comments from the peanut township of Plains, Georgia, caused periodic embarrassment at the White House.

Unabashed by his much-publicised reputation as a buffoon, he often made matters worse by joking at his own expense. A favourite story was that one night he had been drinking heavily and took two cups to bed – one contained bourbon, the other minnows he needed for fishing. Feeling thirsty, he stretched out for the bourbon, only to discover in the morning that he had swallowed the minnows.

It was one of many such anecdotes which confirmed the Anarchist party of Canada's description of him as "a preacher of gross consumerism".

At a time when Colonel Gaddafi was on the State Department's list of public enemies Billy Carter headed a trade delegation from Georgia to Tripoli, but President Carter stepped in and ordered government agencies and officials to rebuff any member of his family who might seek dealings with them. The affair became known as "Billygate".

On another occasion he advertised mementoes of his brother's inauguration for sale at outrageous prices, and flogged inauguration postal covers from the Plains post office. Less successful was his introduction of "Billy Beer", a brand which lasted less than a year.

Describing himself as a "beer-drinking good ol' boy", he held court to a ring of reporters and columnists who syndicated his expletive-punctuated observations at times of crisis when the White House could well have done without them.

Even so, his long-suffering brother made patient allowances, furrowing his brow as he ticked him off, but always forgiving him. During Billy's illness he took him into his home.

William Alton Carter II, who was born near Plains in 1937, was the youngest of four children of James Earl Carter, a prominent businessman, and his wife Lillian – Jimmy Carter's other family cross, the opinionated "Miz Lillian".

He married his high-school sweetheart, Sybil Spires, and joined the Marines. After serving in Japan and the Philippines he drove a truck for the peanut business and attended Emory University, Atlanta, but was expelled after submitting an examination paper written by someone else.

He later ran a petrol-filling station from which he also dispensed beer and soft drinks. But on encountering difficulties with federal tax collectors and other inquisitive government agencies he dropped out, living largely off personal appearance fees.

Carter died of pancreatic cancer, the same disease which killed his father and a sister. "I always said what I thought and I didn't hold anything back," he said in a recent interview after he was diagnosed as suffering from the illness.

He is survived by his wife and their six children.

September 26 1988

CHARLES HAWTREY

CHARLES HAWTREY, who has died aged 74, was an endearingly eccentric comedy actor whose bespectacled, spindle-shanked figure and dotty, weedy, often outrageously "camp" characterisations tended to be more familiar than his name.

The name had, in fact, been cheekily borrowed from the celebrated Edwardian actor-manager Sir Charles Hawtrey, who died in 1923, a couple of years before the young Hawtrey (*né* Hartree) began his career as a boy soprano.

He made his mark as Slightly in *Peter Pan*, and then in revue before becoming a regular member of the ageing schoolboy troupe in the Will Hay films; but it was in another series of even broader comedies, the *Carry Ons*, that he achieved his apotheosis. Resembling a mischievous stick insect, with a face curiously reminiscent of an elderly maiden aunt topped by an incongruous toupée, and with a distinctive high-pitched voice verging on the hysterical, Hawtrey cropped up in one absurdly unlikely role after another as the *Carry On* series established itself as a great British institution.

Carry On Sergeant led to *Carry On Nurse*, *Carry On At*

Your Convenience to *Carry On Camping* – though Hawtrey needed little encouragement in that direction. He had an insouciant way with a double entendre which was all his own; somehow he retained an innocently spinsterish persona amid all the tired innuendoes and remorseless allusions to bodily functions. Indeed Hawtrey frequently managed to steal scenes from fellow stalwarts of the series such as Sid James, Kenneth Williams and Kenneth Connor and became one of the most hilarious "turns" in the cinema.

Many will cherish the memory of Hawtrey as the skittish Seer in *Carry On Cleo* popping his head out of an Egyptian urn, with the lid worn like a beret at a jaunty angle, and prefacing his latest vision with a breezy "Stop me if you've heard this before". Or as the fastidious Red Indian Chief, Big Heap, in *Carry On Cowboy*; or as the kilted Private Widdle in *Carry On Up the Khyber* complaining that "the wind fairly whistles *up the Pass*".

George Frederick Joffre Hartree came from a theatrical family, though his father was a motor mechanic. Born at Hounslow, Middlesex, in 1914, he studied for the stage at the Italia Conti School and made his first appearance at Boscombe in 1925 as a street arab in *The Windmill Man*. His London debut as a boy actor was at the Scala Theatre on Boxing Day 1927 as the White Cat and Bootblack in *Bluebell in Fairyland* and the next year he appeared in *Where the Rainbow Ends* at the Holborn Empire.

In 1929 he began his long wireless career which was to include roles in the Will Hay series, the Norman and Henry Bones children's hour comedy and *Just William* – in which he played the snooty Hubert Lane. In 1931 Hawtrey was seen at the Palladium as the First Twin in *Peter Pan* and five years later he played Slightly in another production of Barrie's classic fantasy at the same theatre. He was commended by W. A. Darlington, dramatic critic of *The Daily Telegraph*, for showing "a comedy sense not unworthy of his famous name".

Hawtrey's many other stage appearances included the Shakespearean role of Gremio in *The Taming of the Shrew* at the Old Vic (1939) and the following year he earned rave notices for the Eric Maschwitz revue *New Faces*, particularly for his "chic and finished study of an alluring woman spy".

During and after the Second World War he appeared in the West End in such shows as *Scoop*, *Old Chelsea*, *Merrie England*, *Frou-Frou* and *Husbands Don't Count*, as well as directing several plays at the Q Theatre. But it was in the cinema that he was best known.

He resumed his partnership with Will Hay in *Good Morning Boys* (1937), *Where's That Fire?* (1939), *The Ghost of St Michael's* (1941) and *The Goose Steps Out* (1942). Other film credits included *A Canterbury Tale* (1948), *The Galloping Major* (1950), *Brandy for the Parson* (1952) and *You're Only Young Twice* (1953).

In 1957 he appeared in the popular TV comedy series *The Army Game* as one of the scruffy lead-swinging squaddies stationed at the forgotten transit camp of Nether Hopping. Hawtrey's character found it restful to indulge in the unmilitary pastime of knitting.

The following year he was cast in what seemed a fairly indifferent film comedy, *Carry On Sergeant*, but it turned out to be the precursor of the phenomenally successful series of *Carry On* films. Bawdy, unsubtle and stuffed with atrocious puns, these basic farces were churned out at production-line speed – roughly two a

51

year for almost two decades – and kept to a notoriously low budget.

Laurence Olivier, arriving at the film studios in a limousine, was surprised to see Hawtrey, one of the best-loved stars of the British cinema, proceeding to work on foot in an old mackintosh, carrying a plastic bag.

Hawtrey's preferred mode of parlance was a weird nonsense language, a sort of telegraphese, which few apart from his *Carry On* co-star Joan Sims were able to fathom.

His mother, to whom he remained very close, was equally eccentric. On one occasion at the film studios, during a break from the *Carry On* action, Hawtrey and the other actors were listening enthralled to one of her spirited monologues when he noticed that her open handbag was on fire. He drew this to the attention of his mother who, with the minimum of effort, poured the contents of a cup of tea that she was holding into the reticule, snapped it shut and continued with her anecdote as if nothing had happened – while steam billowed out of the bag.

Hawtrey lived in an old smuggler's cottage near the seafront at Deal, from which he was rescued during a fire in 1984, emerging as a pathetically dishevelled figure, *sans* toupée, but characteristically refusing hospital treatment.

His recreations included playing the piano and collecting antiques. He was unmarried.

October 28 1988

JACK DE MANIO

JACK DE MANIO, who has died aged 74, was a popular broadcaster on BBC radio, notably on Radio 4's early morning *Today* programme which he hosted for 13 years.

His cheery manner won him a large following and set a new fashion for banter and fun on the radio. But his lightness of touch and cavalier disregard of the Corporation's *mores* carried their own perils.

Executives were not amused, for example, when they discovered that the lion he had invited into Broadcasting House for an interview had not been insured. Nor did they appreciate his tendency to scratch his chest while addressing the microphone.

De Manio was also given to verbal gaffes, blundering over his cues – "Now we've got two little boys on the programme . . . No . . . Here! I've got the wrong story! It's one little boy" – or missing them altogether, explaining his failure to his audience with such excuses as, "I was locked in the loo."

He was also notorious for getting the time wrong: a motorist once tried to sue him for damages because he heard de Manio give the time incorrectly, looked at his watch and drove into the car in front. He once warned a broadcasting colleague to be careful if he drove down Park Lane, "because there's a little grey car hanging round there and it's full of coppers".

Blunt and outspoken, de Manio had an impressive collection of *bêtes noires*, including badly driven dustcarts, nodding dogs in the rear windows of cars and garden gnomes. And he read out so many jokes from *The Daily*

Telegraph that the Corporation deemed it necessary to warn him against political bias.

He was an enterprising journalist, however, and in 1969 achieved a broadcasting coup when he obtained the first radio interview with the Prince of Wales. In 1975 his favour with the Palace was confirmed by an invitation to one of the Queen's luncheons.

The qualities which made him successful were summed up by a *Daily Telegraph* radio critic: "He sounds the sort of man you would like to talk to you, and when he does you feel at ease. It's the essence of good broadcasting and worth far more than technical perfection."

A *Sunday Telegraph* critic once compared de Manio's "purring voice" to the sound of a "pre-war Bentley ticking over". A portly man, similar in build to Sir Winston Churchill, he was considered the most English of Englishmen; yet his father was an Italian and his mother Polish.

Giovanni Batista de Manio was born in London in 1914. He once said: "I don't feel anything but English. If I go to Italy I don't feel Italian. I went to Poland in 1928 and hated it."

His father was a pioneer aviator who once crashed on to a roof in Palmers Green. He was killed during an air race to Lisbon just before Jack was born.

De Manio was brought up by his mother and educated at Aldenham, where he loathed school discipline and did "frightfully badly". The chief consolation of his schooldays was the perpetration of practical jokes – on one occasion he put treacle on the organ pedals in church.

His first job at 18 was as a junior invoice clerk in a brewery, but he was dismissed because, as he put it, "I was absolutely hopeless". He then worked as a waiter at the Ritz, in the kitchens of Grosvenor House, at the Miramar in Cannes and the Congress in Chicago. He retained his love of cooking and came to regard himself as a spaghetti specialist, creating a tripe bolognese for home consumption.

After failing an audition for a post as a BBC announcer in 1938 de Manio was commissioned into the Royal Sussex Regiment from the City of London Yeomanry and fought in France and North Africa. Twice wounded, he was awarded the Military Cross and Bar and promoted major.

The Second World War did not diminish his broadcasting ambitions, and in 1944 he was taken on by Forces Radio in Palestine; impressed by this experience, the BBC gave him a job as an announcer on the Overseas Service. He joined the Home Service in 1955, leaving the staff to become a freelance in 1964.

De Manio made gaffes over the air from the start, and felt that he was only saved from dismissal by regard for his war service and rank. Shortly before the *Today* appointment, for example, he had been dismissed after calling an important radio talk, "Land of the *Nigger*" instead of "Land of the Niger".

He landed the *Today* job soon after its inauguration in 1958 and remained with the programme until 1971; he always insisted that he was given the job only because no one else would want to begin work at such an early hour, and that the BBC was "scraping the absolute bottom of the barrel". Such a self-deprecating and throw-away remark gives the clue to de Manio's enduring popularity with listeners.

After leaving *Today* in 1971 he was given his own

programme, *Jack de Manio Precisely*, which ran until 1978, when the BBC dropped him to make way for the broadcasting of Parliament. He returned briefly – and unhappily – to the BBC in 1979 as a contributor to *Woman's Hour*.

His former extravagance left him with little money; as he told one interviewer: "Being out of a real job is the most frustrating thing in the world. I'm hard up and I want to work." But he avoided bitterness and found use for his time in helping the Friends of Queen Charlotte's and Chelsea Hospital for Women.

De Manio published two books – *To Auntie with Love* and *Life Begins Too Early* – and was a frequent contributor to *Punch*. He was voted Radio Personality of the Year by the Variety Club of Great Britain in 1964 and by the Radio Industries Club in 1971.

He was twice married: to Juliet Gravaeret Kaufmann, an American (the marriage was dissolved in 1946); and to Loveday Elizabeth Matthews, a widow, who survives him with a son by the first marriage.

October 29 1988

PETER LANGAN

PETER LANGAN, the erratic Irish-born *restaurateur* who has died aged 47, was celebrated more for the eccentricity and extravagance of his behaviour than for the real merits of the restaurants with which he was associated.

His greatest success was the brasserie in Mayfair's Stratton Street, which bore his name and became a popular haunt of the famous and notorious alike. It

opened in 1976, on the premises of the old Coq d'Or, an
ailing dinosaur of the Maxwell Joseph period, where it
achieved a remarkable transformation. His immediate
success set the standard for a host of imitators, none of
which could match the original in terms of style, consistent quality of cuisine and modish appeal.

Langan's partners in the venture were the actor
Michael Caine, whose association with the restaurant
gave it a show-business presence of British and American
actors and their camp followers – and Richard Shepherd,
formerly chef at the Capital Hotel.

"I'm a great *restaurateur*," Langan claimed, "but busi-
nesswise . . ." The restaurant worked because Shepherd
organised its every aspect, turning out 400 or 500 covers
a day and providing interesting and constantly changing
dishes to a high standard. But the idea was Langan's and
it was his vivid personality and astute awareness of the
uses of publicity – even publicity that others might
think self-defeating – that stamped the Brasserie on the
public consciousness.

Langan's personal notoriety, his reputation for behaviour variously disconcerting, outrageous or disgraceful,
was sometimes justified – especially when liberally
fuelled by his favourite Krug. He could seem a demonic
figure; but the excesses attributed to him often owed
something to the embroidery of certain journalists.

Of the many anecdotes in the Langan canon, few are
printable. He was celebrated for his insults and had a
highly public quarrel with his partner Caine.

It is said that tabloid newspaper editors, when short
of copy, would despatch youngish female reporters to
interview Langan with the express purpose of being
shocked. Langan invariably obliged, though he strenu-

ously denied the allegation that he had vomited into his napkin before one woman journalist. He insisted that a small piece of food had unfortunately caught in his throat: "I'd never vomit. I'm particular about my manners."

Among the tales he did not deny was that of the cockroach which a distraught customer had found in the ladies' room. "Madam," he exclaimed after studying it closely, "that cockroach is *dead*. All ours are alive." He then apparently swallowed it, washing it down decorously with a glass of vintage Krug.

Langan would regularly launch himself at customers he found, usually for some unfathomable reason, offensive. Often he would pass out amid the cutlery before doing any damage, but occasionally he would cruise menacingly beneath the tables, biting unwary customers' ankles.

Not known for his delicacy towards the fairer sex, Langan rejoiced in daring attractive young women to strip naked in the bar in return for limitless champagne. Patrons of Langan's haunts were only safe when he lay like a white whale in his crumpled suit, snoring sonorously by the Colony Room Club's piano, underneath a table, or on the floor in the gentlemen's lavatory at his Brasserie.

Peter Daniel Langan, son of Dan Langan, the Irish rugby full-back and a prominent figure in the Irish petrol industry, was born in Co. Clare in 1941 and educated in Ireland. After a spell working in petrol in Britain, Langan made his first foray into the restaurant world as the chef, and soon the moving spirit, at Odin's in Devonshire Street, Marylebone, in 1966. There he evolved the idiosyncratic style which distinguished his later enterprises.

The virtues of Langan's largely self-taught cooking were soon apparent and the happy chance that his real passion for pictures was complemented by the presence upstairs of the artist Patrick Procktor. The tables of Odin's came to be frequented by what are now the great names of contemporary British painting while their early works hung on the walls.

Odin's became the works canteen of such artists as Francis Bacon, R. B. Kitaj, Lucian Freud and David Hockney, as well as Procktor. In the manner of a Rive Gauche café proprietor, Langan would exchange meals for the painters' work.

Procktor's mural of Venice still hangs in the unfashionable upstairs room at Langan's Brasserie; and he also designed its distinctive menu, on which a blue-faced Langan looks bemused while Shepherd appears concerned to separate him from an admonitory Caine.

Odin's prospered and removed next door; the original site became Langan's Bistro – still, 20 years on, a pleasing setting for simple dishes of unusual merit. The Dublin Bay Prawns, for example, were appropriately and exceptionally good – even if Langan himself would occasionally nod gently off with his head in a bowl of the crustaceans.

Those who condemned his excesses almost always overlooked Langan's intelligence and wit. For all his flaws he could be a charming and kindly companion and a princely host.

That he was often misunderstood is perhaps understandable but for all his occasional grossness he was a man whose delights, in Shakespeare's phrase, "were dolphin-like, they showed their backs above the element they lived in." Langan had a great delight in life and his exuberant vitality, sometimes tinged with melancholy, was an unfailing diversion to his friends.

Latterly, his thoughts had turned towards the franchising of his name in this country and especially in America where, after long years of abortive negotiation, the first transatlantic Langan's Brasserie has opened its doors in Century City, Los Angeles – though Langan himself was barred from the premises.

His wife, Susan, injured in the fire that cost Langan his life, survives him.

December 9 1988

SIR THOMAS SOPWITH

SIR THOMAS SOPWITH, the early aviator and aeroplane maker who has died aged 101, had an extraordinary career which encompassed the design and production of military machines for the Royal Flying Corps in the First World War, the RAF's first modern monoplane eight-gun fighter in the 1930s and the world's first jump-jet in the 1960s.

The creator of the Sopwith Camel and Pup, he also had overall responsibility for the Second World War Hurricane and the present-day Harrier. As if those achievements were not enough, "Tommy" Sopwith perkily confided to the television cameras in a documentary on his 100th birthday that he had also contested the America's Cup.

Thomas Octave Murdoch Sopwith was born on January 10 1888, the eighth child and only son of a prosperous civil engineer. After being privately educated as an engineer, young Tom indulged the pursuit of speed on water and land. Fascinated by the possibilities of the internal combustion engine, he also gratified a compulsive urge to fly.

In retrospect, the smooth progress of Sopwith's career gives the illusion that it was predestined early in the century and that to succeed he had merely to survive the perils of his pioneer flying exploits. In reality, his success was the result of his personal vision, powers of concentration and talent for employing the right combination of apparently unremarkable men, who just happened to be there when he most needed them.

Under Sopwith's leadership Fred Sigrist, Harry Hawker, Sidney Camm and Frank Spriggs, recruited almost haphazardly, provided the engineering, design and managerial skills of Sopwith Aviation and its successor, Hawkers. In 1910 Sigrist, hired as chauffeur and odd-job man, began to care for Sopwith's part-owned 166-ton schooner, *Neva*, six-cylinder 40-horsepower Napier motor car, motor boats and three aeroplanes. By this time Sopwith had already crewed the winning yacht in the 1909 Royal Aero Club race and satisfied a teenage zest for ballooning.

His passion for flying dated from a day in 1910. Putting into Dover from sea he was told that Bleriot had just landed after crossing the Channel for the first time with a passenger. On finding the pilot in a field seven miles away, he decided on the spot to turn from balloons to aeroplanes.

Within hours he arrived at Brooklands where, inside

the concrete motor-racing circuit, flying lessons and joyrides were being offered in a Henry Farman machine. Producing a £5 note, Sopwith booked two circuits.

From that moment he was "terribly bitten by the aviation bug", and paid £630 for a 40-horsepower Blériot-inspired Avis monoplane built under the railway arches at Battersea. It was delivered to him at Brooklands on October 21 1910, and he crashed it the same day.

Alarmed at the rate at which he was spending money, Sopwith decided to make flying pay by winning prizes. Flourishing his flying certificate (the 31st issued in Britain), he contested the Michelin Cup for the longest non-stop flight by a British pilot in a British machine and, more rewardingly, the £4,000 Baron de Forest trophy for the longest non-stop flight from any point in England to anywhere on the Continent.

By the end of 1910 he had landed both, but not without the indispensable assistance of Sigrist. It was Sigrist who, on December 18 1910, produced the engine-coaxing plan which enabled his employer to bank Baron de Forest's £4,000 after completing 177 miles in 3 hours and 40 minutes to land in Belgium.

Confident that he was now financially and technically equipped to compete in America, in 1911 Sopwith organised a tour of "air meets". At first his arrival, accompanied by his sister, May, was far from welcome in the camp of the pioneer Wright brothers, Wilbur and Orville. They attempted to claim the patent on passenger carrying, which would have ruled out May and her picnic basket of thermos flasks. But the Wrights were appeased when Sopwith, after wrecking his Blériot, purchased one of their biplanes.

Beginning to win prizes of as much as $14,000 and

appearing before crowds of up to 300,000 spectators, he polished his performance in the popular quick-start competitions until he could run and jump into the seat of his moving machine in nine seconds.

Having survived a crash into the sea off Manhattan Beach in the autumn of 1911, Sopwith returned to Brooklands where he opened a flying school. Among his earliest pupils were two men whose names were to become better known to the public than that of their instructor.

One was Harry Hawker. Still in his teens and a mechanic since running away from school in Australia, he had hung around the Brooklands perimeter until hired by Sopwith to join Sigrist as another dogsbody. The other was Major Hugh Trenchard, "Father" of the RAF, who urgently needed a certificate before taking up an appointment at the Services' recently established Central Flying School.

As the First World War approached, the nascent Sopwith Aviation Company outgrew its Brooklands shed. Soon Sigrist and Hawker (already Sopwith's test pilot) were chalking the outline of a biplane, known as the Hybrid, on the wooden floor of the disused roller-skating rink Sopwith had bought down-river at Kingston upon Thames.

Early in 1914, Hawker was in Australia demonstrating the Tabloid (a machine which would shortly distinguish itself as a Royal Flying Corps scout). In his absence Sopwith, who had roughed out modifications on the back of an envelope, selected Howard Pixton to fly one of the machines with floats in the Schneider Trophy competition held at Monte Carlo.

Sopwith had designed and built the airframe but

selected his engine in France. It was a 100-horsepower Monosoupape Gnome, which he brought back "almost literally in my suitcase".

Shortly before the outbreak of the First World War Sopwith also designed a side-by-side two-seater modelled on the Tabloid, for Winston Churchill, First Lord of the Admiralty. Called the Sociable, it was popularly referred to as "Tweenie".

As the Tabloid went to war Sopwith stopped flying. It was not a conscious decision, as he later explained: "I was so occupied with design and manufacture that I just didn't have the time to fly and did not pilot an aeroplane for about 16 years."

That was a characteristic understatement which overlooked the continual reinforcement of the RFC, the Royal Naval Air Service and, after April 1 1918, the RAF on the Western Front with Pups, Camels, Triplanes and other machines destined to become museum celebrities.

By the end of the war two of Sopwith's factories were rolling out ninety fighters a week. Sopwith plants had built 16,000 machines in Britain and 10,000 in France. Camel pilots notched up the highest number of "kills" – 2,700.

After the Armistice the market for aircraft contracted almost as rapidly as it had expanded. But amid the gloom one beacon beckoned – the *Daily Mail* Atlantic Flight competition. Sopwith entered the Sopwith B1, which boasted special features designed by Hawker. On May 18 1919, Hawker took off from Newfoundland on the west–east crossing accompanied by Commander Kenneth Mackenzie-Grieve as navigator.

Less than halfway across Hawker was forced to put down in the sea and the pair were presumed lost. King

George V sent a telegram of condolence to Mrs Hawker before it was learned that the *Mary*, a small Danish freighter, had rescued the airmen.

A month later John Lacock and Arthur Whitten Brown achieved the first Atlantic crossing in a Vickers Vimy and were knighted. The following year, Sopwith put the company into voluntary liquidation while it remained solvent. Hawker registered the H. G. Hawker Engineering Company and acquired a motor-cycle business.

Shortly afterwards "the gang", as Sopwith called his pioneering team, met up. Sopwith, Sigrist, Hawker and Spriggs were unanimous in their decision: "Let's make aeroplanes again."

In less than a year Hawker was dead. He had crashed his Nieuport Goshawk while testing it for entry in the 1921 Aerial Derby.

Sopwith put his heart and money into developing the Hawker Aircraft Co., which totally eclipsed the name and achievements of the former Sopwith Aviation Co. This meant that designs which might reasonably have been designated Sopwith's have entered history under the name of Hawker, though – to confuse the matter further – coming from the drawing board of Sidney Camm.

In the 1920s and 1930s Sopwith masterminded the gradual growth of the company as its military and civil designs found markets at home and abroad. The Hawker Hart, Hind, Demon, Fury, Hornet, Audax and Hotspur are merely a few of the best remembered names. There was also the little Tomtit trainer for which Sopwith – and the Duke of Windsor – always had a soft spot.

Sopwith told a favourite anecdote about it. George

Bulman, his chief test pilot, was about to fly the Tomtit to Martlesham Heath for assessment by the RAF when Sopwith climbed in and told Bulman: "Today you are my passenger."

Then, no longer the occasionally impetuous pilot of his youth, he reflected: "George, you had better take her off."

In 1930 Sopwith was elected to membership of the Royal Yacht Squadron. An outstanding helmsman, he sailed *Shamrock V* (which he had bought from the executors of the tea merchant, Sir Thomas Lipton), to win the King's Cup at Cowes in 1932. In 1935 he won it again in *Endeavour I*.

Sopwith was ambitious to repair Lipton's failure to win the America's Cup, but *Endeavour I* was foiled in 1934. His professional crew walked out after a pay dispute and he lost 4–2 to Harold Vanderbilt's *Rainbow*. *Endeavour II*, a new J-class boat, was defeated in four races by Vanderbilt's *Ranger* in 1937.

As *Endeavour* was being towed back to Newport a motor launch came alongside, and the helmsman called out: "You Sopwith? – I'm Fokker." Over a drink aboard *Endeavour* the former plane-making adversaries exchanged 1914–1918 reminiscences.

From 1935 Sopwith was chairman of the Hawker Siddeley group which he had put together with the help of the financier Philip Hill. The merger and reorganisation established Sopwith as Britain's foremost aircraft constructor.

After bringing Glosters, Armstrong Whitworth and A. V. Roe, builders of the Lancaster bomber, into the Hawker family Sopwith provided a foundation for the future British Aerospace. De Havilland was incorporated later.

Hawkers' consolidation and growth owed everything to Sopwith's good judgement and imperturbable coolness. Enigmatic and rarely on the spot (he revelled in nautical and country pursuits), Sopwith maintained control by operating through an ubiquitous managing director, his former sweeper and office boy, Spriggs. Meanwhile, Sigrist, dogsbody at the start, had become the hard man of Hawkers, troubleshooting and dealing with any unpleasantness.

As the business grew Sopwith encouraged each aircraft company to retain its individuality, enabling Camm and his associated designers to produce the fruits of their particular creative talents. His genius for knowing what was going on without interfering is best illustrated by his relationship with Camm.

If at times Sopwith recoiled at Camm's authoritarian manner in the drawing office, he bit on his pipe and remembered that unemployment obliged Camm's men to put up with him. The end product was K 5083, the prototype of the Hawker Hurricane, financed by the company as a private venture.

In October 1935, George Bulman tested her at Brooklands. The Government dallied until the following summer before issuing a first contract for 600 Hurricanes.

Sopwith's investment and belief in the interceptor monoplane, at a time when the Air Ministry still favoured biplane fighters and afforded priority to bombers, reaped its reward in the Battle of Britain. At that stage the Hurricane far outnumbered the Spitfire in RAF fighter squadrons.

As the war progressed and peace came other aircraft followed, the Typhoon, Tempest, Meteor and Hunter each being destined to become part of aviation archaeology in Sopwith's lifetime. Even the revolutionary jump-jet Harrier, which Sopwith and Camm initiated, could be said to be anticipating obsolescence while Sopwith lived.

Always a man of few words, Sopwith observed the motto on his coat-of-arms, "work without talk", to the letter and to the end. But on his 100th birthday, speaking sparingly on television from Compton Manor, his Hampshire estate near Winchester, he acknowledged the tributes of aviation's great and good as they banqueted at Brooklands in celebration.

Blind, and walking on the arm of a nurse in his garden, he lifted his head towards the sound of a replica Sopwith Pup as it circled overhead in salute. Repeating a favourite aside, he murmured: "You know, they were all done off the cuff."

Sopwith was appointed CBE in 1918 and knighted in 1953. He married first, in 1914, Beatrix Hore-Ruthven (who died in 1930), daughter of the 8th Lord Ruthven.

In 1932 he married secondly, Phyllis Brodie Gordon (who died in 1978). Their son, Tommy, also an adventurous all-rounder, survives him.

January 28 1989

EMPRESS ZITA
OF AUSTRIA

EMPRESS ZITA OF AUSTRIA, who has died aged 96, had a unique claim in the contemporary world to the phrase "living history". As the Consort of Karl, the last Hapsburg Emperor, she shared the throne of an Empire that ceased to exist seventy years ago, consisting of Austria, Hungary and what is now known as Czechoslovakia, together with parts of present-day Italy, Yugoslavia, Romania, Poland and Russia.

She shared the historic throne of the Holy Roman Empire; she was crowned Queen of Hungary in Budapest with her husband beside her wearing St Stephen's Crown as Apostolic King. In the First World War, she was at the very centre of affairs, as consort of one of the "Big Four" among the belligerent monarchs – of the other three consorts, Alexandra of Russia was murdered in 1918 and Augusta Victoria of Germany died in 1921; while Queen Mary, the only one of the three to approach the Empress Zita in longevity, died in 1953.

The distinction frequently attributed to the Empress Zita of being the last European Empress belongs, however, to Queen Elizabeth The Queen Mother, one-time Empress of India.

Princess Zita of Bourbon-Parma was born in 1892, fifth of the twelve children whom Duke Robert I of Parma had by his second wife, the Infanta Maria-Antonia of Portugal, having already had 12 children by his first wife. Her links with European history through her parentage were as remarkable as those of her own life.

Her father reigned as Duke of Parma from 1854 to 1859 when his Duchy was still an independent state, before the unification of Italy. Her maternal grandfather, Dom Miguel, usurped the Portuguese throne in 1828, causing the conflict known as the Miguelite War or "the War of the Brothers" – in which he had the sympathy of the British Prime Minister, the Duke of Wellington, who had seen him out with the Buckhounds, when staying with George IV at Windsor, taking "his fences like anyone else".

Princess Zita's aunt, Doña Maria das Neves, was married to one of the Carlist pretenders to the Spanish throne and fought in the Second Carlist War. Her eldest half-sister, Princess Maria Luisa, was the first wife of "Foxy Ferdy" of Bulgaria.

The other consort of a reigning sovereign among her siblings belongs to much more recent history: her younger brother Prince Félix, who married the Grand Duchess Charlotte of Luxembourg.

Princess Zita had a happy childhood and girlhood at her father's castle in Austria and his villa in Italy; the family moved from one to the other in a special train with 15 or 16 coaches to hold the children, the servants, the horses and the baggage, not to mention the scholarly Duke Robert's books. She grew up to be a princess of exceptional beauty and intelligence; it came as no surprise when, in 1911, at the age of 19, she married Europe's greatest Catholic royal *parti*, the 24-year-old Archduke Karl, second in line of succession to the throne of his great-uncle, the Emperor Franz Joseph.

It was a love match; in falling in love with an

eligible princess, Karl differed from most Hapsburg Archdukes of the previous generation. They had either made loveless dynastic marriages, as his father the Archduke Otto and his cousin the ill-fated Crown Prince Rudolf (of Mayerling notoriety) had done, or else, like his uncle the Archduke Franz Ferdinand, found happiness in *mésalliances*.

And unlike the Emperor Franz Joseph's marriage to the Empress Elisabeth, which turned out unhappy even though he had married her for love and never ceased to love her, the marriage of Karl and Zita was an enduring success, blessed with five sons and three daughters. In this, as in other respects, the eventual heir to the throne was eminently satisfactory; he had been diligent in his studies, he was conscientious in his duties; he was a young man of exceptionally sweet nature though he knew his own mind; he inspired affection in everyone he met.

For the first three years of their marriage, the young Archduke and Archduchess lived mostly away from the limelight while he soldiered. Though it was almost certain that Karl would one day be Emperor (the son of Franz Ferdinand, the immediate heir, being excluded from the succession on account of his morganatic marriage) that day seemed a long way off. Franz Ferdinand was in the prime of life.

But in 1914 Franz Ferdinand and his morganatic wife fell victims to the bullets of Sarajevo, making Karl the immediate heir to the throne. It was to Karl and to the Archduchess Zita that Franz Joseph, after hearing the news, made his famous remark: "I am spared nothing."

On that same occasion, the Emperor said to Karl: "At least I can rely on you." And indeed, for the two years that remained of his reign, he worked far closer with his great-nephew than he had ever done with his nephew; at his request the couple and their children moved into Schönbrunn.

Karl's initiation into affairs of state was interrupted by frequent visits to the front; he was, after all, a soldier and the Empire was fighting a war. However much that war may be blamed on Austria-Hungary, the young Archduke was in no way responsible for its making; he loathed the war and on succeeding as Emperor in November 1916 lost no time in trying to bring it to an end.

The Emperor Karl's peace attempt of 1917, in which the Empress Zita's brother, Prince Sixte of Bourbon-Parma, acted as intermediary, was the only serious effort to end the war made by the leader of any of the belligerent powers. It failed, but only just; he had the enthusiastic support of the British Prime Minister, Lloyd George.

Had it succeeded, millions of lives would have been saved and the subsequent history of Europe would have been very much happier. At the same time as he worked for peace, the Emperor Karl set about reconstructing his heterogeneous Empire on federal lines so that he came to be known both as the "Peace Emperor" and the "Emperor of the People".

In these the two objects which, as Emperor, he put before all others, Karl had the full support of the Empress, with whom he constantly discussed them. Happily married to a highly intelligent wife, who was dedicated to her husband and his subjects, it was natural that he should have initiated her into the secrets of state and sometimes taken her advice. There were those who accused the Empress of influencing her husband, but as he and she were so much at one in their views her influence did no more than strengthen his own convictions.

Because of the lack of space in the house which the Emperor occupied when he was at Army Headquarters, the Empress was sometimes present in the room when he held audiences; but she always avoided joining in. In April 1918, however, while the Emperor was laid up with a minor heart attack, she had a confrontation with Count Ottokar Czernin, the brilliant but unreliable Foreign Minister, who had caused a crisis by allowing the Emperor's secret peace overtures of the previous year to be leaked out.

This drew Austria-Hungary closer to Germany, which had a fatal effect on the attitude of the Entente powers; having intended to preserve the Hapsburg Empire, they now wished to see it dismembered. So with the defeat of the Austrian forces in the autumn of 1918, Karl's Empire collapsed around him.

For a brief while, as the outlying states of the Empire fell away in an orgy of self-determination, it seemed that Karl might at least have kept the throne of Austria; but the fall of the German monarchies brought down the monarchy in Austria as well. The Emperor, who refused to abdicate, which he felt would be to renounce a responsibility given to him by God, agreed to withdraw from all affairs of state, while remaining in Austria.

A few months later, when Austria was on the verge of a Communist takeover, and there was a real danger that the Emperor and Empress and their children might suffer a fate similar to that of the Tsar and his family, they were prevailed upon to go into exile in Switzerland. In 1920, after the collapse of a short-lived Communist regime, Hungary was declared a monarchy once again, under the Regency of Admiral Horthy.

Horthy had told the Emperor that he would not rest until he had restored him to his throne in Budapest and Vienna; but having become Regent of Karl's Hungarian kingdom, he showed himself to be in no hurry to bring Karl back as King. So in 1921 Karl made two attempts to regain his Hungarian throne, by going to Hungary himself; but each time he was foiled by Horthy, who on the second occasion used force against him and the Empress.

For the second attempt, the Emperor and Empress flew from Switzerland to Hungary in a rickety monoplane. "I've never liked flying," the Empress remarked more than 60 years later, having travelled to Rome by jet.

As a result of Karl's second restoration bid, which was very nearly successful, he and his family were banished to Madeira. Here, in a damp and primitive villa which was the best they could afford, the Emperor died of pneumonia early the following year aged 34.

Two months later, the Empress gave birth to their youngest child, the Archduchess Elisabeth. She and her children were then living in Spain, where they had been offered hospitality by King Alfonso XIII. Later, the Empress and her family settled in Belgium; she moved to the United States during the Second World War and then, after a period in Mexico, returned to Switzerland.

She spent her long widowhood in retirement, devoting herself to her family and to the memory of her husband, who is so widely acknowledged to have been a saint that the cause for his canonisation has been opened. She travelled frequently; towards the end of her life she paid her first visit to Austria since the fall of the monarchy and was given a tumultuous reception.

She also paid two visits to Rome, being on cordial terms with Pope John Paul II, whose father had not only been a subject of the Emperor's but had been commissioned by him in the Kaiserlich und Königlich Army. Those fortunate enough to be received by the Empress in her extreme old age found someone to whom the adjective "old" could hardly be applied.

She is survived by all her children, except for her eldest daughter, Archduchess Adelheid, who died in 1971. Her eldest son, the Archduke Otto, who prefers to be known as Dr Otto von Hapsburg, is a distinguished member of the European Parliament and author of many books on political science, history and world affairs.

March 15 1989

JACK DASH

JACK DASH, the colourful former unofficial leader of London's dockers who has died aged 82, made a familiar progression in the national consciousness from dangerous firebrand to treasured old "character".

The legendary Communist agitator, whose cry of "All out!" would plunge the docks into crippling inactivity, ended up as an amiable London tourist guide, dabbling in painting and poetry, giving talks to the boys at Eton and campaigning for his fellow old-age pensioners. But behind the folksy *persona* of the mellowed Dash was a man who had made a major contribution to the rapid decline of the Port of London after the Second World War. In less than a quarter of a century he and his fellow Communists appeared to destroy a whole industry through systematic disruption along textbook lines.

Thanks to the loquacious Dash – a shrewd operator who knew how to dominate a committee and to sway a crowd with his rhetoric – the "docker-on-strike" became a music-hall joke. Demarcation disputes seemed to stretch out like cascading dominoes.

Dash – nicknamed "the Red Napoleon" or, on account of his habit of working stripped to the waist, "Nature Boy" – first came to public notice in 1949 during a 25-day stoppage at the docks involving some 16,000 strikers. It was an offshoot of the Canadian seamen's strike which was regarded, and not only by those obsessed with "reds-under-the-bed", as a worldwide conspiracy at the height of the Cold War. Eventually, when 96 ships were idle in the Port of London, including 27 with food cargoes, the Attlee administration sent in the troops.

Dash and the other agitators defied the Government, the National Dock Labour Board and officers of the Transport and General Workers' Union. Three were expelled from the union, and Dash and four others were debarred from holding union office for two years.

When the strike finally collapsed, its committee was reconstituted, and eventually became the unofficial London Port Workers' Liaison Committee, with Dash in the chair. It was better known in Poplar and Canning Town as "Jack Dash and his Merry Men".

Having won the confidence of 8,000 dockers he claimed to represent, Dash became the spearhead of unofficial strike action in the London docks. Figures of working days lost through strikes in the Port of London illustrate the ravages: 1949, 240,000; 1955, 192,000; 1957, 81,000; 1958, 339,000; 1967, 252,000 and 1970 (the year he retired), 221,000.

Striking and Dash were to become synonymous: time after time dockers would stream out of the gates in their thousands to a meeting in some local park without always knowing why. Importers, sick of seeing their ships regularly queuing for handling, abandoned London in numbers which only the most short-sighted union member could ignore.

When it was suggested that his members might follow the example of their Continental counterparts and organise a night shift to accelerate turn-round, Dash is supposed to have replied: "The British docker is not a nocturnal animal."

In the 1960s Dash vigorously resisted the plans of the Devlin committee aimed at improving efficiency and ending restrictive practices; Frank Cousins, the general secretary of the Transport and General Workers' Union, appeared unwilling to intervene. Dash was labelled a wrecker by the committee. He hotly denied the allegations, saying his task in life was to make life better for dockers. That came first, he claimed. His membership and allegiance to the Communists came second.

A true Cockney, Jack Dash was born in the East End on April 23 1907. After the death of his mother when he was a boy, the family broke up and he was sent to a Poor Law School.

He would recall that he became politically conscious

during the General Strike of 1926 and gained his education from books such as Jack London's *The Iron Heel* and Robert Tressell's *The Ragged-Trousered Philanthropists*. He soon switched his allegiance from the Labour party to the Stepney branch of the Communist party.

During a stint as a hod carrier in the building trade he became active in trade unionism and while out of work, as he frequently was in the 1930s, he was an enthusiastic participant in the National Unemployed Workers' Movement. On one occasion he and his colleagues invaded the Ritz Hotel (where Barbara Cartland was among those in the Palm Court); on another he donned funerary garb to process with a symbolic coffin towards St Paul's.

During the Second World War Dash served with the Fire Brigade and afterwards he managed to get taken on in the Royal Docks. In later life he would reminisce about the gruelling conditions: "We casual workers, dockers and stevedores – 'Beef', they called us – would hitch lifts on lorries from one dock to another and hang around for three or four hours hoping for work. In the Royal Docks you'd have 600 to 800 men 'on the stones'. They'd be fighting and kicking to be picked, like seagulls battling over scraps. Accidents were frequent. On average, dockers needed medical attention four times a year." Once Dash fell 50 feet from the top of a ship to the bottom, but survived.

"When we did get work," he said, "it was ten hours a day, seven days a week. There were often times when everything pawnable was pawned. Food got very sparse and the local pigeons often ended up feeding people via the saucepan. Families were big and mothers always ate last. My wife's meals were half the size of the ones she gave the rest of us."

He described the constant industrial battles as his "university education", saying: "I studied an 'ology' all right – dockology." In retirement Dash was much in demand as a lecturer and he published an autobiography, *Good Morning Brothers* (1972), as well as various poems. He also trained as a guide with the London Tourist Board.

A keen student of architecture and history, he brought an individual approach to his conducted tours of St Paul's Cathedral: "Even in those days," he would say, "they had cuts in wages to speed up building. They cut Christopher Wren's salary by half."

Wren's celebrated epitaph, *Si monumentum requiris, circumspice* ("If you would see his monument, look around"), could equally have been applied to Dash if it had been carved amid the ruins of Docklands during the 1970s. After his retirement the power of the liaison committee waned; as containerisation increased, privately owned ports like Felixstowe flourished and ships moved away from the once great Port of London.

Today only Tilbury and some wharfage survives; where once many thousands of dockers teemed, loading and unloading scores of ships, is now the mushrooming Isle of Dogs and other development areas.

This recent regeneration left Dash unimpressed: "Apart from the improvement in housing for some of the people who've always lived there, the only benefits locals are going to get out of it are a few temporary gardeners' jobs on the landscaping schemes."

Latterly Jack Dash had passed into the historical

mythology of the Left, though his death occurred at a time when dock labour troubles were once again in the news.

June 9 1989

LAWRENCE ISHERWOOD

LAWRENCE ISHERWOOD, the artist who has died aged 72, was driven by his muse to abandon a career as a cobbler. To begin with he painted the women of his native Wigan but he later found a more lucrative market with imaginary nude studies of such public figures as Barbara Castle, Field Marshal Viscount Montgomery of Alamein and Mary Whitehouse.

"I would rather paint the women of Wigan than any film star," he said early in his career, "particularly the old women in their shawls. Old faces have more character and colour." His work of that time showed the characters, mills and narrow streets of the town, fitfully illuminated by the eerie light of sulphur fumes.

There were hints of Isherwood's future direction in 1962, when he exhibited a portrait of Princess Margaret with the infant Viscount Linley in her arms, done entirely in blue. The other pictures in the show were painted over a series "of Lady Chatterley in the altogether", abandoned, he explained, because "no one seemed to appreciate them. They were pretty near the bone, you see."

Isherwood's first major celebrity nude was of the singer Dusty Springfield (1966), which infuriated her but was sold to a Hampshire pig farmer for 75 guineas.

Inspired by his frequent difficulties with traffic wardens, he went on to paint a nude of Mrs Castle, who was then Minister of Transport, with her body decorated by such signs as "NO ENTRY", "NO WAITING" and "NO THROUGH ROAD".

A later portrait of Mrs Whitehouse showed her with five breasts; it was bought by Sir Hugh Carleton Greene, a former Director-General of the BBC, which elicited the response from its subject: "I am rather surprised that Sir Hugh wished to have a full-frontal nude of me on his wall: I think it is unreasonable." Subsequent subjects for this imaginative approach included Field Marshal Montgomery naked save for his medals, and George Best, the footballer.

Isherwood himself was plump and bespectacled, with a blond beard and moustache.

The son of a cobbler, James Lawrence Isherwood was born at Wigan on April 7 1917 and studied art at Wigan Technical College from 1934 to 1953. To make ends meet he followed his father's trade.

In 1956 he exhibited at Wigan, to a mixed reception from the locals. Several exhibits were damaged; the titles under portraits of a Nigerian nurse and a coalminer were switched; and a miniature sculpture in wire and plaster, entitled *Wigan's Wire Women*, was entirely crushed. "Must have been somebody who didn't like modern art," Isherwood said.

His output was prolific and eventually he was able to give up cobbling, though his finances remained precarious. He often paid hotel and garage bills with his work and once offered a watercolour of Wigan jetty in payment of a court fine for speeding, though the magistrate declined the barter. In the early 1960s he was asking an average price of eight guineas for his works, though he admitted: "If anyone offers me four I snatch their hand off – it's a couple of beers and bed and breakfast, isn't it?"

Isherwood would paint until he had enough pictures to fill a van and would then set off on a sales tour with his mother, Lily, who frequently sat for him. He had innumerable one-man exhibitions, often at unusual sites – beneath Boadicea's statue at Westminister, for example, or in a lay-by on the East Lancashire Road. He regularly exhibited at Oxford and Cambridge, and when the Prince of Wales was an undergraduate at Trinity he bought a seascape by Isherwood.

The standard critical response to his work was epitomised by the opinion of Lieutenant-Colonel A. D. Wintle (celebrated for debagging his solicitor), who championed the artist at an exhibition in a Trafalgar Square coffee house in 1959. "What I like about Isherwood's paintings," announced the monocled colonel, "is that there is no doubt about which way they hang."

In the late 1970s Isherwood travelled extensively through Europe and established a permanent exhibition of his work at Torremolinos; he also showed in Malta, where in 1976 he painted both the Prime Minister and Miss Malta.

In 1979 he opened the Isherwood Suite at a hotel in Southport and the next year established the Isherwood Gallery in Wigan, which burned down in 1983.

June 14 1989

LARRY PARNES

LARRY PARNES, who has died aged 59, emerged in the late 1950s as the pre-eminent manager and impresario of British rock and roll.

A reluctant rag-trade retailer, beguiled by Soho nightlife, Parnes stumbled into his gold-mine in 1956, when the publicist John Kennedy approached him to finance the promotion of an unknown coffee-bar skiffler called Thomas Hicks. Renamed Tommy Steele, Hicks was soon hailed as England's answer to Elvis Presley; he became an overnight "teenbeat" sensation and the role model for a string of successors, celebrated as "Larry Parnes's Stable of Stars".

Though Steele devised his own stage name, Parnes insisted on renaming such subsequent discoveries as Marty Wilde (Reg Smith), Billy Fury (Ron Wycherly), Johnny Gentle (John Askew), Dicky Pride (Richard Knellar), Vince Eager (Roy Taylor) and Georgie Fame (Clive Powell). The Cockney guitarist Joe Brown, however, refused to become Almer Twitch.

An all-powerful figure in the burgeoning teenage music industry, Parnes's great strength was his ability to exploit star potential. A Parnes management contract practically guaranteed a recording deal, TV and radio exposure and a place in his touring shows, in which half a dozen acts would share the billing.

He had no ear for music and relied on record company arrangers to guide his artists. They often did so ineptly. But pop music was then seen merely as a stepping stone to pantomime, theatre and film: the common goal was to emulate Tommy Steele, and become an all-round entertainer.

There was an element of *Minder*'s Arthur Daley in Parnes's business approach, and his financial acuity earned him the nickname "Parnes, Shillings and Pence". In 1959, for example, he arranged a press conference for Vince Eager's 19th birthday, for which he gave him a new Triumph Herald.

"It's yours, Vince, because you've been a good boy and always been punctual for rehearsals." Eager later complained: "After everyone left, the man who had delivered the car drove it back to his showroom. Then Larry told me the whole thing was a stunt." Parnes later said of his protégé: "The boy's ingratitude appals me."

In the mid-1960s tastes in pop music underwent a dramatic shift. Parnes's supremacy was ended by the Beatles, whose potential he had badly underestimated some years earlier when he grudgingly hired them to make their first foray beyond Liverpool, backing Johnny Gentle on a lacklustre tour of the Scottish hinterlands.

Laurence Maurice Parnes was born at Willesden, London, in 1930. One of his uncles was a pre-war music-hall star called Len Young the Singing Fool.

Parnes left school at 16 and began working in shops, "picking up pins with a magnet". By the age of 18 he was running his own dress shop in Romford, with a half share of a club in Romilly Street and a stake in a touring play called *The House of Shame*.

After a decade as the Svengali of pop, Parnes was eclipsed by the new Merseyside groups and broke up with Steele, who had been his principal earner. In 1967 he announced that he had "outgrown" pop and would be devoting himself to the theatre.

The next year he put on *Fortune and Men's Eyes*, a play about homosexuality in a Canadian prison. After losing £5,000 on the venture he said: "I'm going back to staging family entertainment."

In 1972 he bought a 12-year lease of the Cambridge Theatre, where he concentrated on musicals. Alongside the management of John Currie, the ice skater, this occupied him until 1981, when he retired from show business after a brain haemorrhage.

Parnes is said to have renamed some of his stars for their sexual potential, but though he undoubtedly adored the company of young men he was circumspect about mixing business with pleasure. The greatest loves of his life were two Alsatian dogs, Prince and Duke, whose cremated remains were prominently displayed in his South Kensington penthouse.

August 7 1989

ANN GEORGE

ANN GEORGE, the actress who has died aged 86, earned a huge following for her distinctly idiosyncratic performance as Amy Turtle, the obnoxious factotum in the long-running ITV series, *Crossroads*.

First seen as a shop assistant in the emporium run by the Midlands motel owner Meg Richardson's sister, Kitty Jarvis, in the mid-1960s, Amy Turtle was subsequently moved to the motel itself as a charlady. The bustling, bespectacled beldam of diminutive stature with an impenetrable "Brummie" accent soon developed into the busybody that viewers loved to hate.

For connoisseurs of *Crossroads*, Miss George's some-what erratic grasp of the script lent the programme a peculiar charm. It was thought that Julie Walters's wickedly funny characterisation of Mrs Overall in *Acorn Antiques*, the spoof "soap" on Victoria Wood's television programme, may have owed something to the Turtle *persona*.

In any event, Amy Turtle became one of *Crossroads'* legendary characters, indeed virtually its "Second Lady" after Meg Richardson (played by Noele Gordon). The part was suitably built up and Amy found herself in some singular situations.

She was, for example, accused of shoplifting, and imprisoned. And in one episode she was even accused of being the notorious Russian spy "Amelia Turtlovski".

But in February 1975, Miss George was abruptly dropped from the show ("I heard the awful news from the wardrobe mistress," she recalled. "She just told me to clear out my things as I wouldn't be coming back"). The storyline intimated that Amy Turtle had gone to visit her nephew in Texas. Nothing more was heard of her, however, and some viewers organised a "Bring Back Amy" campaign.

Then, in 1987, Miss George was unexpectedly invited to rejoin the cast of *Crossroads* and Amy Turtle made the occasional appearance before the programme was finally taken off the air in 1988.

Miss George was born Ann Snape at Erdington, Birmingham, in 1903 and trained as an actress and singer. She appeared in operettas and musicals and at one stage was a member of the D'Oyly Carte Company.

On Amy Turtle's return to the *Crossroads* set after an absence of nearly a dozen years the cast and crew burst into applause, reducing the much-loved actress to tears. In retirement Miss George carried on entertaining fellow pensioners at a club near her Birmingham home.

Her first husband died in 1962. She is survived by her second husband, Gordon Buckingham, and by a son of the first marriage.

September 12 1989

BHAGWAN SHREE RAJNEESH

BHAGWAN SHREE RAJNEESH, who has died aged 58 at his ashram in Poona, India – where he had lived since being deported from America – was the notorious "guru" who drew thousands of followers from all over the world by preaching a bizarre blend of Eastern religion, pop psychology and free love.

The Bhagwan, known as Osho Rajneesh in recent years, had a dedicated following in his heyday. His enigmatic *aperçus*, encouraging the guilt-free enjoyment of wealth and sexual licence, were apparently taken as gospel by more than half a million "Orange people", many of them prosperous Europeans – including a not insignificant group of expensively educated Britons.

The journalist Bernard Levin went so far as to describe the Bhagwan as the "conduit along which the vital force of the universe flows". In *The Times* he described the Bhagwan's *sannyasin*, or followers, as "in general an exceptionally fine crop, bearing witness to a tree of a choice, rare nature".

Levin observed that "The first quality a visitor to
Rajneesh's ashram notices – and he never ceases to notice
it – is the ease and comfort with which they wear their
faith . . . The joy with which they are clearly filled is, as
anyone who listens to Rajneesh must deduce it would
be, directed outwards as well as in; I cannot put it better
than in saying that they constantly extend, to each other
and to strangers, the hands of love, though without the
ego-filled demands of love as most of the world knows
it. They have shed their chains, and they demonstrated
their freedom easily and unobtrusively, though the
results at first can be startling . . ."

Among the events organised by the Bhagwan's
British followers was "an explosion of energy and consciousness" at the Napoleon Room of the Café Royal in
Regent Street. But after the Bhagwan had abruptly
decamped from his original commune in Poona in
mysterious circumstances in 1981 – there was talk of
smuggling, drug-trafficking and prostitution, not to
mention tax problems – it seemed increasingly clear that
"the Bagwash" was a charlatan.

The saying was coined: "Jesus saves, Bhagwan
spends". Certainly he managed to accumulate such items
as a Lear jet, 35 jewel-encrusted watches and 93 Rolls-
Royces.

He transplanted his operation to "Rajneeshpuram" in
Oregon where, together with several thousand of his red-
robed followers, he set about constructing a self-sufficient
utopia. The Bhagwan would drive around the site in one
of his Rolls-Royces past lines of chanting, clapping fans,
but the allegedly paradisiacal atmosphere was somewhat
offset by his escort of helicopter and armed guards;

indeed the supposedly loving community was riddled with paranoia and internecine feuds.

The advent of Aids also rather put the dampener on the free love; the Bhagwan ordered his subjects to use rubber gloves and condoms and to wash with pure alcohol before embarking on sexual activity.

The crash came in 1985 when several of the movement's leaders were jailed. The Bhagwan's principal aide, Ma Anand Sheela, left the commune with the parting shot: "To hell with Bhagwan."

The guru alleged that she had bugged his quarters, amassed millions of dollars at the commune and turned the valley into a concentration camp. Soon afterwards the Bhagwan himself was expelled from America and barred from more than 20 other countries – including Britain – as an "undesirable alien" before returning to Poona.

It was there, in 1974, that the Bhagwan Shree Rajneesh had first established his sect. It soon became controversial as a sex cult; an advertisement for the sect appeared in *Time* magazine under the headline "SEX" which urged: "Never repress it! Search all the nooks and corners of your sexuality."

In Poona followers paid to join sexual encounter lessons called *"tantras"* in which participants were encouraged to behave with the utmost licentiousness. The Bhagwan's western followers defied India's strict moral codes as they kissed and fondled each other publicly while dressed in the garb of Hindu holy men.

One Poona editor complained that their behaviour was analogous to a group of foreigners dressing up as monks and nuns and engaging in sexual activity on American streets.

The Bhagwan said celibacy was a crime against nature and that a high sex drive improved a man's creativity. "It is natural for sexual energy to need expression," he said. "You cannot find in the whole history of mankind a single impotent man becoming a great painter or musician or dancer or scientist or poet."

He said it was fortunate that man's ancestors did not listen to "the idiots who preached against sex. Had they done so, none of us would have been here."

On moving to America, the Bhagwan elected to take an oath of silence and spent much of his time watching children's programmes on television. Although by 1985 seven of the Bhagwan's followers were in jail, and fifteen more were on the run, the Bhagwan pleaded divine ignorance of these matters, and was found guilty only of illegal immigration.

Under a plea agreement he received a suspended ten-year sentence, paid a $400,000 fine, and agreed not to return to America for five years without the written permission of the US Attorney-General.

In 1986 the Bhagwan's chief henchwoman, Ma Anand Sheela, was charged with numerous offences including poisoning 750 patrons of local restaurants; illegal wire-tapping; fire-bombing Government buildings; and attempting to murder prominent members of the community, ranging from the district attorney to the Bhagwan's dentist.

Back in India, where he dropped the Hindu honorific of Bhagwan (meaning "Lord God"), Rajneesh continued to deliver religious discourses at his Poona commune and to outrage many Indians with his support for free sex.

In his most recent public statement last November, he told Indian voters that the country did not need political parties and they should refuse to vote. The Bhagwan had a love–hate relationship with India and contempt for its bureaucracy.

January 20 1990

LORD DARESBURY

THE 2ND LORD DARESBURY, who has died aged 87, was a celebrated rider to hounds, earning widespread affection and respect as Master of both the Belvoir and the Co. Limerick.

An immaculate figure in top hat and swallow-tailcoat, "Toby" Daresbury's appearance suggested a Corinthian of the 19th century. He lost two wives in the hunting field, and survived many falls in an adventurous career which gave rise to a legion of anecdotes.

There was the time he cured a "thruster" in a hard-riding Field with the injunction: "Turn round and jump it again!" And in the 1930s Mr Greenall (as he then was) became involved in a celebrated argument with the Master of a neighbouring hunt, Captain Filmer-Sankey.

As related by a London evening paper of the time, "something was said which caused Greenall to challenge Filmer-Sankey to a 'knuckle' fight in the good old English style". Early one morning the two met by appointment beside a fox covert called Blackberry Hill, situated on the border of the two hunting counties. "Filmer-Sankey wore a low-neck jersey, flannel trousers and tennis shoes," noted the diarist. "But Greenall contemptuously retained his collar and tie. They set to it with a will. Weight and experience were in Greenall's

91

favour, and he looked to be winning, when Filmer-Sankey landed a punch between 'wind and water' straight in the *Derby Kelly*. Though Mr Greenall's heart was willing, previous digestive trouble had made his stomach weak. The fight was ended."

A member of the Cheshire brewing family, Edward Greenall was born on October 12 1902, the younger son of Sir Gilbert Greenall, 2nd Bt, Master of the Belvoir and director of the Royal Show, who was created Baron Daresbury in 1927.

Young Toby was educated at Eton and commissioned into the Life Guards, with whom he served during the Second World War. He succeeded to the peerage in 1938 on the death of his father; his elder brother had been killed in a motoring accident.

Daresbury was Joint Master of the Belvoir from 1934 until 1947 when he proceeded to transform the Co. Limerick, where the sport and the fun became fast and furious. A practical man, Daresbury installed an asphalt floor when he moved from Clonshire House to Altavilla so that it could be swilled down.

Daresbury also took a close interest in the family brewery Greenall Whitley and in freemasonry. He was appointed a JP for Cheshire in 1945.

He married first, in 1925, Madeline Sheriffe, who died of injuries sustained when out with the Quorn the next year; and secondly, in 1927, Josephine, youngest daughter of Brigadier-General Sir Joseph Laycock, who died in 1958.

He married thirdly, in 1966, Lady Helena ("Boodley"), formerly wife of Major "Chatty" Hilton-Green and fourth daughter of the 7th Earl Fitzwilliam.

Lady Daresbury was killed out cub-hunting in 1970.

Lord Daresbury is survived by a son of the second marriage, Edward Gilbert Greenall, born 1928, who succeeds to the peerage. The eldest grandson, Peter Greenall, is a former champion amateur rider under National Hunt rules.

Captain Ronnie Wallace writes: Toby Daresbury was one of the famous foxhunters of the 20th century. He liked to give an impression of an unorthodox approach which concealed deep knowledge and ability.

Toby's early influences were his parents – his father ensured all that was best for the Duke of Rutland's hounds and staff, and his mother was a devoted fox preserver – and then a rugged character from Cumberland, "Doggie" Robinson, who persuaded him of the significance of earths and terriers.

The wonderful combination of a Master of Hounds and his Huntsman was seen at its best with Toby and George Tongue, DCM, at the Belvoir. Toby was running the brewery at Warrington with skill but also organised the hunting and nightlife on the high Leicestershire side of the country.

Toby's horsemanship was in a class of its own, mounted on horses which he schooled himself – people still talk with awe of two thoroughbreds, Big Exeter and Little Exeter. Enthusiasts for hunter judging also recall his performance at one Royal Show when the scheduled judge was taken ill and Toby was pressed into service. He rode all those strong, ring-crafty horses in his Homburg hat and a pair of chaps over his suit without ever touching their mouths.

He paid much attention to the fox coverts in his country with the assistance of the family 'keeper from

Cheshire. One spring they were contemplating a wood-land together at Daresbury, with little sign of pheasants. "They're nesting," said Toby. "Aye," was the reply, "in the fox's stomach."

When war came, and Toby was called to the colours, he somehow managed to keep a representative pack. In the last year of the war George broke his leg and Toby carried the horn.

Inspired by this and his knowledge of Co. Limerick from pre-war days, he transferred his allegiance to that pack. At a time of struggle to restore English hunting to its rightful place, his departure was a major loss; but he was able to leave the Belvoir Hounds in good hands and established a regime at Clonshire which can never be forgotten.

He persuaded Boodley Hilton-Green, a legendary figure in her own right, to come over "for the season" – in fact 23 of them until her death – to organise the stables. Then there was Merry Atkinson, of point-to-pointing fame and also bred in a medical family, to look after the whelping bitches. This suited Toby, who was a born chemist.

The atmosphere, with an element of hubbub, was unique. Priceless pictures adorned the walls, delicious food emanated from a none-too-sanitary kitchen, retain-ers dashed in all directions, grooms, too, and top-class horses emerged from every cubby-hole. Toby had a delightful kennel huntsman, Paddy Reagan, but worked in the kennel and walked hounds himself, with long hours of exercise in the summer months.

I remember one breakfast the second morning after a Hunt Ball, when Boodley had failed to negotiate the bridge over a big river when coming home, and Toby, peering over his spectacles, said: "Darling, I haven't seen the Mercedes the last two days."

"To tell you the honest truth, it's in the Maigue."

"Indeed," commented Toby.

No great lover of white hounds and certainly not black ones, he was faithful to the strains from Belvoir and Quorn and the surplus puppies from those establishments were flown over in incubator boxes to establish the Limerick pack.

What fun they had in that wild and varied hunting country, with many like-minded friends settling out there too, and ever a welcome for the stream of guests. Boodley seemed to know of every young horse in Ireland; she was tireless in suiting them to her friends.

Toby established a marvellous rockery outside the sitting-room window by his own hand and crowbar, and some slightly reluctant help from his assistant "Simo", another character. In that category too we must remember Steer, his batman, and Dan the butler.

Sadly, even the best does not last for ever, and Boodley's death in 1970 was a mortal blow. Toby carried on most gallantly, gradually handing over the kennels when Hugh Robards came as Huntsman.

In 1977 Toby left the hounds in the capable hands of his great friends Lord Harrington and Lady Melissa Brooke, though he continued to ride the country in a style of his own, accompanied by the faithful Gerry, until his last illness.

We do not know whether he fulfilled his promise to ask at the Pearly Gates, "Why wind?" but foxhunters and countrymen must be grateful for all Toby Daresbury did to promote the true place of hunting in rural affairs, for great kindnesses and much laughter.

February 19 1990

VINCENT "BIG VINNIE" TERESA

VINCENT "BIG VINNIE" TERESA, the former *capo* in the New England Mafia who has died at Seattle aged 61, spent the last two decades of his life in hiding under the alias of Charles Cantino, having become an FBI informant in return for a reduced prison sentence.

When he was convicted for handling stolen securities in 1969 "Big Vinnie" agreed to be a federal witness against his former associates. In exchange for his testimony – which resulted in the indictment or conviction of more than 50 mobsters, including Meyer Lansky, one of their principal financiers – Teresa's prison sentence was reduced from 20 to five years.

On his release he embarked on a new career under the name Charles Cantino and wrote a best-selling book about his experiences – *My Life in the Mafia*. He became the Mafia's most wanted man – £200,000 was offered to anyone who could find and kill him, and repeated attempts were made on his life.

And yet "Big Vinnie", a vast bulk of a man who weighed 23 stone, had been one of the Mafia's most formidable criminals; he once admitted to having kept a man-eating piranha in a fishbowl to convince his Boston gambling customers that he ran a tough outfit.

His violation of the code of *omertà* – according to which "men of respect" would never reveal their secrets, and to which he had adhered since childhood – was apparently the result of his having been betrayed within the organisation. Teresa claimed that mobsters had stolen some £1,500,000 from him and threatened his children.

But his new identity did not afford him peace for long. In 1977, within two days of his arrival in Australia to give evidence to a citizens' committee supposedly set up to campaign against the legalisation of casinos, he found himself under a deportation order.

Mr Wran, the Labour premier of New South Wales at the time, denounced the citizens' committee as a sham and revealed that Teresa had received a visa under the name of "Santana". Teresa condemned the Australian authorities for "blowing his cover", claiming that 500 assassins would be after his blood.

Two years later he was named by the Australian authorities as head of a ring which was illegally exporting such birds as the galah from Australia to America, where they were sold for as much as £1,500 apiece.

Vincent Teresa was born in 1928, the grandson of a Mafia don who had emigrated from Sicily to America in 1895. Young Vincent was a compulsive thief from his earliest years and spent much of his childhood in the company of his uncle, Dominic "Sandy Mac" Teresa, who was a bodyguard and enforcer to Joseph Lombardo, another Mafia don.

"Big Vinnie" soon worked his way up to the top of the crime empire of Raymond Patriarca (Lombardo's successor), and by 1965 he had branched out of his New England territory to run gambling "junkets" to casinos all over the world – to Las Vegas, London, Antigua and

Haiti (where he presented President "Papa Doc" Duvalier with a Cadillac) – on which the games were fixed by such "mechanics" as "Yonkers" Joe Salistino, a cardsharper of genius. Teresa boasted that he had cheated "suckers" out of millions of dollars.

After he turned FBI informant in the early 1970s Teresa lived in hiding under heavy guard: in 1977 he said that he and his family had moved eight times in half as many years because he feared that he would "one day wake up and find my head in one room and my legs in the other".

In 1978 he published his second book about his experiences in the Mafia, *The Wiseguys*.

March 11 1990

"KIM" DE LA TASTE TICKELL

"KIM" DE LA TASTE TICKELL, the outrageously flamboyant landlord of the Tickell Arms at Whittlesford, near Cambridge, who has died aged 73, was a legendary figure in East Anglia.

Joseph Hollick de la Taste Tickell was born in 1917 and educated at Marlborough. He dabbled with a variety of professions, as well as amateur theatricals, and then settled down to run the Tickell Arms, near the family home of Whittlesford Manor.

Clad in 18th-century knee breeches and silver-buckled shoes and styling himself squire of the village, he presided over a hostelry which became a cult among

98

the *jeunesse dorée* and fashionable dons of Cambridge University.

To his regulars Tickell was Cambridge's answer to John Fothergill, whose Spread Eagle at Thame was once a magnet to Oxford undergraduates; to others he seemed more like the Basil Fawlty of the Fens. "I'm not having south London garage proprietors and their tarts in here!" he would screech at startled patrons, *"Out, out, out!"*

Tickell had many categories of "insufferables" – especially left-wingers, blacks and "modern" women. In 1962 he barred from his pub anyone wearing a CND badge. "They stand for everything I detest," he explained. "They are disloyal to the Crown, despise law and order and cause a great deal of trouble . . . I won't have Communists in the place either."

The same year he became engaged in controversy over a local Christmas decorations factory. He felt that its female workers lowered the tone of the village – "factories attract the wrong sort of girl!" – and refused to serve them.

When he accused them of "shameful language and disgraceful behaviour" a group of them confronted him, claiming that their language was as nothing to that heard outside the Tickell Arms at closing time. "Have you ever heard me use bad language?" asked Tickell.

When the girls all chorused "Yes!" he said: "I only use good old English words like damn, blast and bloody. You never hear me using four-letter Lady Chatterley words." A woman among them called out "I've heard you say 'Get off my *fucking* grass!'" and the cry went up "Debag him!"

In 1970 Tickell found himself charged with malicious wounding and possession of an offensive weapon. He had ordered a barefoot young American woman to put on her shoes, and later was alleged to have slashed at a man in her party with a carving knife.

He then called for the various medieval weapons that decorated his walls – "Give me my mace and my halberd!" – and ran from the inn shouting "I will take on any bugger who disapproves of the way I run my house!"

Tickell appeared in court sporting a pink carnation in his buttonhole and with an eye-glass on a ribbon round his neck. He apparently made a good impression, was acquitted of both charges, and remained unapologetic and unrepentant.

Decked out in opera cape and silk scarf, he was an avid supporter of the Arts Theatre, Cambridge.

"Kim" Tickell bore his long final illness with the same exemplary courage that he had shown during his service in the Second World War. He was unmarried.

June 5 1990

PEGGY SALAMAN

PEGGY SALAMAN, the aviatrix who has died in Arizona aged 82, achieved fame while still a bright young thing when she beat the London to Cape Town light aeroplane record, picking up a couple of lion cubs on the way.

On October 30 1931 – with a "Cheerio, Mummy, I'm determined to do or die and, believe me, I'm going to do" – Miss Salaman waved her mother goodbye and flew off into the night from the Channel coast airfield at Lympne in Kent.

Peggy Salaman's flight captured the imagination of the press; here was "The Girl With Everything Money Could Buy Who Had Got Bored With It All". Such details as the fact that she had packed an evening gown for Cape Town – and that she had brought along packets of chewing gum to seal any petrol tank leaks – were lovingly chronicled.

Five days, six hours and 40 minutes after she left Lympne she landed in Cape Town – accompanied by Gordon Store, her South African navigator and fellow-pilot. Her time knocked more than a day off the previous record of Lieutenant-Commander Glen Kidston, who that spring had completed the journey in six days and 10 hours.

But, taking into account the fragility of her little single-engined De Havilland Puss Moth, it was an even greater achievement than the figures indicate. Kidston had flown a heavier and more powerful Lockheed Vega – in effect, a Mini compared with a Rolls.

Indeed the Moth was hardly more than a standard flying club machine, maximum speed 125 mph. There was, however, an additional fuel tank and a metal propeller to add about 5 mph to the speed. Navigation lights were fitted but there was no radio.

The Moth, which she called the *Good Hope*, was a present from her mother. It was dressed in a livery of Navy blue with a pale blue stripe – "Like the perambulator I had for her as a baby," said her mother.

The daughter of a businessman and property developer, Peggy Louise Salaman was born in London in 1907 and educated at Queen's College, Harley Street, and Bentley Priory (which, in 1940, was to become Dowding's HQ during the Battle of Britain).

Finished in Paris, she did a London Season before, in pursuit of her passionate determination to fly, taking lessons at Hanworth with Captain Finley, a former RFC pilot. She obtained an "A" licence, and in July 1931 she entered the Moth in the King's Cup air race, where – accompanied by Lieutenant Geoffrey Rodd as her pilot – she won the prize for the fastest machine.

That October, as she headed for Le Bourget in Paris on the first leg of her epic flight, Miss Salaman's only sartorial concession to aviation was a helmet. The rest of her attire in the cockpit comprised grey flannel trouserings and a white sweater.

A pith helmet and shorts were packed with the ballgown for the tropics. With Store navigating, she flew the old "Red Route" of the British Empire. After Rome and Athens came Juba, where she was much taken by a pair of lion cubs. She duly bought the cuddly young creatures for £25 and named them Juba and Joker; they were bottle-fed on board as the *Good Hope* progressed towards Entebbe.

Then it was on to Bulawayo, but the combination of nightfall and a hilly area urged caution, and she landed in wild bush country between Abercorn and Broken Hill, Northern Rhodesia.

Came the dawn and take-off was found to be impossible until a strip had been prepared. Fortunately Store had armed himself with a machete and she had a revolver with which she felled some young trees. An elephant trench was filled with earth to clear a runway. Airborne again, Store, as she recalled, "threaded his way through Africa as easily as a taxi-man in London".

In the last stages of the adventure Miss Salaman left the 18-day-old cubs at Kimberley to be sent on by train. They had become too much of a handful.

On arriving at Cape Town and hearing that she had broken the record, she trilled: "How perfectly lovely!" She added: "We could have got here much earlier, but we slowed to 90 mph over gorgeous mountains and admired the magnificent scenery."

Afterwards she was told the Moth was now unfit to fly. Store stayed on in South Africa, but she sailed home with the lion cubs in the liner *Warwick Castle*. At sea she heard that the celebrated aviator Jim Mollison, already chasing her record, had crashed in Egypt. She cabled to him: "Hard lines. You missed our luck."

Back in London she returned to the family in Cambridge Square, Bayswater. The cubs resided in the cloakroom, but as they grew the maids complained. Not only were they considered potentially dangerous but there were disagreeable odours – despite unsparing applications of *eau de cologne* – and ineradicable scratches on the parquet floor. Bertram Mills came to the rescue but he was unable to tame them for his circus; eventually the lions, by now renamed Romeo and Juliet, were housed in a private zoo.

Subsequently she gained a commercial licence in America, where she entered a Los Angeles Air Derby and finished 42nd out of 80.

During the Second World War she served in the WAAF, as a plotter, and then in the Wrens. Afterwards she helped to look after displaced children at a camp in Brittany.

Miss Salaman was married briefly to Denis Flanders, the architectural and landscape artist. During a visit to America in the 1950s she met her second husband, Walter Bell, an electrical engineer and airman with two private aircraft.

Flying around America together, they landed one day at Phoenix, Arizona, and were so enchanted with it that they bought a house in the *adobe* style and settled there.

September 12 1990

HELLE CRISTINA HABSBURG WINDSOR

HELLE CRISTINA HABSBURG WINDSOR, a familiar figure in the Anglo-Portuguese world who has died in Lisbon aged 100, was, even by the standards of pretenders, one of the more bizarre aspirants to the blood royal.

She claimed to have been born at the Court of Spain in May 1890 as a natural child of the future King George V of Great Britain and Queen Maria Cristina of Spain, widow of King Alfonso XII and daughter of Archduke Karl Ferdinand of Austria. "I was born on the steps of the throne," she used to say. "So awkward for her mother," observed one Lisbon wag.

By her own account, Helle Cristina was ferried as a baby to Malta, where an Englishwoman put her on a ship headed for the East. The "royal lovechild" was thus transported to Smyrna, where she was brought up by a certain Dr Salerio. After a two-year sojourn in a convent on the Greek island of Tinos, Helle Cristina, now in her late teens, boarded a ship for Marseille, from where she followed the railway line to Bordeaux, and eventually crossed the border into Spain.

She spent some time working in music-halls before marrying Roberto Cunat, whom she described as the southern "regent" of a large industrial firm. She was said to have had two sons by this marriage, although in later years she never revealed where they were.

Mrs Habsburg Windsor, as she styled herself, liked to recall meeting her mother in adult life: "She was with her son, King Alfonso XIII, and she looked so happy. I was glad for her because I could imagine the sorrow of being separated from her only daughter." (Helle Cristina was apparently unaware that her mother had in fact had two daughters by King Alfonso XII.)

"I never spoke about my father with my mother. We had no opportunity. Besides, I think we were both so transported that we never thought of speaking, just of being together. It was an occasion."

She also remembered meeting her father – as well as her half-brother, the Duke of Windsor – on several occasions. He was willing, she said, to do anything for her. What he did is unclear.

Soon after the outbreak of the Second World War, Mrs Habsburg Windsor arrived as a refugee in Lisbon with neither papers nor passport, though her *Cartao de Residencia* declared her to be British.

It was at this time that she divulged her origins. Nobody took any notice, but her conduct fast made her a thorn in the side of the British Embassy; she would appear uninvited at numerous official functions, claiming to be a representative of the British Government. She was also a regular worshipper at St George's Church, and more than once occupied the British Ambassador's pew, declaring in a guttural German accent that she took precedence.

Mrs Habsburg Windsor, who spoke several languages and had journalistic experience in Egypt, was frequently taken for a spy – although nobody had any idea for whom she might be working. Ostensibly she made her living by teaching English. She was eventually banned from the premises of the British Hospital, where she was accustomed to sit for hours in the waiting room.

September 16 1990

ELDRESS BERTHA LINDSAY

BERTHA LINDSAY, who has died aged 93, was the last Eldress of the Shakers, the American millenarian sect that espoused communal living, equality of the sexes, celibacy and pacifism, but is best remembered for its production of plain wooden furniture and handicrafts.

The sect was founded in Manchester, Lancashire, in the 1770s by "Mother" Ann Lee, who moved to New York with eight followers in 1774. Formally known as the United Society of Believers in Christ's Second Appearing, its congregation was nicknamed the "Shaking Quakers" – and later simply the "Shakers" – for the members' habit of trembling with fervour during church services.

When they received mystical "gifts from on high"
the Shakers shook from head to toe in a bizarre ritualistic
dance, which variously amused and repelled their visitors
– who included Charles Dickens. The celibacy rule was
instituted by Mother Lee herself, who, having lost several
babies in childbirth, had had a vision of Adam and Eve
entwined in carnal union, which convinced her that
sexual intercourse was the root of all evil.

The Shakers were thus able to expand only by taking
in orphans and converts, but the movement soon took
root, and by the mid-19th century numbered some 6,000
members, who lived in a score of communal villages in
New England, New York, Ohio, Indiana and Kentucky.
Life in the communities was strictly regulated, with
different parts of the day set aside for work, study and
prayer. Traditional sexual roles were maintained – the
women would cook, spin and weave, while the men
worked the land and managed the workshops. But men
and women were considered spiritual equals, and the
leadership was shared between Elders and Eldresses.

Living together as "brothers and sisters", they slept
in separate dormitories under the same roof. Couples
suspected of forming attachments were segregated,
expelled from the community or allowed to return of
their own volition to the World.

Eldress Bertha was one of two surviving Shakers at
the Canterbury Shaker Village, New Hampshire – where
Sister Ethel Hudson (born 1896), survives her – and one
of fewer than 10 remaining in the whole of America.

She joined the community at Canterbury in 1905,
when the Shakers were already in sharp decline, and the
Elders and Eldresses had begun to encourage cultural

assimilation. This culminated in 1965, when they formally closed the sect to new members.

As the Shakers' enthusiasm for converting the "World's People" waned, so their material legacy to the world grew. Pioneers in several aspects of furniture manufacture, they were among the first to machine wood; and they invented an astonishing selection of tools, including rotary harrows, water turbines, screw propellers, mechanical threshers, automatic pea shellers, palm-leaf bonnet looms, revolving ovens and contraptions for peeling and coring apples.

Genuine old Shaker pieces – especially ladderback chairs, chests and boxes – now fetch thousands of dollars at auctions at Sotheby's, Christie's and elsewhere; and even Shaker brooms, farm implements and clothes-pegs are much sought after by collectors. The Shakers themselves, however, shunned all thought of making money from their craft. They regarded patents as immoral, and deemed it wrong to appropriate the "gifts of the spirit" for worldly gain.

When asked if she was sad about the Shakers' demise, Eldress Bertha would recall the prophecy of Mother Lee: "When the Shakers diminished to as many as a child could count on one hand, there would be a revival of the spirit."

She was quick to clarify, though, that they would not be called Shakers. "They wouldn't live in communities. But it would be felt and known worldwide. And we think that is coming to pass."

Bertha Lindsay was born on July 28 1897 at Braintree, Massachusetts, and as an infant moved with her family to Laconia, New Hampshire. Orphaned at the age of four, young Bertha lived for three years with an older sister, but was then placed with the Canterbury Shakers according to the wishes of their parents, who had attended services there.

One of Eldress Bertha's favourite anecdotes told of how as a frightened young girl she was comforted by the love and acceptance of the Shaker sisters. She would recall the day after her arrival, when she joined them in an apple celebration, and how she was touched by the beauty and perfume of the orchard in bloom.

She shared the chores, was educated at the community school and on her 21st birthday, having chosen to remain in the community, signed the covenant and donned the white starched bonnet of the Shaker sister. "I felt that I could give as much here as I could anywhere else in the world," she said, "and could have more friends, both men and women. If I had gone into the world and married, I wouldn't have had that."

Bertha Lindsay soon distinguished herself during her shifts in the kitchen and was put in charge of catering to the business leaders of the community and their guests. She also managed the community's fancywork trade – mainly small handkerchiefs and sewing-boxes – from 1944 to 1958.

In the course of the next decade, having watched as other Shaker communities were sold off, she was instrumental in establishing a museum which later evolved into Shaker Village Inc., a non-profit-making educational corporation which now preserves the Canterbury community as an historic site and museum.

In 1967 she was elected second Eldress of the Canterbury Shaker community and on the death of Eldress Marguerite Frost in 1970, she became Canterbury Eldress.

Her final years brought a brief period of limelight from the outside world which her forefathers had eschewed so vehemently. When not planning and overseeing the production of meals, she greeted visitors and gave interviews to schoolchildren, scholars, television and the press. In 1987 she published her cookbook, *Seasoned With Grace*, in which each chapter of recipes is preceded by stories of her life as a Shaker.

Despite appearing to some as old-fashioned, Eldress Bertha was not mired in the 19th century. She loved television, and faithfully followed the news and programmes such as *Jeopardy* and *The Bill Cosby Show*.

Eldress Bertha once said that she wanted to be remembered simply as someone who lived a true Shaker life. She lost her sight after her 90th birthday and then began recording her memoirs on a cassette recorder: "I want people to know we did have fun, and plenty of it."

October 11 1990

COMMANDER "BIFFY" DUNDERDALE

COMMANDER W. A. "BIFFY" DUNDERDALE, who has died in New York aged 90, was a member of the Secret Service for 38 years and was sometimes spoken of as the prototype of James Bond.

But where Ian Fleming's creation was extrovert and flamboyant, in love with the latest technology, Dunderdale – though one of the ablest agents of his time –

really belonged in the *Boys' Own Paper* era of false beards and invisible ink, and was the most reticent of men. To the end of his long life, visitors to his New York apartment could get almost nothing from "Biffy" about his past service.

The son of a Constantinople shipowner, Wilfred Albert Dunderdale was born on Christmas Eve 1899 and educated at the Gymnasium in Nicolaieff on the Black Sea. He was studying to be a naval architect in St Petersburg when the Russian Revolution broke out in 1917.

His father sent him to Vladivostok to take delivery of the first of a new class of Holland-designed submarines, built in America, and deliver it to the Black Sea. To transport a submarine, still in five separate sections, thousands of miles by rail across a country in the throes of a revolution was asking a good deal of a 16-year-old boy – but young Biffy accomplished it.

The submarine was completed too late to serve in the Imperial Navy and was eventually scuttled at Sebastopol in April 1919. By then the political situation in the region was of literally Byzantine complexity. In 1920 British warships operated in the Black Sea and the Sea of Marmara, bombarding shore installations and sending ashore parties of sailors and marines.

With his knowledge of naval engineering – and of Constantinople and the Black Sea ports – his business-like pretext and his fluent Russian, German and French, Biffy Dunderdale made a superb undercover agent for the Navy.

Still only 19, with the honorary rank of sub-lieutenant RNVR and operating under the *nom de guerre* of "Julius", he was twice mentioned in despatches. In 1920 he was promoted honorary lieutenant RNVR and appointed MBE.

Dunderdale joined the Secret Service in 1921 and was at once involved in foiling one of the frequent Turkish plans to infiltrate troops into Constantinople and seize the city from the Allies. This attempt was finally frustrated by "battleship diplomacy" when HMS *Bembow* and attendant destroyers appeared off the city waterfront.

In the autumn of 1922 British and Turkish troops confronted each other at Chanak in the Dardanelles. Fighting was only prevented by the good sense and moral courage of the Army C-in-C, General Harington. The end of the crisis brought the exile of Sultan Mohammed VI, who was taken to Malta in the battleship *Malaya*, and the downfall of Lloyd George as Prime Minister.

Dunderdale's part in these events was domestic rather than epic. He was responsible for arranging and paying for the repatriation of ex-members of the Sultan's harem who were not Turkish nationals – including one *houri* from Leamington Spa, packed off home on the Orient Express.

In 1926 he joined the SIS station in Paris, where he worked with the Deuxième Bureau and established good relations with the French – particularly with Colonel Gustav Bertrand, head of the French Intelligence Service. He was liaison officer in Paris with the Tsarist Supreme Monarchist Council.

Dunderdale was also on good terms with the Poles, which led to a major intelligence coup. The Poles were pioneers in breaking the Enigma machine cyphers which all three German armed forces were using, so it was imperative that British Intelligence obtain an example.

Dunderdale was "the Third Man" at the celebrated meeting under the clock at Victoria Station on August 16 1939 – which might have come straight out of a spy thriller – when "C" himself (head of the British Secret Service) met Bertrand, a member of the Paris embassy staff, and Dunderdale, who had an Enigma machine in his valise. "C" was on his way to a dinner and cut a conspicuous figure as he strode away, in evening dress, with the ribbon of the Légion d'Honneur in his button-hole and the Enigma under his arm.

The day before war was declared Dunderdale was given the rank of Commander RNVR. He was one of the last Englishmen to leave Paris when the Germans entered the city in June 1940.

When he reached Bordeaux an RAF Avro Anson was sent to make sure he escaped. During the war he kept his links with the Poles and was in contact by radio with Bertrand in Vichy France, and with other members of the Deuxième Bureau who had stayed behind.

Dunderdale also had to deal with the notorious prickliness and slack security of the Gaullist Free French in London, and to fight off the attempts of Sir Claude Dansey, "C's" deputy, to dominate both the Free French Intelligence and the Bureau.

His success was shown by the number of different countries who honoured him. He was appointed CMG in 1942. The Poles awarded him the Polonia Restituta in 1943 for services to the Polish Navy; he was made an officer of the American Legion of Merit in 1946 for "Special Services"; he also held the Russian Order of St

Anne and the Croix de Guerre, and was an officer of the
Légion d'Honneur.

Dunderdale served with the SIS in London after the
war until he retired in 1959, but his influence had
declined. Perhaps he knew too many secrets, and realised
that his life in espionage had been an elaborate game;
but he was an excellent host at his apartments in Paris
and New York and his house in Surrey.

He was thrice married: first to June Morse, granddaughter of Samuel B. Morse, inventor of the Morse
Code; secondly to Dorothy Hyde, who died in 1978; and
thirdly to Debbie Jackson, of Boston, Massachusetts.

November 22 1990

ALFRED HINDS

ALFRED HINDS, who has died in Jersey aged 73,
proved himself, in the course of a prolonged struggle to
establish his innocence of a shop-breaking charge, the
most successful prison escaper in English history and also
one of the shrewdest legal minds never to have been
called to the Bar.

His troubles began in September 1953, when, along
with four others, he was charged with stealing some
£30,000 in jewellery and £4,700 in cash from Maple's
store in Tottenham Court Road. That December Hinds,
pronounced by Lord Goddard to be "a most dangerous
criminal", was jailed for 12 years.

Yet, though it took the jury only half an hour to
make up their minds, the evidence against him was
essentially circumstantial. The prosecution claimed that

traces of a fuse used to blow the safe had been found on Hinds, together with material from the lining of the safe.

One of the other men found guilty of the crime had been at Hinds's house the Sunday after the robbery, and he was carrying watches from the store; Hinds maintained, though, that this visitor had called about a car.

Hinds admitted that he had been near Maple's on the night that the robbery was planned, but said he wanted to buy a carpet – though, as Lord Goddard pointed out, 8 p.m. was an unlikely hour for this purpose.

One of the accused gave evidence against Hinds, the night superintendent at Heal's, an "inside" man who later co-operated with the police in their inquiries. He claimed that Hinds had threatened him about giving evidence, and offered him £500 if he failed to pick out his fellow criminal at an identity parade.

Hinds had eight previous convictions, some of them involving safe-breaking. Nevertheless, in recent years it had appeared that he was going straight, living in a house near the Thames at Staines, where he helped his brother in a building and demolition business.

From the very first he protested his innocence, but in December 1953 the Court of Criminal Appeal dismissed his appeal application. Next year Hinds published a pamphlet in which he demanded an inquiry or a retrial.

This was ignored, and in November 1955 Hinds escaped from Nottingham prison. He took a hacksaw blade out of an electrician's toolbag, made a copy of the prison workshop key from brass after memorising its shape, purloined some planks which he used to climb the prison wall, and made off in a lorry provided by a friend. He was already a seasoned escaper.

Alfred George Hinds had been born at Newington Butts, in south London, in 1917. His father, described variously as a general labourer, a street betting agent and a pugilist, was sentenced to seven years as a consequence of a bank raid at Portsmouth in 1935; he also received 10 strokes of the cat-o'-nine-tails which, Hinds believed, contributed to his early death.

At the age of seven young Alfie found himself in Pentonville remand home, from which he made his first break. Subsequently he was brought up by foster parents in the Midlands, where he acquired his considerable skills at metalwork and machine-turning.

In the Second World War he was in the Royal Tank Corps, until he decided to desert. Subsequently, he arranged for friends to create a disturbance while he was being transported in an army truck at Clapham Junction; with the guards distracted, he made his getaway in a car supplied by another accomplice.

In 1945 Rochester Borstal afforded the next opportunity for Hinds to demonstrate his escaping skills. But the escape from Nottingham prison in 1955 was an altogether more ambitious project, and one that he combined with sustained literary endeavour.

Several papers were bombarded with letters. "I made this escape", he wrote to one, "because it was the only way now left open to me in my fight to obtain justice. I am entirely innocent of the crime for which I was sentenced for twelve years."

The letters were all postmarked SW1, as was the parcel containing the musical boxes which Hinds sent his children for Christmas; nevertheless rumour was endlessly fertile, placing Hinds in Turin, in France, in Ireland, in America.

With fine English logic it was reckoned that his letters were too literate to have been composed by someone of his background. But not long afterwards Hinds's voice was heard on Independent Television setting forth his demands in unimpeachable English.

Scotland Yard announced that it was reconstituting its "ghost squad", credited with more than ordinary powers. This move provoked a letter from Hinds to the *Sunday Dispatch* in which he reflected that public money would be much better spent on an inquiry or a retrial.

Not until he had been free for 245 days, on July 31 1956, was the absconder finally caught, in Dublin: he had been living in a cottage which he had bought for £750 at Greystones, Co. Wicklow.

Hinds was charged with prison-breaking and, acting in his own defence, proved himself more than a match for learned counsel – and also for the judge. "My Lord, I think I can help you there," he would helpfully intervene; and indeed the judge was forced to admit that the accused knew more about some aspects of the law than anyone else in the court.

Hinds managed to get himself acquitted of prison-breaking, and he received only 11 days' extra sentence for escaping from custody before returning to serve his longer sentence.

He seemed to have acquired a taste for the law, and in July of that year reappeared before the Queen's Bench Division to argue a point in an action against the prison commissioners for his illegal arrest.

Hinds contacted accomplices who were instructed to smuggle him a padlock into the Law Courts. Once there he asked to go to the lavatory, whither he was accompanied by two guards. When they removed his handcuffs

Hinds and a friend succeeded in bundling the guards into the lavatory and padlocking the door.

He was quickly recaptured and R. A. Butler, the Home Secretary, remained deaf to all demands for a retrial. Hinds was sent to Chelmsford prison where, in June 1958, he fashioned a key that gave him entry into the bathhouse and thence escaped by way of a skylight on to the roof and over the wall into a waiting Morris Minor.

This time he eluded his pursuers for almost two years, again in Ireland, where, under the name William Herbert Bishop, he established himself as a flourishing second-hand car dealer. It was the customs officials who finally caught him, in January 1960, for possessing cars that had been smuggled across the border, an offence for which he received six months at the Crumlin Road jail in Belfast.

On his return to his native land to continue his sentence for the Maple's robbery – he found time, the while, to sell his life story to the *News of the World* – Hinds settled into a prolonged series of battles with the English legal establishment. "My Lord, you are not quite with me," he would tell the judge, though he also dispensed praise – "you have summed up very well".

But appeal after appeal was dismissed, and Hinds's legal manoeuvres seemed to have got him nowhere, until in 1964 he successfully sued Superintendent Herbert Sparks for libel, gaining £1,300 in damages and costs. This civil victory forced a reconsideration of the criminal sentence, and Hinds was released.

Even so, in November 1965 the Court of Criminal Appeal decided that the original conviction had been correct, and once again refused him leave to appeal.

Hinds, now at large, continued his struggle with a book *Contempt of Court* (1966), and took to lecturing at polytechnics and at the National Council for Civil Liberties. The crying need, he explained, was for a more intelligent police force.

Later he retired to Jersey where he established a property business, and in 1973 reached the semi-finals of a contest to discover the most intelligent person in the island. With an IQ of 150 he made an admirable secretary of the Channel Islands Mensa Society.

January 7 1991

SERGE GAINSBOURG

SERGE GAINSBOURG, the controversial French singer, composer and film director, who has died in Paris aged 62, was best known in Britain for his *succès de scandale*, "*Je t'aime moi non plus*", the heavy-breathing duet recorded with his then girlfriend, the English actress Jane Birkin.

"*Je t'aime*" achieved huge popularity in 1969, despite – or perhaps because of – being banned by the BBC and denounced by the Vatican. Peter Cook recorded a spoof version featuring "Serge Forward and Jane Firkin".

Gainsbourg was one of the many French popular performers whose reputation as a "serious" songwriter dissolved in the Channel. In France he was celebrated for his contribution to popular *varietés*, for his film scores and for his *louche* personality

A notoriously heavy drinker, Gainsbourg maintained an awesome intake of alcohol and tobacco. After a heart

119

attack in 1973, he continued to smoke three or four packets of Gitanes *sans filtres* a day.

Gainsbourg was fond of telling interviewers that he was in a better state than his doctors. Indeed, he outlived three of his cardiologists. According to the doctor who was treating him at the time of his heart attack, Gainsbourg stopped smoking only for three days, while he was in intensive care, "because he believed, foolishly, that his Gitane would cause the oxygen cylinder to explode".

It was often supposed that Gainsbourg took drugs, but in truth he was naturally outrageous, and undertook most of his more contentious projects as he was approaching pensionable age. He was finally banned from live television after a series of drunken appearances on chat shows – culminating in the occasion when he made an obscene suggestion, in broken English, to the American pop singer Miss Whitney Houston.

For 10 years Gainsbourg, who had no driving licence or chauffeur, kept a 1928 Rolls-Royce which, he said, he used occasionally "as an ashtray".

Although he became best known for his collaborations with pop musicians in the 1970s, Gainsbourg acquired a considerable knowledge of the decadent movement. His house in the rue de Verneuil, Saint Germain, was furnished in the style of the apartment of des Esseintes in Huysman's *A Rebours*, and was a shrine to decadence: next to paintings by Dali and Francis Bacon, and originals of Chopin's letters, there were pictures of Screaming Jay Hawkins and the Sex Pistols.

In his later years, Gainsbourg – in private a gentle, polite man – cultivated, with increasing success, the public image of the "dirty old man of Europe". In the 1960s –

after his divorce from his Italian wife Françoise Antoinette Pancrazzi, who described him as an aesthete tormented by his own ugliness – he developed a reputation as an unlikely Don Juan. His supposed conquests included Brigitte Bardot.

Having developed, with *"Je t'aime"*, the taste for putting a nation into shock, Gainsbourg set out – with some success – to repeat the experience. In 1979 there was outrage from French traditionalists, led by *Le Figaro*, when he recruited a group of Jamaican reggae musicians and recorded a highly idiosyncratic version of "La Marseillaise". The song was re-titled *"Aux Armes et Caetera"*, and provoked riots when concerts were disrupted by veteran paratroopers.

Six years previously there had been opposition to the release of *Rock Around the Bunker*, his collection of songs about the Third Reich. The LP included a reading of "Smoke Gets in Your Eyes", which many listeners considered to be in questionable taste.

Record buyers who were familiar with Gainsbourg's family history, however, chose to see this and other of his more controversial releases as an indication of the singer's having been born with "a skin too few". As a child, Gainsbourg, the offspring of Russian Jewish refugees, had been made to wear the yellow star, and on several occasions had narrowly escaped death.

The son of a nightclub pianist, he was born Lucien Ginzburg in Paris on April 2 1928 and brought up in the Pigalle. He changed his name for one he considered to be more aristocratic while still acknowledging his Russian origins.

He trained as a painter but by the early 1950s he

came under the influence of the jazz musician, Boris Vian. Gainsbourg began to work as a singer and pianist in the nightclubs of Saint-Germain des Prés.

Towards the end of the decade he began a career as a film actor, playing villains in low-budget European co-productions of varying artistic merit. Gainsbourg's own performances in such pictures, typically set in ancient Rome, drew a mixed response from critics. Of one show-ing, when he was obliged to flee his public at a cinema in Barbes Rochechouart, he recalled that "they were shout-ing at the screen in Arabic: 'Die, you bastard!'"

In the 1960s Gainsbourg, whose own recordings tended towards the cynical, specialised in writing main-stream pop for such luminaries as Juliette Greco and Petula Clark. Increasingly, however, he indulged his fondness for mischief, notably in 1966 when he wrote the highly suggestive *"Les Sucettes"* ("Lollipops") for the young France Gall.

Mlle Gall, only 16, had won the Eurovision Song Contest the year before with a Gainsbourg song, and had no idea of the new song's "hidden agenda".

In the mid-1960s, Gainsbourg wrote "BB" and other "bubble-gum pop" hits for Brigitte Bardot. Then in 1968 he met the coltish Jane Birkin, who had already acquired some valuable experience of minor scandal (as a result of her nude nymphet role in Antonioni's film *Blow-Up*).

Birkin lived with Gainsbourg for more than ten years before leaving him in the early 1980s. "We were a public couple," Gainsbourg recalled. "We went out a lot. The trouble was, I didn't always make it back . . ."

After Birkin left him, Gainsbourg lived with his "little Eurasienne" wife – Caroline von Paulus, whom he addressed as "Bambou". They had a son, Lucien, known as "Lulu". On his last album Gainsbourg prefaced a song: "When I die, at least throw a few nettles on my tomb, my little Lulu."

As his career progressed into the 1980s, Gainsbourg discovered that his capacity to outrage was increasingly hindered by public tolerance. But nevertheless he achieved his aim in 1984 with "Lemon Incest", an unusually sensual reading of Chopin's Étude No 3 in E Major, Opus 10. The video for the song showed Gainsbourg in bed with his 14-year-old daughter, Charlotte, who subsequently embarked on a successful career as a film actress.

By the time he released *You're Under Arrest*, in 1987, Gainsbourg was visibly suffering the effects of his four decades of hard living. In 1989 he was rushed to hospital for a six-hour emergency operation on his liver.

Although an enthusiastic Anglophile, Gainsbourg never made concessions to the English-speaking market. Apart from *"Je t'aime"*, none of his witty, urbane songs ever achieved significant success in Britain.

His films like *Je t'aime moi non plus* (made in 1976, starring Gérard Depardieu), or *Equateur* (1983), were mainly screened in pornographic cinemas in Britain.

Perhaps surprisingly for a man widely supposed to be on terms of only nodding acquaintance with his face flannel, Gainsbourg also directed advertisements for Lux soap and Woolite.

Though he enjoyed moments of spectacular public disgrace, Gainsbourg was also celebrated for his extravagant acts of kindness and generosity. Bardot described him as "the best and the worst. He struck me as a little Jewish Russian prince reading Andersen and Grimm, who came face to face with the tragic reality of life: a Quasimodo, touching or repugnant depending on his mood."

Gainsbourg was appointed an officer of the French Order of Arts and Letters. The Minister of Culture, Jack Lang, called him "one of the greats of French music and poetry".

March 4 1991

ADMIRAL SIR FREDERICK PARHAM

ADMIRAL SIR FREDERICK PARHAM, who has died aged 90, commanded the heavy cruiser *Belfast* during the dramatic chase and destruction of the German battle cruiser *Scharnhorst* by ships of the Home Fleet off the North Cape of Norway on December 26 1943.

Scharnhorst had sailed from a Norwegian fjord on Christmas Day to attack convoy JW55B on its way to Murmansk and the next morning encountered *Belfast*, wearing the flag of Rear-Admiral Bob Burnett, commanding the 10th Cruiser Squadron, and two other cruisers, *Norfolk* and *Sheffield*.

It was *Belfast* which first detected the enemy by radar at 8.40 a.m. at a range of 16 miles; and some 30 minutes later *Belfast*'s star shell bursting overhead caught *Scharnhorst* completely by surprise. After a brief gun action, *Scharnhorst* broke away.

Burnett decided not to try to follow but to fall on the convoy – a decision which was later criticised. At the

124

time Burnett was greatly distressed to receive a somewhat sharp signal from his C-in-C, Admiral Sir Bruce
Fraser, flying his flag in the battleship *Duke of York*,
some distance away.

Burnett asked Parham if he'd done the right thing.
"Poor old Bob," said Parham later, "he was a terribly
emotional chap, he was jolly near in tears about it. I was
able to reassure him and tell him he had done *exactly* the
right thing."

Both men were vindicated when *Scharnhorst* threatened the convoy again and *Belfast* had another radar
contact just after midday. For the second time the
cruisers caught *Scharnhorst* by surprise.

After another gun action, in which *Norfolk* was hit,
Scharnhorst turned to run for home, closely followed by
the cruisers and Home Fleet destroyers. But *Norfolk*
dropped back to put out a fire, and *Sheffield* suffered a
main engine defect, so *Belfast* was soon alone.

In what Fraser called an exemplary piece of shadow-
ing, *Belfast* broadcast her own position, course and speed,
and *Scharnhorst*'s range, course and speed, every 15 minutes for the next three and a half hours. Throughout that
time Parham marvelled that *Belfast* was never attacked.

"*Scharnhorst* was a much bigger ship than us," he
said. "She'd only got to turn round for minutes and she
could have blown us clean out of the water."

So accurate was *Belfast*'s reporting that Fraser was
able to ponder whether he should have the battle before
or after his tea and to decide on the latter option. It was
forecast that *Scharnhorst* would appear on the flagship's
radar screen at 4.15 p.m.: the actual time was 4.17.

Duke of York's star shell caught *Scharnhorst* by surprise
for the third and last time, and in the final act of the

drama the enemy was brought to bay and sunk by gunfire and by torpedoes from the destroyers, with only 36 survivors from her total complement of over 2,000. Parham was awarded the DSO.

Belfast had covered several Arctic convoys in 1943, and in October sailed with the Home Fleet to accompany the American carrier *Ranger* for an air strike on the Norwegian port of Bodo. In April 1944 *Belfast* was in the Home Fleet covering force for the Fleet Air Arm carrier aircraft strike on the German battleship *Tirpitz* in Altenfjord. At 5.30 a.m. on D-Day (June 6) she was off Juno beach, Normandy, carrying out a two-hour bombardment of a German howitzer battery.

When the Green Howards overran that battery later they found the guns out of action and the crews sheltering in concrete bunkers. For the rest of that day and the next week *Belfast* supported the 3rd Canadian Division and by June 14 had fired 1,996 six-inch shells. When she left to reload with ammunition, Parham was delighted to receive an appreciative signal from the Force commander, praising *Belfast*'s gunnery in verse.

On June 25 *Belfast* was back to bombard railways and bridges near Caen, and on July 8 she supported the Royal Marines at Port-en-Bassein and the assault on Caen the next day. Parham was mentioned in despatches.

Frederick Robertson Parham was born on January 9 1901 and joined the Navy as a cadet in 1914, going to Osborne and Dartmouth. His first posting as a midshipman was to the battleship *Malaya*, which he joined in the Grand Fleet in 1917.

From 1925 he specialised in gunnery and after early promotion was appointed Experimental Commander at

HMS *Excellent*, the gunnery establishment at Whale Island, Portsmouth, in 1934. Three years later he commanded the destroyer *Shikari*, which controlled by radio the movements of the old battleship *Centurion*, used as a gunnery and bombing target ship by the Mediterranean Fleet.

While *Centurion* kept a steady course, bombing results were good, but as soon as Parham varied course and speed accuracy fell off markedly. As a result the Fleet Air Arm largely abandoned high-level bombing of ships and concentrated on torpedo and dive bombing.

In 1938 Parham took command of the brand-new Tribal-class destroyer *Gurkha* and commanded her for the first months of the war – until February 1940, when he went to the Admiralty, first as assistant and then as deputy director of Naval Ordnance. He was closely involved with the application of radar to surface fire control – techniques which were to prove so effective against *Scharnhorst*.

After *Belfast* he went to the Admiralty again, as director of the Operations Division (Foreign) and then as director of the whole division. His last seagoing command was *Vanguard* – arguably the most beautiful battleship ever built for the Navy.

He took her over in May 1947, after she had returned from the royal tour of South Africa, and commanded her at home and in the Mediterranean until July 1949. He was Deputy Chief of Personnel from 1949 until 1951, when he was Flag Officer Flotillas and second-in-command Mediterranean Fleet.

Parham would have been Second Sea Lord in 1953 but was prevented by illness. In 1954 he presided over an investigation into the deployment of warships. Pre-war foreign commissions of two years and more were no longer acceptable.

Parham arrived at a solution, generally welcomed in the Service, of splitting a ship's time between foreign and home stations, with no ship having to spend more than nine months on average abroad.

He was Fourth Sea Lord and Chief of Supplies and Transport from 1954 to 1955; and his last appointment was C-in-C The Nore from 1955 until his retirement in 1959.

Parham was vice-chairman of the British Waterways Board from 1963 to 1967. He was appointed CBE in 1949 and CB in 1951, and promoted to KCB in 1955 and GBE in 1959. He also received Portuguese, Iraqi and Italian orders while acting as host to visiting heads of State as C-in-C The Nore. He was Naval ADC to King George VI in 1949.

Parham married first, in 1926, Kathleen Dobrée Carey, who died in 1973; they had a son. He married secondly, in 1978, Mrs Joan Saunders (*née* Charig).

John Winton writes: "Freddie" Parham was never tested as a fleet commander but as a wartime sea captain he was second to none.

In *Belfast* he had "a very green lot of sailors". Many of her company of 900 had never been to sea before, and some of her RNVR officers were at sea as officers for the first time, but Parham welded them all together into a most efficient fighting unit.

As a man, he was a most agreeable shipmate, gener-ous with praise, sparing with criticism and intensely loyal to those above and below him. He never set out to attract attention to himself but rose steadily through the Navy by sheer merit.

As the senior survivor of the Battle of North Cape he was always ready to give information and interviews. He would recall with humour that long and anxious day of battle, the bitter cold and very bad weather with only pale daylight for a short time around noon. "The best way to get the feel of that day", he said, "would be to read the despatches in a refrigerator, being heavily rocked, by the light of a single candle, with occasionally someone banging on the outside with a very large hammer."

March 27 1991

WILFRID HYDE WHITE

WILFRID HYDE WHITE the actor, who has died in Los Angeles aged 87, made a point of never seeming to take his profession seriously – the important business of his life, he would assert, was racing – but he never succeeded in disguising the fact that he was one of the most accomplished light comedians of his time.

Probably he achieved widest recognition as the genial old buffer Colonel Pickering in the film of *My Fair Lady* (1964). Although this role was essentially that of foil to Professor Higgins – exclaiming "Nonsense!" and "Disgraceful!" at appropriate moments – it seemed entirely credible that Hyde White should share a house with Rex Harrison.

In "You Did It", the song they sang after the ball, Hyde White discovered the same ability as his co-star to transcend the demands of musicality. And in so far as the part afforded him any opportunities – when, for example, Pickering rang up his old chum in the Home Office – his comic timing was equal to Harrison's, with the bonus of understatement.

Between 1934 and 1983 Hyde White appeared in more than 100 other films, many of them forgettable, although there were notable exceptions. In *The Third Man* (1949) he played some sort of British Council representative in Vienna; in *Two Way Stretch* (1960), with Peter Sellers, he was a phoney vicar; in *Let's Make Love* (1960), with Marilyn Monroe, he was Frankie Vaughan's agent.

But he took scant pride in his work for either the large or the small screen, and complained that he was entirely at the mercy of directors and editors. He was a man of the stage to his fingertips, one of the last great practitioners of the drawing-room comedy epitomised by Gerald du Maurier and A. E. Matthews.

Hyde White more or less dispensed with acting, making his entries as if he had no idea what kind of play he had wandered into, but all the comic points were effortlessly taken, and when it came to scene-stealing not even a dog or a child stood a chance against him.

Sleek, natty and silver-haired, Hyde White required no more than a gleam in the eye, or a gesture with a cane, to convey the sly and sinister underside to characters of apparent probity. If he generally played lovable cads, there was a suggestion that not so lovable ones would have been well within his compass.

The indolent style he cultivated on stage bordered on narcissism; the yawning laugh was not so far removed from a sneer; the rich, fruity voice froze out emotion in the style of an affable clubman.

Yet the charm survived because Hyde White was incapable of conducting his life to any lasting advantage. Even his choice of plays was capricious, liable to depend less on the quality of the piece than on the proximity of a racecourse or a good hotel.

He turned down the opportunity to appear in two successful plays by his friend William Douglas Home, *The Jockey Club Stakes* and *The Secretary Bird* (although he later took over from Alastair Sim in *The Jockey Club Stakes*). On the other hand he eagerly seized the opportunity in 1971 to act in James Bridie's *Meeting at Night*, which closed after six weeks, despite considerable critical approbation for Hyde White's performance.

"This famous charmer must have been the original strolling player," wrote John Barber in *The Daily Telegraph*. "His silken good manners and his whimsical low chuckle are well known – a player who could give lessons in relaxation to a sleepy cat."

The son of a canon of Gloucester Cathedral, Wilfrid Hyde White was born at Bourton-on-the-Water, Gloucestershire, on May 12 1903, and educated at Marlborough, which he detested. "We were all frightfully unattractive individuals," he recalled, "embarrassingly self-conscious, hateful products of a hateful system."

In reaction, young Wilfrid opted for the stage. Alarmed at this decision, his family packed him off to London to receive cautionary advice from an actor-uncle, one J. Fisher White. When, however, Hyde White found this worthy living, not in the company of his aunt but with a young girl who evinced a particular enthusiasm for breakfast and champagne in bed, he was confirmed in his thespian ambitions.

Hyde White proceeded to the Royal Academy of Dramatic Art, where, he said, he learnt two things: in his first year that he had no histrionic talent whatsoever, and in his second that this did not matter a damn.

His first professional stage appearance was at Ryde on the Isle of Wight in 1922. Known in those days as "Dasher" White, he remained in the provinces until 1925 – "the year Manna won the Derby with Steve Donoghue up" – when he made his West End debut in *Beggar on Horseback*, with A. E. Matthews.

Over the next half-century he was seldom out of work. In 1936 he gave up the theatre for four years to make films, but then returned to the London stage in the revue *Rise Above It*.

Hyde White made his first New York appearance in 1947 as Sir Alec Dunne in *Under the Counter*. In the 1950s he enjoyed a string of West End successes, notably in *The Reluctant Debutante* (1955) by William Douglas Home, and *Not in the Book* (1958), which ran for 500 performances at the Criterion.

On the whole he steered clear of the classical repertoire, although he did act with the Oliviers in their 1951 season at the St James's, as Euphronius in *Antony and Cleopatra*, and more appropriately, as Britannus in Shaw's *Caesar and Cleopatra*. Later he enjoyed himself as Ralph Bloomfield-Bonnington in Shaw's *The Doctor's Dilemma*, and as Lord Augustus Lorton in Wilde's *An Ideal Husband*.

Hyde White's life took another turn after 1960 when George Cukor lured him to America for *Let's Make Love*. Marilyn Monroe's displays of temperament kept him in

Hollywood for eight months instead of the eight weeks that had been envisaged, and during this time American producers marked him down as the perfect celluloid Englishman.

The job offers flowed in: "I couldn't turn them down," Hyde White declared, "particularly when you consider what a lousy actor I am." A more convincing reason was that he was eternally in debt to the bookmakers.

He had also acquired an American wife, whom he had met during the Broadway run of *The Reluctant Debutante*, so it seemed natural to settle in Palm Springs. It was a decision he never ceased to lament. "If I've made one big mistake in my life," he said, "it was leaving England. Because once an Englishman leaves his home he is never quite the same."

However great his income, it never kept pace with his rate of expenditure. In 1977 the Inland Revenue started bankruptcy proceedings against him for a claim of £10,000. "Is it only £10,000?" Hyde White imperturbably inquired. "I thought it was much more." He showed some reluctance to attend the proceedings, which eventually led the Registrar to declare that he was "trifling with the court".

When he did eventually appear his dealings with the court lost nothing in the telling. Apparently the Official Receiver asked: "If you cannot tell us how you spent such a large sum in so short a time, perhaps you can tell us what will win the Gold Cup at Ascot this afternoon?"

"Of course, dear fellow," Hyde White replied, and named the winner, although he warned the Receiver to limit his investment. "We don't want to have to change places, do we?"

American television helped to rescue Hyde White from financial catastrophe. He starred as Emerson Marshall in the series *The Associates* about a New York lawyer's chaotic practice, and also portrayed Dr Goodfellow in *Buck Rogers in the 25th Century*.

At the end of his life Hyde White declared that he had been too materialistic. "I've owned 12 horses, seven Rolls-Royces, and I've had mistresses in Paris, London and New York – and it never made me happy."

Wilfrid Hyde White married first, in 1927, Blanche Aitken, who died in 1960. He married secondly, in 1957, Ethel Korenman (whose stage name was Ethel Drew); they had a son and a daughter.

William Douglas Home writes: My first recollection of "Uncle Wilfrid", as I always called him, is of the first night of *The Reluctant Debutante*'s pre-London tour in Brighton. He was sitting at the breakfast table with Celia Johnson as the curtain rose, after which there was a long silence broken by Wilfrid's voice shouting to the prompter: "Come along, boy, give me the line, boy, give me the line."

From then on until the final curtain fell he did not put a foot wrong, although I learned later that as he came forward at the end of the play with Celia and Anna Massey to take a curtain call he whispered to the former: "Let's get in front of that bloody girl, she's too damned good for us."

One other memory of him is not so happy – of his performance as Claude Johnson, the middle man between Rolls and Royce in my play *Rolls Hyphen Royce*. Although I had written an introductory speech for him he decided to ignore it on the first night, preferring to come on and say: "I'm surprised to see you all here tonight with all these one-way streets around the theatre. In fact I doubt very much if you'll ever get away afterwards, so we'll look forward to seeing you again tomorrow night."

And not content with that, he went on to say: "By the way, they tell me the roof fell in on this theatre last year. Let's hope it doesn't do it again tonight." Then he reverted to the text – in my opinion far too late.

But I forgave him for it, as one always forgave Wilfrid, disarmed as one always was by his incomparable charm. Sometimes one had to bargain with him – as, for example, in *The Jockey Club Stakes*, when he came on stage one night saying "Anybody seen my hat?" knowing full well that it was on his head.

He only agreed to abandon this regrettable addition to the script after I allowed him to rename some of the fictitious horses mentioned in the play with the names of some of those he had owned himself during a lifelong flirtation with the Turf.

"Do you know when I met my first bookie, me boy?" he said to me once. "Well I'll tell you. I was playing with my bricks when I was a little boy at home in Gloucester when the front door bell rang and my father said: 'Go and tell him I'm not in, me boy.' Down I went, and there was a fellow on the doorstep in a check suit holding my father's betting account."

But my favourite tale of all concerned an occasion when he and I both lunched with Robert Morley at Buck's Club, and Wilfrid started talking very loudly during the meal, much to Robert's embarrassment. "Lower your voice, Wilfrid, for God's sake," he said. "This is a gentlemen's club."

135

"Is it, me boy?" said Wilfrid. "Nothing written up to say so anywhere."

From now on, alas, there will be no new stories to recount about him, although happily he left behind enough to last a lifetime. Dear old Uncle Wilfrid was full of eccentricity and charm, and could put it all across whenever he felt like it.

This was not always the case. I told him once that I thought he had underplayed the part of Colonel Pickering in *My Fair Lady*. "Well, why not?" he answered. "What's the point of trying to compete with that old bugger Rex?" Of course he managed to compete with everyone in his own inimitable way.

May 8 1991

HARRY RÉE

HARRY RÉE, who has died aged 76, had two distinguished careers – first in the Special Operations Executive during the Second World War, and then as Professor of Education at York University, after which he went back to school as a classroom teacher, an almost unheard-of self-demotion.

Rée – like Francis Cammaerts, another of SOE's best agents – had begun the war as a conscientious objector, before a change of heart led him to sign up as a gunner. In 1942, after a spell in Intelligence, Rée was recruited by Major Peter Lee, who had created SOE's No 2 Field Section, and commissioned with the rank of captain as a field security conducting officer.

This entailed keeping an eye on radio operators.

Among Rée's duties was to assess the operators' reliability on a booze-up, as well as their ability to resist temptation by women. In London this test was taken a stage further when the men were given the addresses of enthusiastic amateurs, who took them to bed and reported their susceptibility to seduction by female Gestapo agents.

All this whetted Rée's appetite to operate in the field himself and he badgered Lee to let him train as an agent. Lee was horrified, telling him: "You know far too much about the system to risk capture, torture and interrogation."

When Lee was posted to North Africa, however, Rée was able to persuade SOE's "F" Section to parachute him into France. His arrival, in April 1943, was disconcerting. A container accompanying him was caught on a pylon; his first safe address turned out to be a hotel the Gestapo had occupied two weeks earlier.

Moreover, the agent whom Rée had been told to contact at Clermont-Ferrand, on hearing Rée's French, advised him to pack it in: the SOE had hoped that Rée's Mancunian accent might pass for Alsatian. Nevertheless he remained in France for most of 1943, training and operating with the *maquis* in the Jura mountains.

Operating under the codename "César" and the assumed identity of "Henri Rehman", itinerant watchmaker, Rée was a brilliant saboteur. His invention of what became known as blackmail sabotage at the Peugeot works at Sochaux, near Montbeliard, has assumed textbook status in the literature of subversion.

The peacetime car factory was busily engaged producing arms for the Luftwaffe and Wehrmacht. Rée went to see Roger Peugeot, who ran the works, and suggested he co-operate with internal sabotage in return for an agreement with the RAF to call off attacks on the plant – attacks which were costing civilian lives.

The subsequent explosions within the factory destroyed a 600-ton press vital in the construction of tank turrets. Later, when the Germans sought to replace it with a press delivered by canal, Rée sank the barge.

Eventually rumbled, Rée hit the German military policeman sent to arrest him over the head with a bottle of Armagnac, but was shot in the process: one bullet penetrated a lung, another grazed his heart. After a 20-minute struggle during which he bit off the German's nose, Rée escaped. He managed to cross a river and crawl several miles through the countryside to the Swiss border.

Harry Alfred Rée was born at Manchester on October 15 1914, the youngest of eight children. His grandfather had emigrated from Germany in the 1870s; his mother was French.

Young Harry was educated at Shrewsbury and St John's College, Cambridge, where he read economics and modern languages. His first job was as a French master at Penge Grammar School, and after the war Rée returned to teaching.

In 1947 he went to Bradford Grammar School as French master; four years later he became headmaster of Watford Grammar School; and in 1961 he co-founded the seminal "Agreement to Broaden the Curriculum", a movement against "the undesirable degree of specialisation" in the public and grammar schools.

In the same year Lord James of Rusholme, the first Vice-Chancellor of York University, invited Rée to become Professor of Education. He took up the post when the university opened its doors to students in 1963.

At York, Rée established himself as a leading contributor to national debates about the role of education: he was no respecter of received wisdom, of pedants, or of teachers and academics unduly preoccupied with their own prestige. When the Bachelor of Education degree was launched, for instance, he spoke of trainee teachers suffering from "unwanted and indigestible academic teaching which they mistake for scholarship".

In 1965 Rée announced the creation of SASSD, the Society for the Abolition of School Speech Days. Four years later he was the moving spirit behind SPERTTT, the Society for the Promotion of Educational Reform Through Teacher Training – which pressed, among other things, for a regular interchange of functions between teachers and college lecturers. "We teachers", he declared, "must come off our pedestals."

Before he went to York Rée had been a militant supporter of the grammar school and wrote a well-argued book on the subject, *The Essential Grammar School*. He later underwent an almost Pauline conversion and became an equally vigorous advocate of comprehensives.

Thenceforward Rée was firmly aligned with the progressives. The rallying cry among them was "relevance", and Rée's thinking was undoubtedly influential in disseminating that hard-to-define concept. But he gradually began to realise that he had had no experience of meeting the real challenge of secondary school teaching – educating the large majority who had no motivation to go on to higher education.

He therefore left York in 1974 to become the lowest grade of language teacher at Woodberry Down Comprehensive School, London, arguing: "People who've been in the teacher training business *should* go back into the schools."

Rée was rising 60. The crowd-control aspect of teaching in a comprehensive came as a surprise to him, and later he frankly admitted that his attempts to teach French to unacademic, unmotivated pupils with wildly varying levels of ability were a failure; but his zest was undiminished. He remained at the school for six years until finally retiring in 1980.

Rée then took up the cause of "Community Education" – "raising the school leaving age to 90", as he put it – and for seven years edited the Community Education Development Centre Monthly Bulletin, *Network*. He greatly admired and was much influenced by the educational eccentric Henry Morris, who pioneered the pre-war "Village Colleges" in Cambridgeshire.

In 1973 Rée published a notable book about Morris, *Educator Extraordinary*, in furtherance of his strong belief that schools should not shut themselves off from the rest of the community, and should "consciously encourage the formation of an educated public opinion, without which democracy cannot survive the cultural pollution by which it is increasingly threatened".

Rée, who had a house at Ingleborough, grew to love the dales and moorlands of Yorkshire: he wrote *Three Peaks of Yorkshire* (1983), with photographs by Caroline Forbes, as a tribute to the landscape of Ingleborough, Penyghent and Whernside.

For his work with the Resistance Rée was appointed OBE in 1945 and awarded the DSO and the Croix de Guerre.

Shortly before his death he spoke at Valençay at the

unveiling, by Queen Elizabeth The Queen Mother, of a memorial to members of the SOE's French section.

Rée married, in 1943, Hetty Vine, who predeceased him; they had two sons and a daughter. He married secondly, in 1965, Peta Garrett.

May 20 1991

EDWINA BOOTH

EDWINA BOOTH, the American film actress, who has died aged 86, shot to fame after starring as the "White Goddess" in the classic African adventure *Trader Horn* (1931), but never appeared before a camera again.

For the next six years Miss Booth was confined to her bed in a darkened room, plagued by a series of mysterious tropical maladies she claimed to have contracted while making the film in the African jungle; and she was dogged by rumours of her death.

A doctor's daughter, she was born Constance Booth Woodruff at Provo, Utah, on September 13 1904, and began her career as a Hollywood extra in silent movies.

In 1928 Metro-Goldwyn-Mayer embarked on a film version of *Trader Horn*, the story of a white trader overcoming tribal hostility in Africa. The director, W. S. Van Dyke, announced that he wanted "a milk-white blonde with a brunette's temper, or better yet a redhead's" to take the female lead.

After days of fruitless auditions, Van Dyke recalled that Edwina Booth had a "temper like a spanked cat". She got the job, and duly set sail with the company for Mombasa.

The trouble started at Murchison Falls, near Victoria Nyanza on the River Nile, where the first scenes were shot. Clad only in a monkey skin, she was bitten mercilessly by insects while crawling through long elephant grass. The sun scorched her body, and she was frequently laid low by sunstroke.

Miss Booth rejoiced when a cloudburst destroyed their camp but, after hippopotami trampled on the debris, Van Dyke ordered the company to remove to the Belgian Congo. There Miss Booth, still wearing garments of singularly sparing cut, was assaulted by the malignant tsetse fly; she fell ill with malaria and then with dysentery; and hardly had she recovered when she fell out of a tree and nearly fractured her skull.

To make matters worse, the picture, initially intended as a silent movie, was transformed mid-production into a "talkie", and cast and crew had to wait for many weeks in the jungle while new sound units were shipped from Hollywood.

On her return home Miss Booth suffered a nervous breakdown, and then collapsed completely. Specialists were summoned from all over America to her bedside, to no avail.

Nor was the patient's condition improved when, in 1933, she was sued by the wife of Duncan Renaldo, who had played the lead in the film. Mrs Renaldo alleged that during their protracted stay in the African jungle Miss Booth had played the role of vamp all too well and stolen her husband's heart.

The jilted wife claimed £12,000 damages, though the "White Goddess" was absolved. "I have won my case," she said afterwards. "I have even forgiven the woman who caused me such misery."

The next year Miss Booth filed a claim for more than $1 million against Metro-Goldwyn-Mayer on the grounds that her health had been ruined by the hardships she had been subjected to.

She alleged that during the 9-day voyage from Naples to Mombasa she had been ordered to sunbathe naked on the ship's deck, and that the film's company had failed to provide her with protective clothing in the jungle.

Still languishing behind closed shutters in her bedroom, Miss Booth drew up a list of 10 separate ailments caused by her ordeal: "Impairment of metabolism; depletion and partial destruction of nerve centres; sunstroke; low blood pressure; malaria; dysentery; wounds on the head and back; contusions of feet and legs; loss of vitality, vivaciousness, beauty of form and other physical attributes essential to motion picture actresses."

Miss Booth's lawyers attempted to speed up her case, explaining that their client was by now almost destitute and urgently required financial assistance. The result of the case was never disclosed; it was thought that MGM made an out-of-court settlement.

In 1935 Dr Woodruff, who had been forced to take early retirement to care for his daughter, brought her 7,000 miles on a stretcher to Britain for treatment at the London Hospital for Tropical Diseases.

Her condition appeared to improve during the eight months she spent convalescing at a flat in Marylebone. Every day Dr Woodruff would wheel his daughter, black-veiled against the sun which had destroyed her nerve centres, to Regent's Park. "She is slowly emerging from the darkness of the tomb," a friend told *The Daily Telegraph*.

But in 1936 Miss Booth suffered a relapse, and her father was obliged to take her to Europe to consult a physician in Vienna. By 1937, seven years after her return from Africa, Miss Booth – now a brunette – could finally pronounce herself cured.

She immediately declared that she would be dedicating all her future leisure and a large proportion of her earnings to the alleviation of human suffering. "My years of illness have not been wasted," she informed the national press. "I have learned to love mankind."

Miss Booth never revived her cinematic career, although she continued to receive fan-mail right up to her death. Latterly she worked at a Mormon temple in Los Angeles.

Booth was twice married. Her first husband, Anthony Schuck, annulled their marriage soon after her return from Africa; her second husband, Reinold Fehlberg, died in 1983.

May 24 1991

RONALD ALLEN

RONALD ALLEN, the actor who has died aged 56, spent 16 years in the role of David Hunter, the debonair motel manager in the legendary television soap opera *Crossroads*.

Before it folded in 1988 – after disastrous attempts to rejuvenate both its script and cast – the twice-weekly series, which recounted the ups and downs of life in a motel somewhere outside Birmingham, enjoyed a faithful following of about 26 million viewers. Even in its heyday, though, *Crossroads* was not distinguished by polished performance – for years it was made on such a punitively low budget that it was shot virtually "live", and ham acting was par for the course.

Characters supposed to be away on business would reappear inexplicably in crowd scenes; and almost invariably the person on the other end of Meg Richardson's telephone could quite clearly be heard talking from the other side of a thin partition wall. But "Ronnie" Allen, with his male model good looks, his transatlantic smile, his wide Seventies suits and his perfectly coiffed hair – just a hint of grey at the temples – was in his element amid all the bland roadside sophistication.

He first joined the motel staff in 1969, and was promoted manager in 1981, when Noele Gordon's part – as the tight-lipped manageress Meg Richardson – was written out. From then, until Hunter was himself written out in 1985, Allen glided gracefully through a welter of farcical tragedies – fires, blackmailings, murders, kidnaps, armed robberies, frauds, threats and inter-staff tiffs – without having so much as to straighten his tie.

The crises were sometimes extreme – as, for instance, when his son Chris plotted the successful kidnapping of Hugh Mortimer, the millionaire husband of the proprietor of the motel, Meg (by now Mrs Mortimer). But even at the height of the tension Allen – whose acting technique was characterised by frequent pauses between phrases, often supplemented by sighs – contrived to seem blissfully unaware.

As Hilary Kingsley put it, in her seminal study *Soap Box*: "David was the most famously dull character in the history of soap operas . . . with the charisma of an ashtray

and all the life of Sooty without Matthew Corbett's hand
... To describe him as wooden would bring a libel suit
from the Forestry Commission." But if Allen had doubts,
he was careful never to show them. Far from lamenting
lost opportunities, he always maintained that he preferred television serials to stage plays: "You get a real
sense of involvement with the audience."

Certainly, Allen received letters daily from viewers
seeking a job at the Crossroads Motel, and enclosing
details of their work experience. Most of his correspondence, though, was from fans asking, "How much is David
Hunter Ronald Allen?"

To this he would reply: "How do you divide personality from appearance? I look the same way and I talk
more or less the same way. Those things are an important
part of what personality is like, but the character qualities are very, very different indeed."

His protests seemed less convincing, though, when
Allen proposed marriage to his screen wife, Barbara,
played by Sue Lloyd (of *The Bitch* and *The Stud* fame).
Six months later the wedding was called off, though the
couple finally married earlier this year.

When the Hunters were dropped from *Crossroads*,
Allen did not conceal his bitterness. But he could console
himself with having had his role immortalised in Noele
Gordon's *Crossroads Cookbook*. Introducing "Beef Chasseur", she pointed out that the French word "*Chasseur*"
translated into English as "Hunter" – adding, "but I
don't mean *you*, David!!"

Ronald Allen was born at Reading, Berkshire, in
1934, and trained at the Royal Academy of Dramatic
Art, where he won the John Gielgud Scholarship.

He worked in repertory before joining the Old Vic

146

company, where he played Benvolio in *Romeo and Juliet*, Mountjoy in *Henry VI* and Paris in *Troilus and Cressida*, which went to Broadway. Back home, Allen appeared in a number of television plays and made a notable impression as the honeymooning husband in *A Night to Remember*, a poignant film about the *Titanic*.

Allen's first big television break came in the late 1960s in *Compact*, the twice-weekly soap opera in which, for more than three years, he played the editor of a women's magazine. He then spent seven months in the rather less probable role of the manager of a football club in the serial *United!*.

After leaving *Crossroads*, Allen's matinée-idol demeanour endeared him to a new wave of comedians, and he made frequent guest appearances in the Comic Strip television films, notably as the lubricious Uncle Quentin in *Five Go Mad in Dorset*; as the Dracula-crazed policeman in *Supergrass*; and, more recently, as the denim-clad English don in *Oxford*. That he performed these roles with such relish said much for his sense of humour and gallant self-parody.

In recent years Allen also went to Hollywood, where he gained a part in the serial *Generations*, as an English tycoon who spent his time clinching impossible business deals. But the period was not a happy one; unable to obtain a work permit, he had to return home.

Allen was highly regarded by his fellow actors, who thought it a pity that for much of his career he never quite fulfilled the promise of his early classical roles. Only last year he returned to the London stage and showed theatregoers what a fine and underrated player he was, with a bravura performance as the leading man in Tom Stoppard's sunny play, *Rough Crossing*.

Allen's hobbies included gardening and collecting antiques. He is survived by his wife.

June 20 1991

RUSSELL "BIG RUSS" HINZE

RUSSELL "BIG RUSS" HINZE, the Queensland politician, who has died aged 72, became known as "the minister for everything" during the free-booting reign of Sir Joh Bjelke-Petersen.

"Big Russ" was a kind of natural wonder: built on the scale of Ayers Rock, he possessed a hide seemingly impervious to considerations of public propriety. From the time he became a cabinet minister in Bjelke-Petersen's National Government in 1974 until he resigned from politics in 1988, he was continually the target of corruption allegations – although, in the tradition of Queensland politics, he laughed them off.

Hinze once described himself as "the roughest, toughest bloody politician you could come across". He gained nationwide notoriety for his keenness to enter beer-belly competitions, his habit of stirring his tea with his finger, and his regular nomination as one of Australia's worst-dressed men.

A large, rumbustious man, grossly overweight in his later years, Hinze pulled no punches. He called for rapists to be castrated, murderers to be executed by firing squad, and "dole bludgers" to wear dog tags.

He was, in fact, the consummate populist, whose

148

larrikin style and amiable nature earned him genuine affection among many of his political foes. Cabinet colleagues respected him not only as an able administrator, but also because he was one of the few figures in the National party prepared to stand up to Bjelke-Petersen. Indeed, he spoke openly of his ambitions to become premier.

Hinze could have flourished nowhere but in Bjelke-Petersen's Queensland, where the dreams of entrepreneurs were endlessly indulged, corruption was a way of life, and civil liberties and social justice received short shrift. As Minister for Police, Hinze was asked what special qualities he brought to the post. "I've got big feet," he volunteered, "no brains, and I'm 21 stone."

Pulled over once by a young traffic constable, he allegedly opened up a map of Queensland and said, "Right, son, where would you prefer to go, Birdsville or Bedourie?" – referring to two remote townships in the far outback.

As Minister for Local Government, Hinze was also a land developer; as Minister for Main Roads – known as the "Colossus of Roads" – he was a major supplier of gravel for road works; and as Minister for Racing, the proud owner of more than 100 racehorses. Questioned about conflicts of interest, he would insist that his public and private lives were entirely separate. "Say what you like," he would laugh, "I'm a good bloke."

For the inaugural Queensland Beer Belly Championships in 1984 Hinze stood shirtless and laughing, his arms around two men whom he described as "only kids – I'm 24 stone and the biggest of these blokes is only 22 stone". As the crowd cheered he added: "Aren't they the sexiest pair of bastards you've ever seen?"

Hinze's downfall, and that of the National party Government, came a few years later, after the 1987 Fitzgerald report into corruption in the Queensland police force. Hinze was charged with having accepted $A520,000 in bribes from three property developers and an accountant. He was one of seven Queensland cabinet ministers, including Bjelke-Petersen himself, to be charged with a whole range of crimes.

Hinze, who was due to appear in court at the time of his death, had strenuously denied everything from the start. In 1979 he declared his annual income to be $A360,000, and claimed that he was far too rich to be interested in bribes.

"I've got my sentence," he said in one of his last public appearances. "No matter what they do to me, I've been sentenced by the Lord."

Russell James Hinze was born in Brisbane in 1919, and left school at the age of 12 to help his father to run cows and haul logs behind what is now the surfers' paradise – the Gold Coast strip of southern Queensland.

He milked cows seven days a week for 15 years, but managed in the interim to educate himself in his spare time, and also acted as secretary of the local cricket club.

By 1952 he was a member of the local shire council, and subsequently served for nine years as chairman. He was elected to the Queensland parliament in 1966.

Even in those early years Hinze's frankness disarmed his enemies. Soon after being appointed a cabinet minister he said, with apparent seriousness, "I told the Premier, 'If you want the boundaries rigged, let me do it and we'll stay in office for ever. If you don't, people will say you are stupid.'"

150

As it was, the Nationals stayed in power for 32 years, mostly in coalition with the Liberal party.

Hinze brought a rare light moment to the Fitzgerald inquiry when, during eight days in the witness box, he was asked about allegations that as a minister he had been seen in a brothel. This was impossible, he replied, since his knees had been giving him trouble at that time; he had been on crutches and could not have got up the stairs.

Altogether, the commission was told, Hinze had received millions of dollars in loans and payments. He replied that he borrowed money only from friends and always paid it back.

Hinze appeared in public occasionally after he was forced out of the cabinet. Latterly, suffering from cancer, he was a gaunt shadow of his old self.

Hinze married first, in 1947, Ruth Byth; they had three sons and three daughters. He married secondly, in 1981, Fay McQuillan, his secretary, who appealed to him, he said, "because she never drinks or smokes or swears and, if anyone tells a smutty story, she'll walk out of the room".

July 2 1991

FRANK "BIG BAMBINO" RIZZO

FRANK "BIG BAMBINO" RIZZO, the former mayor of Philadelphia who has died aged 70, promised on his election to that office: "I'm gonna be so tough as mayor, I gonna make Attila the Hun look like a faggot."

Rizzo did not disappoint his supporters, who were the poor whites of his native "South Philly", disturbed by the racial and student unrest of the 1960s and 1970s, caught between the derision of rich white liberals and the fury of radicalised blacks. It was typical of Rizzo's street-brawler's bravado that soon after he became mayor in 1972 he left a Boys' Club banquet to quell a potential race riot with a billyclub tucked in the cummerbund of his dinner jacket.

In his previous role as Police Commissioner he had vowed to "crush black power", challenged the Black Panthers to a duel and sent his men to raid their headquarters at night, with orders to strip them naked and photograph them. "Imagine the big Black Panthers with their pants down," he was reported to have gloated.

In an earlier incident Rizzo had mobilised the city's entire police force of 7,000 for a minor disturbance in a black area. His declared intention was to stamp out violence before it spread, and during the bicentennial celebrations in 1976 he asked President Gerald Ford for 15,000 federal troops because he feared riots – the request was declined.

Neither the style nor the substance of Rizzo's policies endeared him to civil libertarians, and the allegations against him became so serious that in 1979 the Justice Department filed a suit against the Philadelphia Police Force, citing evidence of beatings with brass knuckle-dusters, lead pipes and telephone directories. Rizzo dismissed these charges as "hogwash" and told critics that "Philly's Finest" were strong enough to "liberate Cuba with air support".

It was, none the less, a substantial achievement that under his leadership America's fourth largest city avoided the large-scale troubles of its counterparts. Even when the black ghettos exploded over the assassination of Martin Luther King, Rizzo kept things quiet by sending in his men disguised as clergy to pacify the crowds.

The son of Italian immigrants, Frank Rizzo was born on October 23 1920 and educated at South Philadelphia High School. He recalled his upbringing with fondness: "There was no question as to who was right or wrong. There were no democratic formulas. Boom! You got knocked down. It was a good system."

He left school early to enlist in the US Navy, and after joining the Philadelphia police in 1943 rose through the ranks to become Commissioner in 1967. He never ceased to be a "cop's cop", and this reputation was enough to ensure his election as mayor in 1971, with the support of 90 per cent of voters in South Philadelphia.

Black Northern Philadelphia did not respond with such enthusiasm. But Rizzo counted on the fact that the majority of Italians, Jews and Irish in the city, who traditionally voted Democrat, were moving towards the right. "A conservative", he remarked, "is a liberal who's been mugged."

Richard Nixon knew that Rizzo was disgusted by the sharp leftward trend of the Democratic party, and by George McGovern's successful campaign for the Democratic nomination. The President pumped money into the city and flattered Rizzo ceaselessly; and Nixon's aides were shocked at how easily he slipped into profanity when conversing with the Mayor.

The approach paid off, and Rizzo became one of the traditional working-class Democrats to endorse Nixon, so earning himself the accolade of "the President's favourite Democrat". Rizzo later defected to the Republican side, taking with him 60,000 "Rizzocrats", and became the Philadelphia chairman of George Bush's 1988 campaign.

Rizzo's term of office (which ended in 1978) was dogged by accusations of racism and corruption. A feud over patronage with Peter Camiel, the Democratic city committee chairman, attracted national attention when the two men, at Rizzo's suggestion, took a lie-detector test over charges of political kickbacks in the award of city contracts to architects: Rizzo failed the test.

When the *Philadelphia Inquirer*, the city's leading newspaper, published a satirical interview with Rizzo, Rizzo denounced it as "garbage, filth and treason", and launched a $6m lawsuit.

Rizzo was re-elected in 1975, against the wishes of the local Democratic organisation and two out of three city newspapers. Their preferred candidate in the primary, Senator Louis G. Hill, challenged Rizzo to a debate. Rizzo declined, so Hill appeared with a live chicken on an empty chair. "Lou Hill", countered Rizzo, "is the only politician who can debate with a chicken and lose."

The City Charter debarred anyone from running for a third term, but Rizzo campaigned for its repeal. His forthright appeal to his constituents to "vote white" cost him some support, but won him the Ku Klux Klan's "racist of the month award" in April 1978.

Rizzo failed in two later comeback attempts against Wilson Goode, the first black to be elected mayor of the city. Rizzo called him "the Bomber" in reference to the disastrous battle with the radical MOVE cult that ended with the deaths of 11 people and the destruction of 61 houses when the city police bombed the cult's headquarters in 1985. "There goes the neighbourhood," observed Rizzo.

Rizzo was the most quotable Philadelphia politician since Benjamin Franklin, and polarised public opinion until the end of his life. But his bark was often worse than his bite.

During his mayoralty more blacks than ever before were appointed to city jobs, and by the time he retired the police force was 25 per cent black. Rizzo inspired fierce loyalty among his friends, to whom he was known as "the Italian John Wayne".

Sporting a slicked-back coiffure, standing at 6 feet 2 inches and weighing 17 stone, he looked a caricature of the Italian-American working man. But he dismissed his reputation as a Lothario.

"The newspapers have made me pure," he declared. "I can't get away with anything. Listen, if I wanted to cut a caper with a promiscuous broad, I'd have to find one who's an Eskimo and meet her in an igloo – and I'd probably have to wear a beard for a disguise."

The epitaph he yearned for was "You'd better hope he's really dead."

He married, in 1942, Carmella Silvestri; they had a son and a daughter.

July 18 1991

"SADIE" BARNETT

"SADIE" BARNETT, a Cambridge legend, who has died aged 80, was one of the last of the great Dickensian landladies – and certainly the sole surviving private landlady in King's Parade.

She presided over the most splendid digs in the University at No 9 King's Parade, overlooking King's College Chapel and the Gibbs Building.

Mrs Barnett's social expectations of her lodgers were as traditional as the ambience of her rooms – and in this respect she was perhaps more of a Trollopian than a Dickensian figure. She would frequently ask Gonville and Caius College, from which she held the leasehold, to supply her with "proper young gentlemen". When Caius undergraduates became too *bourgeois* for her liking, she turned to Magdalene and Pembroke.

She greeted the representative of one noble family with the words: "The last time we had a lord here, he hanged himself in room four." To another upon receipt of his Coutts' cheque at the end of his first term, she declared: "You're very modest, aren't you? You didn't say you was no *Hon*."

In later years Mrs Barnett took in undergraduates from less exalted backgrounds, but she took a dim view of their career prospects when compared with their landed coevals'. "*Nah*, he's labour," she would say dismissively – though it was unclear whether by this she meant that he was destined for manual labour or was merely perceived as a supporter of the Labour party.

Mrs Barnett never entertained doubts about the

rectitude of her grander residents. "He was such a gent," she once said. "When he was sick he was always sick out of the window."

One recent resident, Simon Sebag-Montefiore, set much of his fictional university memoir *King's Parade* (1991) at her house; but the publishers are said to have found the character based on Mrs Barnett beyond belief, and she was duly excised.

Mrs Barnett was always very proud of the achievements of her "boys", who latterly had included the historians Andrew Roberts and Michael Bloch. She regularly corresponded with her *alumni* all over the world, and would sometimes stay with them on her travels.

She was born Sarah Wolfschaut on January 3 1911 in Stepney, east London, the daughter of a Jewish fruit and vegetable trader in Aldgate.

Young Sadie was the seventh of 10 children and began life in the rag trade, as a dressmaker. At the age of 15 she met a waiter, Michael Barnett, whom she married in 1932.

They moved to Cambridge where Mrs Barnett began her career as a landlady. They separated during the Second World War but their childless union was never dissolved.

From the late 1940s Mrs Barnett enjoyed the leasehold at King's Parade. Although *kosher* herself, she cooked breakfast of eggs and bacon for her lodgers, and had strict rules about women and hours of residence.

She regretted the passing of the more deferential undergraduates and after the upheavals of the 1960s felt sorely tried by her more high-spirited lodgers, who preferred an unsupervised existence.

Some claimed that Mrs Barnett was an unconscious

exemplar of enlightened despotism, but in reality she was a maternal neo-feudalist who exercised great care over her wards. She could display an almost Plantagenet *"ira et malevolentia"*, which concealed a fundamentally good heart.

This fierce protectiveness manifested itself when the constabulary arrived to arrest one tenant after some undergraduate excess: "You leave him alone, he's not a burglar. He's not a murderer. He's one of my nice young men."

On another occasion, when some anti-"blood sports" campaigners, enraged by the sight of a brace of pheasants hung out of her window by one of her lodgers, sought to gain entry to the house, she gave them short shrift. "He can kill what he likes," she told them. "He's a *sportsman*, you know."

Attired in a quilted dressing-gown, Mrs Barnett would sit in her room for much of the day watching the trade test transmission card on BBC. "I am waiting for the Royals to come on . . . I know they will be on soon – Ascot and all that," she would say, whatever the season.

When some undergraduates tried to disseminate the "free Mandela" message to her lodgers, she showed them the door with the parting shot: "Who is this *Nelson Piquet* anyway?"

Mrs Barnett could always detect the tread of women's feet on the stairs and would display remarkable swiftness in bounding after them in order, prematurely, to enforce the official curfew.

She was intolerant of the ways of the Modern Girl and when introduced to two of the species at a tea party declared: " *'Pickle'* and *'Pooh'*? What sort of names are those? Get out of here, you brazen hussies! You're here for one thing – and for one thing only."

On one occasion she was found on her hands and knees outside the door, eavesdropping. Within, a lodger had a "punk" girl friend with dyed green hair, whom he hid under a blanket when Mrs Barnett suddenly entered.

Mrs Barnett poked the bedding with a broomhandle, thereby revealing the naked punk. She threw out the tenant, observing: "I wouldn't have minded if it was only the hair on her head that was green."

Sadie Barnett was an efficient landlady who was capable of great kindnesses to those in need – particularly foreign students, who for years afterwards would write her grateful letters.

But not for nothing did the university newspaper describe her as "King's Parade's Boadicean landlady".

August 15 1991

LAURA RIDING

LAURA RIDING, the American poet who has died aged 90, was as remarkable for the mesmeric force of her personality – and in particular for her influence upon Robert Graves – as for her literary achievement.

Yet she abandoned both Graves and poetry before she was 40. Poetry, if not Graves, was dismissed as "humanly inadequate"; she chose instead to dedicate the remainder of her life to "direct linguistic handling of the truth-problem".

Year after year Riding's *Who's Who* entry proclaimed the imminence of "a book . . . to be entitled *Rational*

Meaning: A New Foundation for the Definition of Words
(publishing arrangements pending)".

Now, it seems, they will pend perpetually. "History",
Riding once declared, had "finished" – for she herself
was "Finality". Such claims were advanced without the
least tincture of irony or humour, but if, at a distance, it
is tempting to snigger, few presumed on such *lèse-majesté*
in her presence.

All who encountered Riding attested to her intelligence – a fierce, harsh intelligence, that sought to
dominate, never to ingratiate. Once she had pronounced
on a subject she never suffered any appeal.

Undeniably there was substance in her self-belief. No
less a judge than W. H. Auden described her as "the
only living philosophical poet".

But Riding found no pleasure in such praise. Auden,
she felt, was a "magpie", who had stolen quite shame-
lessly from her work. At least, though, he was preferable
to Yeats who, in editing the *Oxford Book of Modern Verse*,
failed to ask Riding for a single contribution; his death,
in 1939, caused her an unholy satisfaction.

As for the public, Riding admitted in the preface to
her *Collected Poems* (1938) that it found the greatest
difficulty in understanding her work. This, she
explained, was because people read her poems for the
"wrong" reasons.

Only one person, it seemed, adequately assessed her
talent. In 1924 Robert Graves came across Riding's poem
"The Quids" in an obscure American literary magazine:
"The little quids, the monstrous quids, / The everywhere,
everything, always quids", and so on and so forth.

Graves wrote to express his appreciation. Some transatlantic correspondence ensued; and at the end of 1925

Riding was invited to accompany him to Egypt, where he had taken a Chair in English Literature.

The Cairo venture was a fiasco, from which Graves beat a speedy retreat, but his relations with Riding proved more enduring. From the moment of her arrival the newcomer dominated the poet's household.

Graves's confidence at that time was at a low ebb – his poems poorly received, his finances in permanent crisis, his marriage, albeit productive of four children and conducted on the most arduously libertarian principles, heading towards disaster.

Riding's appearance heralded a new and more promising era. The complete intellectual superiority she established – "Laura is sweet to me, and is gradually teaching me to ratiocinate clearly," he wrote in 1926 – had the positive effect of enabling him to maintain a healthy independence *vis-à-vis* the rest of the world.

For a while even his relations with his wife improved. Nancy Graves liked Riding, whose feminist views reflected her own: "Mothering innocents to monsters is / Not of fertility but fascination / In women."

"It is extremely unlikely that Nancy, Laura and I will ever disband," Graves told Siegfried Sassoon in March 1925. Yet by May 1927 he and Riding had moved to a flat at St Peter's Square, Hammersmith, while Nancy and the children were installed nearby in a barge on the Thames.

The year before, through Graves's good offices, the Hogarth Press had published a volume of Riding's poetry. Now, flush with the proceeds from Graves's book, *Lawrence and the Arabs*, the two of them founded a small publishing company of their own, the Seizin Press.

But Graves's dog-like devotion soon diminished his

attractions as a lover. Sexual intercourse, Riding explained in her essay *The Damned Thing* (1928), obliged women "to enliven the scene with a few gratuitous falsetto turns", but no one should confuse these noises with any form of pleasure.

But though Graves was now allowed in her bed only to dispense comfort during thunderstorms, Riding had by no means exhausted her interest in the monstrous male. In 1929 she declared that "three-life" had become "four-life" – her way of indicating that an Irish poet called Geoffrey Phibbs, who had been discriminating enough to praise her poetry, had been summoned to the *ménage* in Hammersmith.

Phibbs was received "with open arms"; not so his wife. "Laura," Mrs Phibbs later recorded, "as cold as the cheap sparkling trinkets with which she was covered, accompanied Geoffrey, and they brought me to the Regent Palace Hotel – thrust a bottle of brandy into my hand and said, 'Drink this and forget your tears.'"

Yet Phibbs still showed some disposition towards matrimonial loyalty. He fled with his wife to France, and remained recalcitrant even when Riding, Graves and his wife swept across the Channel in pursuit.

In the public lounge of a French hotel Riding threw herself on the floor and screamed – "you seemed to die", Graves tactfully recorded. When, a few weeks later, Phibbs sneaked back to London Graves announced that he would "kill Geoffrey if he wouldn't return to Laura".

Riding herself, unable to contemplate life at St Peter's Square without Phibbs, drank a disinfectant called Lysol, and when this tipple failed to bring oblivion, leapt with a "doom-echoing shout" from the fourth-floor window of the flat, landing on the stone below. Graves, sympathetic but cautious, ran downstairs and ejected himself from a window on the third floor.

Amazingly Riding survived – which she appeared to regard as further proof of her divinity. With Phibbs and Nancy Graves (whom the Irish poet unaccountably seemed to prefer) now cast as demons, "four-life" dwindled pretty sharply into "two-life". In October 1929 Graves and Riding removed themselves to Majorca, where they settled into a life of primitive simplicity, courtesy of an industrious maid.

Their house, Canelluñ, in the fishing village of Deya, and indeed their entire life in Majorca, was financed by the success of Graves's autobiographical *Goodbye to All That* and, later, by *I Claudius* and *Claudius the God*.

But those who visited Canelluñ soon discovered that it was dangerous to offer any praise of Graves's books. When a guest asked Riding whether she would consider writing a historical novel herself, she retorted that she "didn't think she could sink so low" – a statement which would later be borne out by her fictional assault on the Trojan War.

Though such put-downs appeared only to increase Graves's admiration, the sexual strain was beginning to tell; and in 1931 he impregnated a lusty German girl called Elfriede. Riding grandly assured him that the event was insignificant, but insisted on an immediate abortion, standing at the bottom of the bed in order to ensure that the operation was carried out.

Riding's attention turned next to Tom Matthews, an American journalist who had come to Majorca in 1932 with his wife and children in order to work on a novel. For a time she helped Matthews with his work – paring his novel down to the bare conjunctions. Then one day she handed her baffled disciple a letter in which she explained that she perfectly understood the effect that she had on him; but, if he could not control his feelings, he should get up and go; she would quite understand.

Such distractions did not prevent Riding applying herself with grinding industry to her own literary endeavours, until in 1936 a Fascist takeover in Majorca forced her and Graves to flee at short notice on a British destroyer, carrying one suitcase each.

Back in London, they began to develop the idea of a new kind of dictionary, which would give definitions "not only exact but poetic". This was the first seed of the project that came to dominate Riding's life, though it was Graves who did most of the early work.

Meanwhile Riding's attention drifted towards international affairs, which she held to be closely linked with "the woman question". The "outer, predominately male, world", she explained, had become "recklessly disconnected from the world of the personal life and thought".

These reflections found expression in her *Letter on International Affairs* in 1937; and next year Riding called a meeting "to decide on moral action to be taken by inside people: for outside disorders". *The Covenant of Literary Morality* was duly drawn up, but unfortunately the document never came to Hitler's attention.

In 1938 Riding's *Collected Poems* were published, to a stunning display of critical indifference. In January 1939, however, a poetaster called Schuyler Jackson reviewed the poems in *Time*. Jackson's opinion that the work was "the book of books of the mid-20th century" seemed to Riding to betray an uncommon insight. Plans were now laid for an American visit.

Graves was graciously, if somewhat superfluously,

granted his sexual freedom. Shortly before their departure for America, he was summoned to Riding's bedroom to receive her latest revelation: "Love is a beautiful insincerity; and true."

When she and Graves arrived in America at the end of April 1939 they went to live on the Jacksons' farm. Tom Matthews, who was there, watched in horrified fascination while Riding and Jackson, after their own peculiar fashion, fell in love. Matthews was reminded "of two basilisks, motionless and staring, the rest of us . . . immobilised into cramped stone until the predetermined affair was ready".

It was unfortunate that Jackson was married, but after Laura had subjected Katherine Jackson to a series of "talks" this difficulty was removed. Mrs Jackson, who had initially professed a high regard for her interrogator, now cracked up, became violent and was removed to an asylum.

Poet and critic duly retired, with an absolute minimum of discretion, into a single bedroom – until Riding, as if sensing that this development represented a backsliding of principle, emerged to issue a bulletin: "Schuyler and I do."

Yet, for all the satisfactions which Jackson afforded, Riding had suffered an irreparable loss. Graves's return to England without her did not limit her intellectual ambition; it did, however, portend the end of her literary achievement.

Laura Riding was born in New York on January 16 1901, the daughter of Nathan Reichenthal, a tailor of Austrian extraction, and his second wife Sadie, a native of Manhattan whose parents had been born in Germany.

Nathan Reichenthal's ill-fated business enterprises

turned him into a ferocious anti-capitalist, and he dreamed of bringing up his daughter as "an American Rosa Luxembourg".

Young Laura was educated at the Girls' High School in Brooklyn and Cornell University, where she fell in love with Louis Gottschalk, an assistant teacher in ancient history, whom she married in 1920.

Mrs Gottschalk abandoned her own studies to follow her husband to various teaching posts, but by 1923 their marriage was failing, and she was throwing herself with increasing enthusiasm into writing. As Laura Reichenthal Gottschalk seemed a bit of a mouthful to inflict on editors, her middle name was changed to Riding, which she felt carried "a certain identity weight".

Her poems began to appear in various literary journals – notably in *The Fugitive*, a publication produced by an eponymous group of poets centred on Vanderbilt University at Nashville. Riding-Gottschalk was much taken by the Fugitives and determined by hook or by crook to attach herself to their number. But the hectoring manner in which she delivered her tirades about the poet's role – his task was "to take the universe apart . . . and then reintegrate it with his own vitality" – understandably alarmed the Southern *littérateurs*.

Riding removed in disgust to New York, where she gained something of a reputation as a man-eater, without, however, losing her concern that Americans did not take poetry seriously enough. This was never a fault that could be imputed to Graves. Yet it was Schuyler Jackson who established himself as the strong man who lurked in the shadow of her feminist ideals.

They married in 1941, and went to live in a small house standing on stilts amid the stagnant waters and scraggy Australian pines of Wabasso, in Florida. Jackson bought a grapefruit grove, but the venture failed; indeed, everything that Jackson touched tended to fail, including, fortunately, his attempts to break into the trust fund bequeathed to him by his father. But Riding gratefully fell into the role of fetching his slippers.

She also beavered away at the *Dictionary*, the one project which she had been determined to salvage from the wreck of her relations with Graves. But in the 29 years of her marriage, Riding, previously such a hive of literary activity, published only a handful of articles in obscure magazines.

Her prose style had always been freakish, but at least, in Matthews' memorable phrase, it had once been "thunderous with unshed meaning . . . capable of fierce (and clarifying) lightning flashes". Now, whether in letters she penned to chastise critics for their mistaken views of her work, or in the lectures which she visited upon her acquaintances, her writing became ever more impenetrable.

After Jackson died in 1968, her output of articles increased somewhat; she even, on one occasion, broadcast on the BBC: "I judge my poems to be things of the first water as poetry," she vouchsafed.

No doubt there will be disciples eager to maintain this claim. Yet in the last analysis the life of Laura Riding must serve chiefly as a cautionary tale – of cleverness unsanctified by humility, of power unredeemed by benevolence, and above all of human presumption swallowed up in the vast indifference of eternity.

September 5 1991

JEAN ROOK

JEAN ROOK, the journalist, who has died aged 59, revelled in describing how she had "clawed and scrambled" her way to become "the First Lady of Fleet Street . . . Britain's bitchiest, best known, loved and loathed woman journalist".

Rook also owned up to having been the original model for *Private Eye*'s female columnist, Glenda Slag. "I never minded the *Eye*'s caricature of me as the scurrilous hackette Glenda Slag," she wrote, "mainly because I didn't regularly read it. I daren't. It was too near the mark. If any more of wittily written Glenda had rubbed off on me, I'd have ended up as the carbon copy, instead of the other way round."

And in truth Rook never did allow the parody to outstrip her original self. She loved the privileged position of a newspaper columnist, and if she dressed in extravagantly brassy style – legendarily clanking with chunky accessories – she had the opinions and language to match.

In her weekly column in the *Daily Express*, crammed with superfluous punctuation and an excruciatingly alliterative mixture of mangled metaphors, she wrote exactly what she thought of those in public life. Lefties and feminists – indeed any manifestation of post-Sixties Britain – aroused particular scorn: "Those women who go boobing and bouncing around with hairy legs make me feel *yuk*!"

The fact that Rook's own success in a male-dominated world could be seen as a feminist victory – where hairy legs failed, furs and fragrance were sure to succeed – was neither here nor there. But then Rook was nothing if not inconsistent. Her never less than outrageous column became the vehicle for wild swings of opinion – a vacillation she considered necessary to reflect the public mood.

Thus, one week Rook would hold Prince Philip in favour; the next she would think nothing of describing him as "a snappish OAP, with a temper like an arthritic corgi". The Duchess of York was treated with similar schizophrenic hyperbole. "Sarah Ferguson looks like an unbrushed red setter struggling to get out of a hand-knitted potato sack," wrote the rancorous Rook – only to temper her description with the revelation that she was also "great fun, powerfully sexy, tremendously boisterous and thrilling to men"; as for the Duke of York, his taste, "let's face it, is about as subtle as a sat-on whoopee cushion".

Even Rook's adoring readers sometimes professed to find her unashamed vulgarity too much to bear. She received her heaviest mail-bag after referring to Mary Whitehouse as "a whited sepulchre who hands out black marks to programmes she doesn't watch through her half-closed fingers". Of 1,000 letters, six expressed agreement with this view, but 994 wanted Rook sacked. Of course this only added to her provocative reputation.

During nearly 20 years on the *Daily Express*, Rook remained a much-vaunted institution. Besides producing her column, she interviewed scores of public figures – ranging from Margaret Thatcher and Indira Gandhi to Elizabeth Taylor and Barry Humphries – and adopted what she referred to as "the same down-to-earth approach" with them all. "You know why I'm popular with the readers?" she once said. "Because I'm as ordinary as they are. They like me because I have the same reactions, the same simple view of the world. I ask the same questions. If they were interviewing Elizabeth Taylor, they would look at her hands to see if she was wearing the Krupp diamond."

Sometimes, though, for all the stylistic infelicities, traces of Rook's degree in English literature could be descried. On one occasion she launched into a discussion about W. H. Auden and Sir John Betjeman, which resulted in another sackful of abusive letters, notably from a reader who derided the article as "Literary Criticism for imbecile housewives in the same gushing but ill-natured style".

But Rook was happy to admit she had no great novel to write. She simply believed that if people chose to preach to the public, then they must expect counter-attacks. She could certainly take it herself.

For all her faults and vanities, Jean Rook was an indispensably conscientious member of every team on which she worked – someone who gave as good as she got, with true Yorkshire grit. She missed her deadline for her *Express* column only twice in two decades – once, when her son was born, and the second time, when she was diagnosed as suffering from cancer.

In typically candid and courageous style, she went on to announce her illness to her readers in her next piece. She wrote her last column only two weeks ago.

The daughter of an engineer and an usherette, Jean Rook was born in Hull on November 13 1931. She enjoyed a carefree childhood in the East Riding, and later in life would sometimes dream about giving up

Fleet Street to return to a more peaceful existence in the North.

She was educated at Malet Lambert Grammar School and Bedford College, London, where she became the first woman to edit the student newspaper, *Sennet*. She began her career on the *Sheffield Telegraph*, where she met her future husband, Geoffrey Nash.

Rook moved on to the *Yorkshire Post* and then to *Flair*, a fashion magazine, and in 1964 launched herself on Fleet Street as fashion editor on the new *Sun*. She recalled that when the woman's editor told her to check out a photograph of a skinny teenager called Lesley Hornby, she did not bother. Next week the *Daily Express* had renamed the unknown girl from Neasden, "Twiggy".

Already, though, Rook's "killer style" was in evidence. In 1965, when it was still customary to describe royalty with glowing respect, her remark about Princess Margaret's "fuddy-duddy feet" caused a sensation.

Next she moved, as woman's editor, to the old *Daily Sketch*, where she distinguished herself by her "Save our Mini-skirt!" campaign. When the *Sketch* was subsumed in the *Daily Mail*, Rook became woman's editor of the new tabloid. But after 18 months on what she described as the "morose *Mail*", she crossed the Street, amid recriminatory heat, to become woman's editor of the *Daily Express*.

Over the next 19 years, she survived eight editors; she was also the first journalist to enter the same cage as a pair of man-eating Bengal tigers. With uncharacteristic modesty she denied having actually "discovered" Mrs Thatcher, but she did not forswear to note that back in

1974 she had predicted her potential as "Britain's first woman Prime Minister".

She also described her as "the English rose who, in her dew-drenched days, looked like a long-stemmed thornless pink bud, still in its Cellophane wrapper". Denis Thatcher was apostrophised as "a balding golf-ball".

Some felt that Rook met her match in Larry Lamb, who took over the *Express* editorship in 1983. Relations were fraught from the start. As she put in her lively memoirs, *The Cowardly Lioness*: "I bear three scars – my Caesarian, my lumpectomy and Larry Lamb."

In that book Rook also showed a touchingly vulnerable streak. She led two lives: one as Jean Rook, the abrasive columnist, the other as an understanding wife, mother, daughter and friend. She could play "Fleet Street's First Bitch" because it was a professional act, and she often said she would have preferred to have been an actress. She would dress up for the role every day, play it way over the top, then go home to a blameless family life.

But last month, talking to Anthony Clare on BBC Radio Four's *In the Psychiatrist's Chair*, she also confessed to being addicted to work. If she had the choice between time with her husband (who died in 1988) or an assignment, the assignment always won.

After discovering that she had cancer Rook made a resolution to lead "a good and pure life", but this was not her style: "You have to be superhuman to do that," she said. "Anyway it's boring."

She is survived by her son, who was educated at Eton.

Dame Barbara Cartland writes: Jean Rook was a close friend of mine for many years. I admired her courage – and she had a great many difficulties in her life.

I admired also the way she always told the truth even if it was not particularly pleasant, and, above all, the way in which she managed to give those who knew her some of her own enjoyment and zest for life.

She will be a loss to the Press, which she raised to a very high standard of journalism, and her friends will never forget her.

September 6 1991

SIR EWAN FORBES OF CRAIGIEVAR, BT

SIR EWAN FORBES OF CRAIGIEVAR, 11th Bt, doctor, magistrate, landowner and farmer, who has died aged 79, was embroiled in a three-year dispute during the late 1960s to establish his claim to the baronetcy.

For Sir Ewan had been registered as a girl at his birth and went by the name of Elizabeth Forbes-Sempill until 1952 when – by that time a much-loved GP in his native Aberdeenshire – he re-registered his birth and changed his name to Ewan Forbes-Sempill.

He was born on September 6 1912 and baptised Elizabeth as the third and youngest daughter of the 18th Lord Sempill, head of the Forbes-Sempill family, a long-established Scottish dynasty holding a 15th-century Barony and a Baronetcy of Nova Scotia, created in 1630.

173

Young "Betty" (as she was known) was educated at her home by a tutor after having refused to go away to a girls' school. Her girlhood was dominated by general gender insecurity. Sir Ewan was later to remark that he thought "everyone realised my difficulties but it was hard in those days for anyone to know what to do."

The greatest ordeal came towards the end of the teenage years, when Betty Forbes-Sempill was taken to London "to go through with that ridiculous convention, the coming-out season". She "hated every minute of it" and longed to return to her horses and dogs in Scotland.

The recalcitrant Betty was sent abroad – where she attended Munich University – before her dearest wish was granted and she returned to Scotland. There she recruited a team of Scottish country dancers from Donside. They were dubbed the "Dancers of Don" and delighted audiences all over Scotland. Miss Forbes-Sempill was also a talented harpist and clarsach player.

On the death of her father, the 18th Lord Sempill, in 1934, both the barony and the baronetcy passed to her elder brother, who entrusted the management of his Fintray and Craigievar estates to his sister.

Miss Forbes-Sempill's little beige van – "Betty's Covered Wagon" – containing produce from the farms and game from the moors was a familiar sight in the neighbourhood. She left the fashionable world of London far behind as she took to speaking and reciting in broad Scots. Her usual attire at this time was a mannish kilt – although she eschewed the masculine fashion of turning down her stockings.

During the Second World War she went to Aberdeen University to study medicine and, after graduating in

1944, worked for a year as a senior casualty officer at the Aberdeen Royal Infirmary.

In 1945 she took up practice in the Alford district and it was from this point onward that Elizabeth Forbes-Sempill looked and behaved liked the man she knew she really was. Her practice was one of the largest in north-east Scotland and "the Doctor" (as she became generally known) was tireless in her efforts to reach her patients. In the winter months she often had to travel through ten-foot drifts of snow to reach isolated hill crofts – hazardous journeys which she undertook in an ex-Army caterpillar-tracked Bren-gun carrier specially procured for the purpose.

Dr Forbes-Sempill went about her change of gender in the quietest possible manner. She applied to the Sheriff of Aberdeen, and acquired a warrant for birth re-registration.

Then, on September 12 1952, there appeared a notice in the advertisement columns of *The Press and Journal*, Aberdeen, which stated that henceforth Dr Forbes-Sempill wished to be known as Dr Ewan Forbes-Sempill.

The patients at his medical practice were loyal and supportive when sought out by the press. "The doctor has been telling us for some time of his intended announcement. We admire his courage in taking this step," said one. And the 100-year-old Mrs Isabella Grant waxed lyrical in his praise: "the doctor's a fine craitur [*sic*] – I wouldn't change for anything."

Dr Forbes-Sempill himself was extraordinarily candid: "It has been a ghastly mistake," he told one reporter. "I was carelessly registered as a girl in the first place, but of course, that was 40 years ago ... The doctors in those days were mistaken, too . . . I have been sacrificed to prudery, and the horror which our parents had about sex."

Some three weeks later the doctor announced that he was to wed Isabella ("Pat") Mitchell, his housekeeper. It was a fairly quiet ceremony.

On the death of his brother, the 19th Lord Sempill, in 1965, the barony passed in the female line to the 19th Lord's eldest daughter. It was assumed that the baronetcy would be passed to Ewan Forbes-Sempill, but his cousin, John Forbes-Sempill (only son of the 18th Lord Sempill's youngest brother, Rear-Admiral Arthur Forbes-Sempill), challenged the succession to the baronetcy.

The case was taken to the Scottish Court of Session. The court ruled in favour of Ewan Forbes-Sempill, but when his cousin continued with his challenge the dispute was taken to the Home Secretary, in whose office the Roll of Baronets is kept by Royal Warrant.

The Lord Advocate was consulted by the Home Secretary, James Callaghan, and eventually in December 1968, Mr Callaghan directed that the name of Sir Ewan Forbes of Craigievar (he had dropped the name of Sempill) should be entered in the Roll of Baronets.

The Doctor had given up his medical practice in 1955, after which he devoted himself to farming. He was appointed a JP for Aberdeenshire in 1969. In 1984 he published *The Aul' Days*.

There were no children of Sir Ewan's marriage. His cousin, John Alexander Cumnock Forbes-Sempill, born 1927, now succeeds to the baronetcy.

October 1 1991

BRIGADIER "SPEEDY" BREDIN

BRIGADIER "SPEEDY" BREDIN, who has died aged 80, won an MC in Normandy and a DSO in Holland, both in 1944, and was mentioned in despatches in Malaya in 1956.

A soldier who led from the front, "Speedy" was always particularly careful to preserve an immaculate appearance – for the sake of regimental morale. In Normandy in 1944, when moving forward with his radio operator, he was caught in the open in the middle of an enemy artillery barrage. Observers felt that this must be the end of him and, when the barrage lifted, went in to bury the remains. To their considerable surprise they found "Speedy" not only standing up but demanding of his radio operator: "Brush me down, brush me down!"

Ten years later, commanding the 1/6th Gurkhas at Ipoh, Malaya, Bredin wore the starched shirting and shorts so characteristic of the period. As he was the CO, the *dhobi wallah* starched and creased his shorts to such perfection that when he sat in his office he would take them off and stand them up in the corner: none of his visitors was the wiser.

Before emerging to inspect the lines, "Speedy" would step into the crisp shorts, giving no sign that he had been working at his desk in a temperature of more than 90°F, with accompanying humidity.

Scion of an Anglo-Irish military family, Alexander Edward Craven Bredin was born in 1911 in Rangoon;

his father was a colonel in the Indian Army. He was educated at King's, Canterbury, and Sandhurst. Commissioned into the Dorsetshire Regiment in 1931, he soon acquired the nickname "Speedy" for his ability to arrive on parade just on time.

In 1936 the regiment moved to Palestine, where the Arab rebellion had begun; but after a year restoring order, a draft commanded by Bredin sailed for India, where it joined the 1st Battalion in the Khyber Pass. The valleys were stiflingly hot and the peaks bitingly cold. Fighting was as natural as breathing to the tribesmen, who were expert marksmen, and a careless move could offer a target which a sniper was unlikely to miss.

When the battalion moved to Nowshera, Bredin became the brigade intelligence officer under the future Field Marshal Alexander; and in 1939 Bredin served as air liaison officer during the Waziristan operation. While on the North-West Frontier he travelled through Afghanistan to Bamian, and through Chitral and Gilgit to Kashmir; much of the country he traversed had peaks which ranged up to 20,000 ft.

On the outbreak of the Second World War the regiment was withdrawn and stationed at Malta, but as there was no imminent threat from Italy, Bredin and others were sent back to Dorset.

In the autumn of 1940 Bredin was sent to Gibraltar, where he found himself on the staff. He managed to reach a more active area by travelling on a Halifax bomber through enemy-infested airspace to 18th Indian Brigade.

Next he went to the 10th Indian Division, before returning to the 1st Dorsets, brigaded with the 2nd Devons and 1st Hampshires in 231st (Malta) Brigade.

After training in amphibious landing techniques on the Suez Canal, Bredin, now a company commander, landed in Sicily. Later in the battle for the island he became second-in-command of the 1st York and Lancaster Regiment, with which he landed and fought in Italy.

He was then permitted to rejoin the 1st Dorsets; they trained in the West Country before landing in Normandy on D-Day and capturing Arromanches. From then on it was heavy fighting, first through the Normandy Bocage and then up to the "island" between Nijmegen and Arnhem.

Although the 50th Division (of which the 1st Dorsets were a part) was returned to England after nearly two years of continuous action, Bredin was soon back in the thick of the North-West Europe campaign, in command of the 5th Dorsets. He led them in the Rhine crossing and into Germany.

After the war Bredin was on the staff of Western Command; AQ in the Middle East; and OC, Company Commanders' Division, at the School of Infantry, Warminster. Then, in 1954, he was selected by Field Marshal Sir John Harding, Colonel of the Regiment, to command 1/6th Gurkhas in Malaya, which he did for two years.

From 1956 to 1959 Bredin commanded 156 (Lowland) Infantry Brigade (TA) – a singular appointment for a Sassenach of Irish extraction. Later he became Inspector of Physical Training at the War Office and Commandant of the APTC. From 1967 to 1977 Bredin was Colonel of the Devonshire and Dorset Regiments, and made four visits to Northern Ireland.

He became president of the Dorset Regimental Association in 1962, and was the first president of the D-Day and Normandy Fellowship. On his visit to Normandy in

1978 the grateful villagers of Hottot renamed the square *"Place du Dorset Regiment – A E C Bredin Commanding Officer"*.

He was the author of several books, including *Three Assault Landings: the 1st Dorsets 1939–45*; *The Happy Warriors: The Gurkhas*; *The History of the Devonshire and Dorset Regiment 1958–83*; and *The History of the Irish Soldier Throughout the Ages*.

"Speedy" Bredin was above all a fighting soldier who took a great pleasure in the fact that most of his service was with the troops and little of it spent in the War Office. In his younger days he was an excellent athlete and cricketer, and rode to hounds with the Cattistock.

In retirement he was active in local affairs and a faithful contributor to the correspondence columns of *The Daily Telegraph*, where he expounded on the virtues of the infantry and the old county regiments, while excoriating politicians bent on defence cuts. "I am sure I speak for many," he declared in 1964, "if I say I would rather pay for British infantrymen than for 'false teeth for foreigners' and other luxurious trappings which go towards making us an effete as well as an affluent nation."

Bredin was a Deputy Lieutenant for Devon.

He married Desiree Mills. They had a son, now serving in the Guards, and a daughter, who predeceased him.

November 8 1991

LORD MOYNIHAN

THE 3RD LORD MOYNIHAN, who has died in Manila, aged 55, provided, through his character and career, ample ammunition for critics of the hereditary principle.

His chief occupations were bongo-drummer, confidence trickster, brothel-keeper, drug-smuggler and police informer, but "Tony" Moynihan also claimed other areas of expertise – as "professional negotiator", "international diplomatic courier", "currency manipulator" and "authority on rock and roll".

If there was a guiding principle to Moynihan's life, it was to be found on the wall of his office in Manila, where a brass plaque bore the legend, "Of the 36 ways of avoiding disaster, running away is the best."

Moynihan learnt this lesson at an early stage. The first time he ran away was in 1956, to Australia. There were two reasons for his flight. The first was to elude his father's fury over a liaison with a Soho nightclub waitress.

The second was to escape his wife, an actress and sometime nude model; they had married secretly the previous year, and she had now taken out a summons against him for assault. Her father had made a similar complaint – "I regret to say I gave him a swift right uppercut," Moynihan announced from Australia.

The idea was that he should work on his uncle's sheep farm in the bush, but after five days he ran away to Sydney, where he made his debut as a banjo-player and met the Malayan fire-eater's assistant who was to become his second wife. The next year he returned to

181

London, where he effected a reconciliation with his first wife and found a job as manager of the Condor, a Soho nightclub. The job did not last, and in 1958 he married the former fire-eater's assistant, by now a belly-dancer working under his management.

"Of course," Moynihan explained, "it means I shall have to become a Mohammedan first." To this end, at dusk each day he kneeled to the setting sun with a cloth draped over his head.

His father was displeased by the marriage, but Moynihan was unabashed. "Actually," he confided to a journalist, "I only see the old man when I'm a bit short."

Soon after the wedding he made his first court appearance, accused of the larceny of two bedsheets. He was found not guilty, but as he walked from the court he was presented with another summons, this one over a lease. It was time to run away again.

With his new bride, Moynihan moved to Ibiza to set up a nightclub; when this failed he left his partner to pick up the pieces and fled to the mainland, before returning home once more. His next venture was a coffee bar called El Toro, with a Spanish bull-fighting theme, at premises in Beckenham, Kent. But that, too, failed, so Moynihan set off with his wife on a belly-dancing tour of Europe and the Far East. In 1961 the two of them converted to the Persian faith of Baha'ism: "It propagates Oneness of Mankind," Moynihan explained.

On their travels he occasionally challenged people to duels, but nothing came of these. An Italian declined to fight: "Moynihan's behaviour is founded on exhibitionism. It has nothing to do with gentlemanly conduct."

In Tokyo he challenged an American journalist who

had disparaged his wife's dancing; the critic elected martinis or cold noodles as weapons. In 1960s London Moynihan cut a rather ridiculous figure in Kaftans, and worked for a time for Peter Rachman, the slum landlord, driving his maroon Rolls-Royce.

"I didn't really understand what was involved in those days," recalled Moynihan. "It was quite cruel. They had this big Alsatian dog that had been taught to soil the tenants' beds."

Moynihan later claimed that three years after Rachman was reported dead he met him at an hotel in Izmir, Turkey, where they had a drink together and reminisced about old times.

After he succeeded his father in the peerage in 1965 Moynihan took the Liberal Whip in the House of Lords, where he was principally concerned in arguing that Gibraltar be given to Spain. The House was not impressed. In 1968 Lord Boothby interrupted one of Moynihan's speeches: "My Lords, the noble Lord has bored us stiff for nearly three-quarters of an hour. I beg to move that he no longer be heard."

Moynihan's business career and personal finances had meanwhile given rise to a number of misunderstandings. By 1970 he faced 57 charges – among them fraudulent trading, false pretences, fraud against a gaming casino and the purchase of a Rolls-Royce motor car with a worthless cheque. To avoid disaster he fled once more, this time to Spain.

"I knew of my impending arrest 48 hours in advance," he claimed. "I'd been approached by a CID man who told me that for £50,000 the case against me would be dropped. Because I believe in God and England I told him to get stuffed." His extradition was sought from Spain, but he disappeared, to resurface the next year in the Philippines.

In 1968 he had married for a third time – another belly-dancer, this one a Filipino – and the new Lady Moynihan's family had a chain of massage parlours in Manila, where Moynihan remained for much of the rest of his life. At the Old Bailey in 1971 he was named in his absence as "the evil genius" behind a series of frauds. "This is a case of *Hamlet* without the Prince of Denmark," declared the judge. "The Prince figuring behind all these offences is Lord Moynihan."

As the 1970s wore on Moynihan found employment in the narcotics trade, as well as in fraud and prostitution. The first hint of this came in 1980, when he was named by an Australian Royal Commission as an associate of Sydney's "Double Bay Mob", engaged in the import of heroin from Manila.

No charges were brought, however, and Moynihan continued his life as a Filipino pimp under the patronage of President Marcos – "my drinking chum", as he called him. Marcos apparently shielded him from prosecution over the murder of a nightclub owner (who had married one of Moynihan's ex-wives). At one stage he ran a brothel within 100 yards of the British Ambassador's residence.

After the coup against Marcos in 1986, Moynihan's position became exposed, and the next year he was forbidden to leave the Philippines pending investigations of his links with drugs and prostitution.

Moynihan was thus vulnerable to pressure from Scotland Yard and the American Drugs Enforcement Agency to help them catch Howard Marks, a Balliol man who at that time controlled an estimated sixth of the global market in marijuana, and with whom he was already on friendly terms.

He approached Marks with a bogus offer to sell him an island in the Philippines, on which he could grow marijuana; and in return for his own immunity agreed to wear a secret tape recorder to ensnare his friend. Marks was duly convicted in Florida, with Moynihan as chief witness for the prosecution.

The DEA gave him refuge and protection in the United States for a time, and hailed him as "a hero, one of the good guys". Marks saw things differently. "I feel terribly betrayed," he said. "He's a first-class bastard."

Perhaps the most charitable judgement of Moynihan was one offered by a friend: "Tony could never see wrong in himself, only in others. He thought he was just having harmless fun."

Antony Patrick Andrew Cairne Berkeley Moynihan was born on 2 February 1936, the eldest son of Patrick Moynihan, a barrister and stockbroker who succeeded to the Barony of Moynihan later that year.

Patrick's father, Sir Berkeley Moynihan, an eminent surgeon who introduced surgical rubber gloves to Britain from America, had been created a baronet during Lloyd George's final administration, and then a peer in 1929.

Young Tony was educated at Stowe and did his National Service with the Coldstream Guards; it was his last contact with respectability, and he was inclined to reminisce over it in his cups.

His father, the 2nd Lord Moynihan, died in 1965, financially embarrassed and facing charges of homosexual importuning. He had been chairman of the Liberal party executive from 1949 to 1950 but resigned from the party in 1963; his decision was announced by the

Freedom Group, in which he was associated with Edward Martell.

Colin Moynihan, Conservative MP for Lewisham East and currently Minister for Energy, is the son of his second marriage, and thus the half-brother of the 3rd Lord Moynihan. The two were never close, but in 1985 they fell out when Tony Moynihan announced that he intended to sell the Victoria Cross won in 1855 by their great-grandfather, Sergeant (later Captain) Andrew Moynihan. Colin Moynihan is said to have raised £22,000 to pay off his errant half-brother.

In Manila, to which he returned after his sojourn in America, Moynihan lived in the suburbs in a heavily fortified house with a swimming pool, and had as his base in the city a brothel named the Yellow Brick Road. "I just sit back and collect the money," he said. "The girls do all the work."

He frequently spoke of returning to England – "to clear my name", as he put it. "I miss things like decent roast beef and good newspapers, the civilised way of life."

In 1988 he claimed to have secured immunity from police prosecution, and announced that he looked forward to taking his seat on the Labour benches of the House of Lords.

Giving evidence at Marks's trial in 1989, Moynihan told the court that he had been appointed to the Order of Don Quixote by General Franco, whom he much admired. The court seems to have believed him, but no such order exists.

In *Who's Who* his recreation was listed as "dog breeding", but when pressed on this matter he strenuously denied it: "As for breeding dogs, I can tell you I don't. Like every Englishman I like dogs, but that's where it ends."

Moynihan is reported to have been married five times, and to have fathered various children. The heir to the Barony appears to be his son Daniel, born in February this year.

November 26 1991

TOM BAKER

TOM BAKER, a singular Suffolk character, who has died aged 96, looked after the celebrated duck decoy on the Pretyman estate of Orwell near Ipswich.

When the late Sir Peter Scott took over the decoy he held out his hand, with what he hoped was a modest smile, and said: "Is this the man who knows more about duck than I do?" Baker replied in his direct Suffolk way: "I reckon I do." After this exchange the *rapport* between the two men was never quite what it might have been.

Baker had begun work as decoyman on the Orwell estate after serving throughout the First World War in the Suffolk Regiment. In one year, 1925/26, he caught 9,500 ducks.

When the late Mrs Pretyman (elder daughter of the 2nd Lord Cranworth, KG, a shooting companion of King George V) was first married in the early 1930s, she watched a catch and said:

"Oh Tom, how can you? The poor things. And they're so pretty." To which Baker responded: "You'll be lucky, madam, when your time comes, if you go as quick."

A gamekeeper's son, Thomas Baker was born in 1895 and volunteered for the Suffolks in 1914.

While training at Colchester he defeated the British Army champion at the rifle range. In France he became a renowned sniper.

On one occasion he stayed up for a week, watching for a German sniper who had killed many men. At last he saw a slight movement in a haystack; he fired at it and out toppled the German sniper.

When Colonel Maxse took over the Suffolks he complained of their scruffiness: "I wouldn't mind in the line, but here it looks dreadful." At this point Baker put his hand up and the Sergeant-Major gestured fiercely. "No," said the Colonel, "let that young man speak. I want to hear what the men think."

Baker spoke out: "We'd be a sight cleaner, Sir, if we had any soap or cleaning materials. We ran out a year ago, and you know you can't always afford 'em and you can't always steal 'em."

The Colonel was silent for a while, and then said quietly: "I'll see you get them." The men took it for the usual easy promise, but ample cleaning materials arrived next day and the Suffolks became so smart that other regiments copied them.

Baker would also recall how the Suffolks trained for Gallipoli, brought amphibious warfare to a fine art and were then sent back to France while untrained men were sent to take their place. "And when we heard what happened to them poor boys, we wept."

He had total recall of everything he had ever seen, so to talk to him was to be on the Somme. His account of the First World War was exact, dramatic and fascinating

– except in one particular: he would never tell how he won his Military Medal.

He celebrated his 91st birthday by going pigeon shooting, and brought down three high birds. At 94 he was still digging and scything, and always took a walk every day; his notion of a walk was seldom less than a mile and often about five.

Tom Baker was a good Christian but preferred not to talk about it.

He is survived by a son and three daughters.

December 2 1991

WALTER HUDSON

WALTER HUDSON, who has died at Hempstead, New York, aged 46, was once listed in *The Guinness Book of World Records* as the heaviest man on earth.

About 6 feet tall and 9 feet around, with cherubic features set off by pigtails braided in the Cherokee style, he long devoted himself to the pleasures of the table. Four years ago Hudson – then tipping the industrial scales at his top weight of 85 stones – gained worldwide notoriety (as "Whopping Walter") when he became stuck in his bedroom door. He was wedged there for some four hours; it took eight firemen to free him.

Walter Hudson was born at Brooklyn in 1945 and, as he recalled, "began gorging at the age of six". At 15 he was so obese his legs collapsed underneath him and he was confined to bed.

Indeed, except for the time when his family moved

to Hempstead in 1970 and he was transported by motor car (his then 42 stones broke the seat), he remained inside. "I'm just a foodaholic," he once confessed. "I have no excuse."

Hudson's eating habits were fuelled by food brought in by members of his family. He would generally start his day with a breakfast of two pounds of bacon, 32 sausages, a dozen eggs, a loaf of bread, jam and coffee.

For luncheon Hudson favoured four Big Macs, four double-cheeseburgers, eight boxes of fried potatoes, six pies and six quarts of Coca-Cola. He would dine off six corns on the cob, three ham steaks, half a dozen yams and another six or seven baked potatoes, ending with a whole apple pie.

Between these principal repasts he would despatch a fowl or two, chased by macaroni, string beans, six large bottles of soda, not to mention colossal sandwiches and copious snacks such as Ring-Dings, Yodels, Yankee Doodles, Twinkies and assorted candy. "All I cared about," he recalled, "was food, *food*, FOOD!"

When not eating and sleeping he would watch television, listen to tapes and read the Bible – he had a particular penchant for the Psalms and was apt to recite Psalm 121: "I will lift up mine eyes unto the hills . . ." Hudson, though, was advised against sitting up for longer than five minutes because of the risk of being smothered by flab. The only exercise he engaged in was when he attended to his ablutions; it took him an hour to negotiate the six yards to the bathroom from his bedroom.

Then, in 1987, he found himself wedged in the doorway. "The day I got stuck in that door," he recalled, "that's when the Lord got me the help I needed." The help to which he referred was offered by Dick Gregory, a comedian who masterminded the Slim Safe diet scheme.

"We think what might have happened," said Gregory about his new client, "is that in 27 years of lying around he might, because of the reading of his Bible, have taken on the same characteristics as Buddhist monks – slowed down the biological processes. But we don't know."

Gregory placed Hudson on a 1,200-calorie-a-day diet of raw fruit and orange juice. For exercise he was advised to lie in bed waving his arms about like a conductor.

Hudson soon lost some four inches off his knees, and within three months had shed 28 stones. It began to look as if he might fulfil such ambitions as visiting his mother's grave, riding on the New York subway, driving into the country – and even flying to a clinic in the Bahamas, from which he envisaged emerging as a sylph of thirteen stones.

But it was not to be. At the time of his death, of an apparent heart attack, Hudson reportedly weighed 80 stones. Rescue workers had to cut a large hole in the wall of his bedroom to remove the body.

He was unmarried.

December 28 1991

THE DUKE OF MONTROSE

THE 7TH DUKE OF MONTROSE, who has died aged 84, was a Rhodesian farmer whose presence in Ian Smith's rebel government gave it a faint whiff of Ruritanian respectability.

A Gaelic-speaking giant of 6 feet 5 inches, of great charm but with opinions noticeably stronger than his executive abilities, Montrose regarded the Beatles, Carnaby Street and long hair as part of a Communist plot to subvert the West.

"It is a common observation that the African is a bright and promising little fellow up to the age of puberty," was his considered opinion submitted to an official inquiry. "He then becomes hopelessly inadequate and disappointing, and it is well known that this is due to his almost total obsession henceforth with matters of sex."

Montrose squared his loyalty to the Queen and support for Smith's Unilateral Declaration of Independence by claiming that the rebels were merely taking power from British ministers which would be returned to her when she reclaimed it personally.

Montrose was refused permission to enter Britain during the rebellion. If he had come he could have been charged with treason, thereby evoking memories of his ancestor, the great Marquess of Montrose, who was executed in 1650 for his brilliant but unsuccessful military campaign in defence of the Stuarts.

The modern Montrose – plain Angus or Lord Graham as he liked to be called in Rhodesia – found himself prevented from attending the weddings of two of his children. It was claimed that he was particularly upset at the Government's veto on his appearance as Chief of the Grahams at a clan gathering in 1977.

The British Government was adamant in refusing him a passport, although his sister Lady Jean Fforde pointed out in a letter to *The Daily Telegraph* that he still received the Queen's command to attend the opening of Parliament.

James Angus Graham was born on May 2 1907, the elder son of the Marquess of Graham, who was in turn heir to the 5th Duke of Montrose.

The Graham family had seen its fair share of fortune, bad luck and eccentricity. The 1st Duke had promoted the Union of Scotland and England; the 3rd Duke was credited with obtaining permission for Highlanders to wear the kilt again after the Jacobite Rising of 1745; and the Duchess of the 4th Duke had publicly booed Queen Victoria for listening to gossip about her husband.

The 6th Duke was the inventor of the aircraft carrier and an early supporter of Scottish nationalism – until he realised that it threatened the Union. Death duties reduced his estates, which consisted largely of uncultivated tracts of land producing no income, from 130,000 acres to some 10,000 in forty years.

Young Angus Graham was born into straitened circumstances for his rank. He was sent to Eton, where he seemed an impressive figure in the boxing ring – but 40 years on there was rather more interest in a Wall Game where he had bitten Quintin Hogg in the hand. Montrose claimed that the future Conservative Lord

Chancellor and fierce political opponent had been cheating.

From Christ Church, Oxford, where he rowed, played rugby and distinguished himself with his fine singing voice, Graham joined a British contingent which travelled around Canada helping with the harvest. His next job was with Imperial Chemicals in Newcastle upon Tyne from which he would fly himself home for the weekend to Brodick Castle on the Isle of Arran.

For his wedding in 1930 to Isobel, daughter of Colonel T. B. Sellar, 450 estate workers came by special steamer from Arran to the Edinburgh ceremony, at which he wore the red cloak and carried the sword of the 1st Duke.

Lord Graham's financial position, however, prompted the couple to move first to Johannesburg and then to Salisbury where he worked first as a seed salesman. In his spare time he took boxing lessons from the ex-heavyweight boxing champion and future federal prime minister Roy Welensky who judged him an indifferent pupil.

He then bought a 1,600-acre farm at 16s an acre, and settled down to proving himself as an excellent farmer, rising at 5 a.m. each day to supervise his labourers. After about three years he was forced to sell up by a mining exploration company, which owned the mineral rights. But he began again and successfully built up both a 3,000-acre farm outside Salisbury and a ranch 100 miles away.

Montrose made periodic visits home – on one occasion giving an address on the wireless in Gaelic – and he also went to Germany several times where he witnessed the Nazi Youth rallies.

It was hardly surprising that Montrose's name should have appeared among the list of supposed members of the German-sympathising Right Club which mysteriously surfaced in 1990, although he later declared that he knew nothing about the organisation.

At the outbreak of war, Montrose immediately rejoined the Royal Naval Volunteer Reserve, in which he had enrolled at 21. He served in destroyers involved in the evacuations of Greece and Crete, and was later given command of *Ludlow*, an American "lend–lease" warship which was on convoy duty first in the Atlantic and then in the North Sea.

Graham, who attained the rank of lieutenant-commander, asked the Admiralty for some Gaelic-speaking crew and adopted as his ship's mascot a jackdaw which would fly unhindered around the upper deck and sit on a man's hand when summoned.

After the war he returned to Rhodesia, where he found the farm growing prosperous but the colony's politics changing. A spirit of retreat had set in at home with Labour's victory in 1945 and he was unimpressed when the Tories launched the last great imperial venture: the Central African Federation of Nyasaland, Northern and Southern Rhodesia.

Graham stood as an unsuccessful Confederate party candidate bent on protecting the white-dominated *status quo* in the 1953 general election.

When he succeeded to the Dukedom of Montrose in 1954 on the death of his father (who left an estate of £802), he saw little reason to come home, preferring to leave the Scottish properties to be run by his 18-year-old son, the Marquess of Graham.

The new Duke's only public gesture was to protest

about the Walt Disney film *Rob Roy* which showed the
1st Duke's men murdering the outlaw's mother. His
grandfather had made a similar protest about a silent
film.

As the Federation's prospects declined, with the
growth of an African nationalism fuelled by Westminster
funk, Montrose had no doubts about where the blame
lay. After being elected an MP in the 1958 federal
election, he declared that South Rhodesia's Premier,
Winston Field, should replace Welensky as federal Prime
Minister in order to ensure that there would be "no
miserable compromise with London".

When the Macmillan Government proposed an
inquiry into unrest in Nyasaland, Montrose joined Viscount Malvern, the former Rhodesian Prime Minister,
and Lord Robins, President of the British South Africa
Company, in flying to London for a Lords debate.

Montrose made his mark in a speech calling for the
colony to be given the independence of full Dominion
status and talked of the 60 to 100 Africans he employed
on his farm. Those who lived in Rhodesia "had a great
faith in at least 99½ per cent of the African people and
are prepared to entrust our wives and children to them
and the country far from our nearest European neighbour," he explained.

"If our trust is misplaced, and our families become
objects of violence, we feel that is our lookout. But we
are not prepared to be made sitting ducks for agitators,
egged on by people living 6,000 miles away in safety."

In 1961 he returned to the Lords, where he joined
the 5th Marquess of Salisbury in attacking the British
Government's policy on Rhodesia. When Salisbury called

Iain Macleod, the Colonial Secretary, unscrupulous, Montrose began by trying to cool the temperature in the House: "Perhaps I may use a term that will bring less odium on him when I say that I have evidence that will persuade you that he at least is a fast worker in his political aims."

Then, with characteristic bluntness, he declared that the Government's proposed constitutional changes were "breakneck and slap-happy" and that Macleod's lack of candour had created "a complete lack of trust".

Although Montrose's style of address involved frequent pauses and references to papers, he commanded a certain respect from his fellow peers that he could not always expect from his fellow legislators in Salisbury when he became Agriculture Minister in Field's Southern Rhodesian Government. Always interested in crop developments, he was at first frustrated that his responsibilities were restricted to white farms, but after independence he was able to bring to bear his experience when dealing with the realities of subsistence farming.

As a conductor of ministerial business, it was remarked, he sometimes seemed rather slower at grasping a point than many of the Africans about whom he had reservations. His manner in answering parliamentary questions would bring cries of despair from his fellow MPs: "No, no, Angus. Not that one . . . Look at the bottom of page 64."

Nevertheless, with his unflinching belief in the leading part to be played by the white man, he became an important factor in the election of Ian Smith as the Rhodesian Front Prime Minister. As the situation deteriorated and Southern Rhodesia demanded independence

– like the black-dominated Northern Rhodesia (renamed Zambia) and Nyasaland (Malawi) – he was even mooted as a possible Regent.

The suggestion did not appeal to Harold Wilson, whose supple mind was the least likely to appeal to the increasingly exasperated colonists. At a dinner on a visit to Salisbury, Wilson expected the bargaining to continue but Montrose, believing it to be an opportunity to relax from the strain of negotiations, proceeded to sing a "blue" song about a dancer, with illustrative movements. "I now understand", the Labour Prime Minister observed in broadest Yorkshire, "what qualifications you have to be Regent."

When Montrose gave public support for UDI, a Labour MP proposed that the law should be changed to prevent him taking his seat in the Lords. Wilson replied: "You don't use a steamroller to crack a nut; not this nut, anyway."

Although Montrose found little difficulty in agreeing to UDI, he remained concerned that his colleagues might eject his friend the Governor, Sir Humphrey Gibbs, from Government House. "It would be over my dead body," he declared, "that they would put a hand on the representative of the Queen."

Whatever the doubts Smith privately shared with Wilson about the ducal intellect, he recognised Montrose's public relations value by making him External Affairs Minister. When Montrose rather than Smith greeted Herbert Bowden, the Colonial Secretary, at the airport, it indicated that the colony now considered itself an independent country.

Montrose's reputation also played an important part in attracting what Ken Flower, head of Rhodesian

Intelligence, called the "Nuts in May". Among the visitors were an armorist styling himself The Gayre of Gayre and Nigg, who believed the Zimbabwe ruins were too sophisticated to have been produced by Africans; Captain Henry Kerby, an eccentric Tory MP with many Intelligence connections; and L. Ron Hubbard, leader of the Scientology cult.

The trouble was that, as the consequences of the constitutional act of madness became apparent to Smith, the Rhodesian leader found Montrose still in no mood to compromise. Montrose played a key role in the Cabinet rejection of the offers made by the Wilson Government on HMS *Tiger* and HMS *Fearless*.

One Salisbury joke had it that Smith took half an hour to explain the British offer to colleagues and they then took 12 hours to explain it to Montrose.

After the *Fearless* talks failed Montrose was involved in an attempt by Cabinet right-wingers to introduce formal apartheid. It failed; two colleagues resigned, but Montrose continued in office several more months.

In the 12 years of independence, Montrose was an increasingly ignored figure. An attempt to persuade the party to drop Smith as its president in 1972 failed, and he was defeated when he stood for the new Senate.

When the Rhodesian rebellion ended in 1980, Montrose moved to Natal and paid a visit home to Scotland, where he attended a retirement party on the family estates for a gardener, a gamekeeper and a shepherd which had been put off until he could attend.

"I did all I could for Rhodesia. I cannot do any more. I did my best for my country," he told a reporter. Later he took the oath of allegiance again by taking his seat in the Lords.

As the sands of time began to run out for South Africa, Montrose finally returned home in 1988 after 57 years in which he had witnessed the full sweep of Britain's imperial decline. The Duke, who spent his last years in Kinross, was Hereditary Sheriff of Dunbartonshire.

His first marriage was dissolved in 1950; they had a son and a daughter. He married secondly, in 1952, Susan, widow of Michael Gibbs and daughter of Dr J. M. Semple, of Kenya; they had two sons and two daughters.

The heir to the dukedom and subsidiary titles is his eldest son, James Graham, Marquess of Graham, born 1935.

February 12 1992

PRINCESS BROWN THRUSH

PRINCESS BROWN THRUSH, a leader of the Matinnecock Indian nation, who has died at Flushing, New York, aged 79, dedicated her life to the territorial and cultural rejuvenation of the last native American tribe organised within the New York metropolitan area.

The Matinnecocks were part of the once-mighty Algonquin family which held most of the country east of the Mississippi, from Virginia in the south to Hudson Bay in the north. Before the arrival of the *Wissunkies* ("white men"), the Matinnecocks were one of 13 tribes that roamed Long Island: their lands extended around

200

Oyster Bay and modern-day Queens, where they subsisted, *inter alia*, on beached whales.

Their totem was the wild turkey. "We are the Turkey People," said Princess Brown Thrush's sister, Sun Tama, "famous for manufacturing wampum and loghouses, and for the beautiful singing voices of our women."

Partly on account of the small size of the tribe – but also because of their extensive intermarriage with the local black population – the Matinnecocks were little noticed by the white authorities. One United States government survey early this century stated that the tribe had disappeared altogether in the 1860s.

While the formal tribal structure had disintegrated, Matinnecock families none the less remained in contact with one another. They claimed the survey had been designed to cover up a land grab, for which they had received no compensation.

But from the 1950s onwards a series of dynamic leaders – Chief Wild Pigeon, the 102-year-old Chief John Standing Waters and Princess Brown Thrush's siblings, Princess Sun Tama and Chief Bald Eagle – reorganised the tribe, which was formally reconstituted at Douglaston, Long Island, in 1958.

In attendance were Indian chiefs from the Four Corners of Mother Earth, including Chief One Arrow of the North American Council of Indians and that body's formidable medicine man, Chief Flying Squirrel. At the ceremony, Princess Brown Thrush – who hitherto had been known as Lila Elizabeth Harding – was installed as Keeper of the Wampum (or treasurer).

She had been born in Flushing, New York, on June 5 1912 and educated at the local high school. For much of her life she worked for the New York Board of Education, serving school luncheons.

Along with her colleagues on the 14-member tribal council – who included, among others, Chief Little Moose as Junior Chief, Chief Thunderbolt as Serjeant at Arms and Princess Heatherflower as Keeper of the Long Count, or secretary – Princess Brown Thrush carried high the torch of Indian rights at a time of passivity and inactivity among Native Americans. Although their cause has since become fashionable, when Princess Brown Thrush began her campaign it had a rarity value on the East coast (Indian issues having endured in the public consciousness mainly in the western states).

Princess Brown Thrush met both Governor Averell Harriman and his successor, Nelson Rockefeller, to press the land claims: after one meeting at a fairground in Queens, Rockefeller graciously gave orders that Princess Brown Thrush should be conveyed to her home in the gubernatorial limousine. But the Princess was not seduced by the attentions of the establishment, and in 1964 she and other members of the tribe protested vigorously when the town of North Hempstead sought to expand a hospital in Manhasset, next to a sacred tribal burial ground.

"Desecration!" cried Princess Sun Tama at a town meeting, with Princess Brown Thrush at her side. "We want you to know you are dealing with the landlord!" As a direct result of their efforts, the construction project was abandoned, as were many subsequent ones.

Foremost among Princess Brown Thrush's duties was the maintenance of the tribal longhouse, or gathering place. She spoke fluent Algonquin, and devoted much time to teaching ritual dancing, cooking (especially the medicinal "bone set" tea) and tribal law to the younger generation.

When Princess Sun Tama died in 1969, Princess Brown Thrush became chairman or spokesman of the tribe: she was also regarded as *sachem* (or medicine man) and, as an Earth Mother, had the task of ensuring harmony in the tribe.

Emboldened by the successful land claims of other Native Americans, Princess Brown Thrush again went "on the warpath" in the 1970s and 1980s. In an attempt to create a semi-autonomous society, she and other members of the tribe claimed ownership of as much as one per cent of Suffolk County and 25 per cent of Queens County. This covered some of the choicest real estate in America, including Oyster Bay, Flushing Meadow Park, the National Tennis Stadium and the New York Mets' Shea Stadium.

As an interim measure, however, Princess Brown Thrush and the tribal leadership were prepared to accept a small reservation on the old Flushing Meadow World Fair Ground, which she hoped would be transformed into a centre for Indian crafts.

It appeared that some of the Matinnecocks' claims might be acknowledged, because of New York State's violations of the Indian Non-Intercourse Act of 1789. This was the first piece of legislation passed under George Washington's presidency, and stipulated that no Indian lands could be alienated without the consent of the federal government. But their efforts have not enjoyed much success.

This is partly because the tribe – which still totals only 250 families – does not have the resources required to launch a suit; but also because the prerequisite of a successful action is federal recognition, which the Matin-necocks do not currently possess, and which would be costly to obtain.

However, Princess Brown Thrush could claim to have played a large part in combating the massive urbanisation of Long Island.

To the moment when she "left this world", Princess Brown Thrush, who was unmarried, remained true to Matinnecock tradition. She was buried upon sprigs of pine needles, in a red satin dress specifically made for her passage by Chief Little Fox, while the choir of her local Episcopal church (of which she had been an enthusiastic member) sang "What a Friend We Have in Jesus".

Although their old hunting grounds are now filled with highways, corner delicatessens and Chinese take-aways, the recent validation of Mohawk land claims in upstate New York and the continuing work of her successor, Chief Osceola Townsend, offer some hope.

March 11 1992

COLONEL FRANK "MONOCLE" MORGAN

COLONEL FRANK "MONOCLE" MORGAN, who has died aged 99, served with the Imperial Camel Corps in the campaigns against the Turks in the First World War, and with the Royal Corps of Signals in the Second.

Morgan – variously known as "Monocle" and "Pin-point" – was chief air formation signals officer in France in 1940 and in the Middle East and Italy from 1943 to

1945. Between the wars, and after the second, he farmed in west Wales. When blindness compelled him to give up farming in 1966 he learned Braille and carried on with his public duties, being much in demand as a witty public speaker.

Morgan had a broad range of knowledge which included literature, history, law, mathematics, agriculture and science; he contributed articles to newspapers and magazines and throughout his life wrote light verse.

Frank Stanley Morgan was born in 1893 at Seoul in Korea, where his father, a commissioner of the Imperial Chinese Customs, was on a tour of duty. His mother was a niece of his father, and young Frank claimed this relationship made him his own great-uncle.

He spent much of his childhood in China but returned home to school at Marlborough. He then read law at Christ Church, Oxford.

In 1914 he enlisted in the Pembroke Yeomanry but two years later was seconded to Signals, then a branch of the Royal Engineers. He subsequently served as signals officer with the Imperial Camel Corps, taking part in cavalry battles against the Turks in Egypt and Palestine.

Of the Imperial Camel Corps he would say that it comprised an aristocratic element among its officers and complete ruffians in the ranks; all they had in common was a disdain for danger.

When he asked once for a volunteer bugler, a particularly blackguardly fellow stepped forward. "Can you blow the bugle?" asked Morgan. "Oh, no," replied the man. "I thought you said *burglar*. I am very good at that."

When the major objectives of the Palestine campaign had been achieved Morgan was transferred back to France to serve in the trenches as an expert on telephone communications. Hundreds of miles of telephone cables were laid in France, sometimes by horses, sometimes by men and sometimes by dogs with small drums on their backs. Lines were often cut by shell fire, and in repairing them it was not easy to know whether one was joining one's own line or one of the enemy's.

Morgan was the first to learn of the Armistice in the trenches, where he intercepted instructions from the German GHQ ordering the generals to lay down their arms.

After the war he returned to farm his estate in Wales. In 1920 he joined the newly formed Royal Signals (TA), and then transferred to the Supplementary Reserve in 1925.

During this period he was active in public service in the Principality, and devoted himself to the development of scouting, and became a friend of Sir Robert Baden-Powell, the founder of the Boy Scout movement. He was awarded the Order of the Silver Wolf for his services to scouting.

In 1939 Morgan went to France as OC2 Air Formation Signals and played a key role in organising telecommunications between the French and British forces: for this he was appointed CBE. Just before leaving France in 1940 he had given a final dinner party at the Ritz in Paris to members of his unit, but had inadvertently left without paying the bill. When dining there again in 1945, after the Liberation, he found the old bill laid respectfully beside the new bill by his plate, without comment.

After the fall of France he had become chief signals officer, Aldershot Command. He was deputy chief signals officer, Western Command, from 1941 to 1942; and then CSO Air Formation Signals, Home Forces, in 1943.

Next Morgan was posted to the Middle East and from 1944 to 1945 was CSO, Air Formation Signals, Middle East. During the period he had also taken part in the invasion of Italy.

He retired from the Army in 1948 and returned once more to his estate at Bishopton, where he devoted himself to farm improvements. He became a county councillor, sat on the Gower Bench, served on innumerable committees (including the governing body of the Church of Wales) and was appointed a Deputy Lieutenant for Glamorgan in 1948.

A volume of his light verse, appropriately called *Lines of Communication*, was published on his 80th birthday. At the age of 98 he contributed a preface to the biography of Colonel De Lancey Forth, of the Imperial Camel Corps.

Morgan was honorary Colonel of 50 and 80 Air Formation Signal Regiments from 1952 to 1960 and was awarded the ERD.

Frank Morgan was a tall, hawk-like figure, noted for certain eccentricities. He had lost an eye as a child and wore an eyeglass in the remaining one. He could eject this by jerking his head upwards, and then catch it again in the socket. He said he found this a useful trick when addressing restive or sleepy audiences.

Perhaps the most remarkable feature of "Monocle" Morgan was his adaptability. Brought up at a time when military aircraft would have seemed a fantasy, he later became an expert on one of the most complicated of signal functions, air–land co-operation. Yet he never forgot that when the Pembroke Yeomanry had been mustered in 1914 the occasion had all the marks of a medieval call to arms.

He married first, in 1918, Gladys Joan Warde, who died in 1953; and secondly, in 1956, Lieutenant-Colonel Helen Pine, WRAC.

April 6 1992

COLONEL MAURICE BUCKMASTER

COLONEL MAURICE BUCKMASTER, who has died aged 90, led the French section of the Special Operations Executive for most of the Second World War.

After the Dunkirk evacuation in the early summer of 1940 Churchill's directive to SOE "to set Europe ablaze" was hardly more than an act of faith. Even a year later, as Buckmaster contemplated empty "in" and "out" trays at SOE's Baker Street headquarters, sabotage and subversion across the Channel seemed almost an impossibility.

"The fact is," Buckmaster was told when he first reported to Baker Street as information officer, "everything's highly embryonic here." So he busied himself with self-imposed duties; initially it seemed sensible for him to remember what he could about French factories which he had visited while working as the manager of the Ford Motor Co. in France before the war.

Then, late one night when Buckmaster was responsible for security of the building, he challenged a dimly lit figure in a doorway. "My name's Hambro," the shadow said. "I happen to be the No 2 in this SOE set-up."

And so Sir Charles Hambro, the banker, settled down to question Buckmaster. The upshot was that, in July 1941, Hambro was instrumental in Buckmaster receiving temporary control of the Belgian section.

That September Buckmaster was promoted to head the French section, almost certainly the hottest seat in SOE. For the next three years he masterminded the training and despatch of agents to France.

Buckmaster faced a formidable task in their selection. Not the least of the crosses he had to bear was the abiding suspicion of General de Gaulle, who insisted that SOE would not be allowed to recruit French nationals but only French speakers with British passports, Quebecois – whose accent was usually unmistakable – and Mauritians. So, for the most part, he picked and trained half-French men and women or others with a good knowledge of the language and the country.

Buckmaster's agents were to provide a roll of honour second to none in the story of British wartime undercover operations. Their stories inspired a host of books, films and television series. Some agents, such as Violette Szabo, were tortured and shot. Others, like Odette Churchill, suffered at the hands of the Gestapo, but survived.

The high losses of the men and women whom Buckmaster sent to France have since raised questions about his methods. In retrospect, and with hindsight, Buckmaster has been unfairly criticised for running an "amateurish" organisation and incurring unnecessary loss of life.

But this was emphatically not how it seemed in the years when Europe was occupied by a ruthless Nazi regime – and when sabotaging railways and communications, attacking road convoys, supporting and arming the Resistance were considered paramount.

As M. R. D. Foot, the least partisan of SOE's historians, has observed in connection with Buckmaster: "Was it not Turenne who said, the general who made no mistakes has commanded in remarkably few battles?"

Charges of amateurism were particularly misplaced coming from the Secret Intelligence Service, which was not averse to obstructing Buckmaster's section. For his part Buckmaster did his best to turn such rivalries to good purpose and looked upon the competitive element in such relations as encouraging each group to seek to outdo the other. He described such liaison as existed with de Gaulle as owing everything to the tact and charm of SOE officers – "the only weapon against jealousy and intransigence".

Amid such arrows, it comforted Buckmaster that, when it was all over, Eisenhower credited his French section with contributing significantly to shortening the war by six months. "It was", Ike said, "the equivalent of 15 divisions."

Perhaps the most telling tribute of all came from Hitler, whom Buckmaster quoted as saying: "When I get to London I am not sure who I shall hang first – Churchill or that man Buckmaster."

Early in life Buckmaster had been steeled by the vicissitudes of fate: home life was precarious as his father's business fluctuated between prosperity and decline.

Maurice James Buckmaster was born on January 11 1902. He went to Eton, but it was touch and go in his last year whether the fees could be found. When his father was made bankrupt the school recognised his prowess by giving young Maurice a scholarship.

He had already demonstrated a remarkable facility for speaking French and was particularly influenced by a master named Robert Larsonnier whom he used, in later years, to describe as "a wonderful man". The verdict was characteristic, for Buckmaster tended to divide the world into three categories: "Wonderful men", "Splendid girls" and "Not my cup of tea".

After school he was sent to France where he perfected his command of the language working as a journalist on *Le Matin*. There followed six years with the merchant bank J. Henry Schroder & Co.

Then, in 1929, he joined Ford, first as assistant to the chairman and thereafter as their manager in France and then the whole of Europe. Buckmaster's European contacts and linguistic abilities inevitably led, on the outbreak of the Second World War, to a job in the Intelligence Corps. He claimed, aged 37, to be the oldest second lieutenant in the Army.

His task was to arrange suitable French billets for 50th Division, a job which led to a lifelong friendship with Paul Krug, head of the celebrated champagne house.

At Dunkirk in 1940 Buckmaster was ordered by the future Field Marshal Templer to stay behind with the rear-guard on the grounds that when the Germans arrived Buckmaster would have only to divest himself of his uniform to pass himself off as a native Frenchman for the duration. In the event, he managed a spectacular escape, and was reunited with his division and his batman, who had inadvertently made off with his puttees.

"Thank God, sir," Buckmaster used to recall the man saying. "You're safe, sir. Your puttees, sir!"

In the autumn of 1940 Buckmaster's fluency in

French secured attachment to "Operation Menace", an ill-fated Anglo-French enterprise designed to wrest Dakar, capital of French West Africa, from the Vichy government and hand the port over to the Free French under de Gaulle. Buckmaster recalled this fiasco as "sitting in the Bay of Rifisque and being bombarded and dive-bombed for 24 hours, and torpedoed". In 1941 50th Division was posted to North Africa, where Buckmaster reasoned that his French would be of little use, so he presented himself at the War Office, hoping to find more relevant employment. There he bumped into Templer again.

"Ah, Buckmaster," he said, "you speak French. Got a job for you. Start this afternoon. No 64 Baker Street."

Once in the hot seat – after succeeding H. A. R. Marriott, a director of Courtauld's French company – Buckmaster, ably assisted by Vera Atkins, worked up to 18 hours a day. He would occasionally give himself a break by bicycling home to Chelsea for an early dinner before returning at 8 p.m. to Baker Street, where he would remain until 4 a.m.

Buckmaster was acutely aware of the loneliness of his agents and of their doubts about those such as himself understanding or even caring about their problems. So he made a point of presenting them, as they were leaving for France, with personal gifts – for instance, gold cufflinks or cigarette cases for the men, powder compacts for the women – carefully manufactured to disguise their origin. "You can always hock it," he used to say, "if you run out of money."

By the end of the war Buckmaster had been responsible for the training and despatch of some 500 people.

He was devastated by the loss of men and women whom he regarded as close personal friends and felt keenly the responsibility of sending them, however unwittingly, to their deaths.

He was always fiercely loyal to his operatives, who included men like Richard Heslop, codenamed "Xavier", who sent a fusillade of boulders on to a Panzer division on the Route Hannibal, delaying its arrival in Normandy until a crucial 17 days after D-Day. Then there were the two schoolmasters, Francis Cammaerts and Harry Rée (*q.v.*). By the summer of 1944 Cammaerts had been so successful in the South of France that Buckmaster could claim that he had 10,000 men under his orders – at least half of whom had been armed by his efforts.

Rée immobilised the tank turret production factory at the Peugeot works at Sochaux. It was his demolition exploit which gave Buckmaster the satisfaction of calling on "Bomber" Harris at Bomber Command HQ with photographic evidence. Harris had hitherto been sceptical of SOE's ability to blow up targets which, he maintained, were better left to his aircrew.

Buckmaster found it intensely frustrating that he himself was not allowed to go into enemy territory. None the less, this did not prevent him on one occasion – so the story went – from flying to France in a Lysander in order to make essential voice-to-voice contact with George Starr, one of his agents in the Gers.

As they approached the rendezvous Buckmaster's pilot remarked crisply: "Look at those bloody awful lights."

At which Starr's inimitable Staffordshire voice cut in over the plane's radio: "Your lights would be bloody awful, too, if you had the Gestapo less than a mile away."

Starr merged into occupied France so successfully that he became mayor of his local village.

Perhaps the most characteristic story of Buckmaster was his reaction to General de Gaulle's post-war attempt to expel Starr on the grounds that he did not hold a French passport. Starr replied that he only answered to his Colonel and asked Buckmaster for orders. Buckmaster cabled: *"Tu y es, tu y reste"*, which he himself translated gruffly as "Don't budge an inch". This rather impressed de Gaulle who relented at once and gave Starr the Légion d'Honneur instead.

Although SOE was wound up after the war Buckmaster worked resolutely to ensure that the French section's connections with the Resistance lived on through an old comrades' association, the Amicale Libre de Résistance – more popularly known as the "Amicale Buck".

In 1945 Buckmaster returned to Ford, first in his old job as head of Europe and subsequently as director of public relations. Then, in 1960, he went freelance.

He was best known in the field of public relations as an appropriately effervescent PRO for the wines of Champagne. Certainly this account was his first love and consumed most of his time, enabling him to retain his close links with his beloved France and with men like Krug.

A trip to Champagne with Buckmaster was a privileged opportunity to see a rare example of the *Entente Cordiale* in action – as well as being an intoxicating and stylish *caves*-crawl, in which the various houses vied with each other in doing honour to the legendary Colonel Buckmaster and his friends.

Buckmaster divided his later years between a small

flat in Chelsea and a country hotel in Sussex. Although he became increasingly frail, his spirit was always indomitable and his speech forthright.

France honoured Buckmaster as a Chevalier de la Légion d'Honneur in 1945 and raised him in 1978 to the rank of Officier. He was also awarded the Croix de Guerre avec palmes and the Medaille de la Résistance, as well as the American Legion of Merit. Britain appointed him an OBE in 1943, which many felt to be less than generous.

He wrote two volumes of autobiography, *Specially Employed* and *They Fought Alone*.

Buckmaster, who described his recreation as "family life", married first, in 1927, May Dorothy Steed; they had a son and two daughters. He married secondly, in 1941, Anna Cecilia Reinstein, who died in 1988.

April 20 1992

ALBERT PIERREPOINT

ALBERT PIERREPOINT, who has died aged 87, was Britain's leading executioner for 25 years, but later campaigned for the abolition of the death penalty.

Short and dapper, with mild blue eyes, a pleasant singing voice and a fondness for cigars and beautiful women, Pierrepoint was fascinated by bar tricks with coins and matchboxes – which were in plentiful supply at the oddly-named Help the Poor Struggler, a pub he kept in Lancashire. While employed as a hangman he never spoke of "t'other job", and he hated the thought of any impropriety, unseemliness or vulgarity connected with his craft, which he viewed as sacred. After his retirement, however, he spoke of it freely – notably in his autobiography *Executioner: Pierrepoint* (1974).

"Hanging must run in the blood," he explained (his father and an uncle were both hangmen). "It requires a natural flair. The judgment and timing of a first-rate hangman cannot be acquired."

Pierrepoint was undoubtedly a first-rate hangman: "I hanged John Reginald Christie, the Monster of Rillington Place," he wrote, "in less time than it took the ash to fall off a cigar I had left half-smoked in my room at Pentonville."

During his career he hanged more than 400 people – his record was 17 in a day ("Was my arm stiff!"). In 1946 he went to Vienna, where he ran "a school for executioners"; the British authorities had sentenced eight Polish youths, but refused to hand them over to Austrian hangmen, whose methods were brutally unscientific. Pierrepoint hanged the youths at the rate of two a day, and stayed on for a fortnight to give further instruction.

He recalled only one awkward moment in his career. "It was unfortunate. He was not an Englishman. He was a spy and kicked up rough."

In 1956 Pierrepoint resigned, incensed at the meanness of the Home Office, which had granted him only £1 in expenses, and began his campaign against capital punishment.

"If death were a deterrent," he wrote, "I might be expected to know. It is I who have faced them at the last, young lads and girls, working men, grandmothers. I have been amazed to see the courage with which they take that walk into the unknown. It did not deter them then, and it had not deterred them when they committed what they were convicted for. All the men and women whom I have faced at that final moment convince me that in what I have done I have not prevented a single murder."

Albert Pierrepoint was born on March 30 1905 at Clayton, a district of Bradford in the West Riding of Yorkshire, and brought up in Huddersfield and Manchester. His father, Harry, had been an executioner for 10 years, and his uncle for 42. Young Albert was nine when he first conceived the ambition to become an executioner.

When he moved with his mother to Manchester, he spent half a day at school, and the other half working in the local mills, a practice which the law then allowed boys over the age of 12½.

Six months later, he left school and started work as a piecer at the mills. In 1926 he found another job as a horse-drayman at a wholesale grocers, and by 1930 had become a motor-drayman. It was then that he wrote his first application to the Home Office to be included in the list of official executioners, but there were no vacancies.

A year later Pierrepoint was invited to an interview at Strangeways Prison, where he was disappointed to learn that he was the tenth applicant to be interviewed, his chagrin only slightly lessened when he noticed that the previous applicant was clearly drunk. None the less he was accepted.

After a week of intense training by the prison engineer, Pierrepoint was placed on the list of approved assistant executioners – subject to his attendance at an execution to test his nerve.

The first execution he attended was not, however, authorised by the Home Office, but by the Irish government. Tom Pierrepoint (Albert's uncle and then the chief hangman) was contracted privately, and was allowed to select his own assistant. He chose his nephew. Pierrepoint's first British execution was at Winson Green Prison in Birmingham, where the executioner, once again, was his uncle. The role of assistant involved pinioning the condemned man's legs and getting off the trap as fast as possible, but it was the gravity of the occasion that was the real test.

It was 1940 that marked the turning point in Pierrepoint's career. After acting as assistant to an executioner who had been less than competent, he was asked if he would be prepared to be head executioner. His first execution as principal hangman was that of a gangland murderer at Pentonville in London, and further engagements soon followed.

In 1943 he was sent to Gibraltar to execute two saboteurs. During the Second World War there were 16 spies convicted in Britain, and Pierrepoint hanged 15 of them (the 16th was reprieved).

He always maintained that there was no glamour in taking the lives of others and he abhorred all publicity, so he was displeased when General Sir Bernard Montgomery announced from his headquarters in Germany that Pierrepoint received a £5 note in an envelope, with a slip of paper reading simply "Belsen".

At the end of the war Pierrepoint became a publican. His pub attracted ghoulish sightseers by the coach-load, but he denied press reports that he ever discussed "t'other job" with his customers. He did admit, though, to having hanged one of them, a man convicted of the murder of his mistress.

He hotly denied, too, the existence of a sign reading

"No Hanging Round the Bar", though several people claimed to have seen such a sign – among them the late Diana Dors, the actress, who also claimed that Pierrepoint had sung amorous songs to her over the telephone.

In 1954 Pierrepoint himself was "sentenced to death" by the IRA for the execution of a terrorist in Dublin in 1944.

After his resignation, he settled down as landlord of another pub, the Rose and Crown at Hoole, near Preston, which he had taken in 1952, but the ghouls put him off pub-keeping, so he concentrated his energies instead on his small farm.

A keen fan of boxing, he was appointed a British Boxing Board of Control inspector in 1956.

Pierrepoint married, in 1942, Anne Fletcher.

July 13 1992

VISCOUNT MASSEREENE
AND FERRARD

THE 13TH VISCOUNT MASSEREENE AND 6TH VISCOUNT FERRARD, who has died aged 78, was one of the most engagingly eccentric members of the House of Lords.

He held four Irish peerages and one in the United Kingdom which enabled him to sit in the Upper House where he was revered as an institution. His singular contribution to debate and to public life prompted the then Lord Chancellor, Lord Hailsham of Saint Marylebone, to remark in a foreword to Lord Massereene's book,

The Lords: "One hopes that Viscount Massereene and Ferrard will never be reformed."

He was able to enliven debates on almost any subject with personal anecdote and reference to his own experience – although the question was once or twice gently raised whether "Lord Mass of Cream and Feathers" was really of this world.

In a debate on the Brixton riots in the early 1980s Massereene ventured to suggest that he was "the only member who has spoken today who has had agricultural estates in Jamaica", where the only riots he witnessed were "riots of joy, because when I arrived I always gave a big barbecue for all the people".

On unemployment, Massereene was once able to inform their Lordships that the situation was not as bad as they supposed, since he had been trying for months to find an under-gardener at his seat, Chilham Castle, in Kent. He also found it inexplicable that British Rail should complain of shortage of staff while there was widespread unemployment, and that prisons were over-crowded when the problem could be solved by creating jobs to build more of them.

In his preface to *The Lords*, a stirring apologia for the Upper House, Massereene reflected that: "I have witnessed the swift disintegration of everything the word 'British' once stood for and I have seen the world, in consequence, become a poorer place."

Above all he stood, in his sometimes idiosyncratic way, for an old-fashioned common sense which the modern world did not always comprehend.

Massereene was originally in favour of Britain being part of Europe, but latterly he had become distrustful of the French and was a convinced Eurosceptic. Having broken his leg in 1991, he was looking forward to returning to the Lords and "speaking up for Britain".

He had a remarkable range of interests, most of them rooted in the country and country sports. He was never busier in the House of Lords than during the passage of the Wildlife and Countryside Bill in 1981, when he spoke on 77 occasions.

Several of his speeches were about bulls (his coat of arms includes six of them); one recalled his boyhood when he had fired a catapult at a sparrow and hit an old man taking a bath. When the Wildlife (Northern Ireland) Order came to be debated in 1984, Massereene expressed his bewilderment that curlew remained on the quarry list, since they were "filthy to eat", unless it was to give Irishmen the opportunity to shoot something other than each other. The oyster-catcher was another bird that Massereene found indigestible, having once shot one by mistake.

Massereene was responsible for introducing several measures and proposals, including the 1963 Deer Act; two Acts to regulate riding schools and give protection to horses and ponies; and the Protection of Animals (Penalties) Act in 1987.

He also twice tried unsuccessfully to restore the right of Irish peers to a seat in the House of Lords. He once proposed a tax to support the major political parties which was well received in the Lords by the Labour and Liberal parties, but it got no further.

John Clotworthy Talbot Foster Whyte-Melville Skeffington was born on October 23 1914, the only surviving son of the 12th Viscount Massereene and 5th Viscount Ferrard. He spent his early years at the family seat of

Antrim Castle, first built in 1613 by Sir Hugh Clotworthy, father of the 1st Viscount Massereene, who was instrumental in the restoration of King Charles II.

The 6th Viscount (and 2nd Earl) Massereene was a great Irish eccentric. He ordered 60 dogs decked out in mourning attire to attend the funeral of his favourite hound.

In 1922, on his eighth birthday, young "Jock" witnessed the burning of the castle by Sinn Feiners. He was educated at Eton and joined the Special Reserve of the Black Watch in 1933.

A dedicated sportsman, he was a gentleman-rider under National Hunt Rules and contributed to *The Field* from the mid-1930s onwards. A motor-racing enthusiast, he drove the leading British car at Le Mans in 1937.

During the Second World War he served with the Black Watch until invalided in 1940. Later he joined the Small Vessels Pool, Royal Navy. He succeeded to the viscountcy in 1956. In addition to his principal seat at Chilham, where he kept falcons and an imperial eagle, Massereene lived at Knock on the Isle of Mull, where he spent much time observing birds of prey in the wild, and stalking on the 70,000-acre estate.

The pursuits of this most eclectic peer ranged from opera (he presented *Countess Maritza* at the Palace Theatre) to foxhunting (he served as Master of the Ashford Valley). He also kept foxes as pets.

Massereene served as vice-president, and treasurer, of the Ashford Conservative Association and was president of the Monday Club (from which he resigned last year). He once acknowledged, however, that if he had been born in a Liverpool slum, "it might have taken me a long time to become a Conservative".

222

He was Commodore of the House of Lords Yacht Club for thirteen years, and a member of the Worshipful Company of Shipwrights. He promoted the first scheduled air service from Glasgow to Mull, and was concerned with the development of land in Florida which afterwards became the rocket-launching site of Cape Canaveral.

Among many public services for Kent, Massereene presided over the Canterbury branch of the Royal National Lifeboat Institution, and the Kent Hotel & Restaurants Association. He was treasurer of the Kent Association of Boys' Clubs for more than twenty years and served as a Deputy Lieutenant for Co. Antrim.

At the time of his death, Lord Massereene was engaged on a biography of his great-grandfather, George Whyte-Melville, novelist and poet, who died in the hunting field.

He married, in 1939, Annabelle Lewis; they had a son and a daughter. The son, John David Clotworthy Whyte-Melville Foster Skeffington, born 1940, succeeds to the viscountcy.

December 29 1992

LIEUTENANT-COLONEL "TITUS" OATTS

LIEUTENANT-COLONEL L. B. "TITUS" OATTS, who has died aged 90, won a DSO while commanding the Chin Levies in Burma in the Second World War.

His first assignment in 1940 was to penetrate the

Naga Hills, in areas previously unexplored, and put them under the administration of the Government of Burma. This was the only way by which the war-like Nagas could be prevented from raiding such adjoining areas as Assam to obtain slaves and victims for human sacrifices.

"Titus" Oatts's first experience of these jungle people gave little indication of what valuable allies they would later become. They had curious conventions of chivalry and would not fight invaders without a preliminary parley.

On a remote jungle path Oatts would come upon a pile of branches with plantains laid on top; he would then wait with an interpreter, leaving his soldiers 200 yards behind. The Nagas, as he recalled, would then "suddenly materialise as if they had shot up out of trap doors". At the end of the parley they disappeared just as quickly: "One moment they were there, the next they were gone, without even a trembling of a leaf to mark their passage. They went into battle naked apart from spears, bows and an implement like an elongated meat chopper with which they were adept at removing people's heads. They also coated their bodies with lime from head to foot, giving them an extremely ghoulish appearance.

"Against this grey-white background their teeth and lips stood out in crimson paint, making it look as if they had been sucking someone's blood. Fixed to each man's temples, so skilfully that they seemed to be growing out of them, was a pair of immense buffalo horns, tricked out with human hair. However, lack of education did not mean that they were ignorant or stupid; far from it. They understood all about wildlife and the growing of crops. They could weave cloth and tan hides, work in metals, build houses and construct such works as suspension bridges for which a knowledge of mathematics is commonly held to be necessary."

Paths to the remote country in which the Nagas lived invariably ran straight – "one day we would camp in a village at 1,000 feet and the next morning go over a mountain 8,000 feet high. When it rained the paths became rivers." Unpromising though these initial encounters seemed, Oatts and his companions so impressed the Nagas that they became staunch allies against the Japanese.

General Bill Slim subsequently said that "their loyalty even in the most depressing time of the invasion never faltered. Despite floggings, tortures, executions, and the burning of their villages they refused to aid the Japanese in any way or to betray our troops: they guided our columns, collected information, ambushed enemy patrols, carried our supplies and brought in our wounded under the heaviest fire, and then, being the gentlemen they were, often refused all payment. Many a British and Indian soldier owes his life to the naked, head-hunting Nagas".

An officer in the Highland Light Infantry, Oatts had volunteered for service with the Burma Frontier Force in the Chin Hills in 1938, when his regiment had concluded its tour of duty on the North-West Frontier of India. The Chin Hills extend along the Burma–India frontier for 300 miles, stretching from Manipur State to the Arakan. Oatts, who was often surrounded by Japanese in the jungle, had a personal bodyguard which consisted of "a group of 'retired' bandits of extreme villainy but unsurpassable jungle craft".

An indigo planter's son, Lewis Balfour Oatts was born on April 4 1902 and educated at Bedford and Sandhurst. He was commissioned into the Highland Light Infantry in 1922. Much of his early service was spent on the North-West Frontier.

His Chin Hills battalion consisted of numerous warlike peoples who had little in common and often spoke such different dialects that they could barely understand each other.

When the Japanese carved their way through Burma in 1941 they did not at first press into the hills; when they did they met the Chin Levies and got the worst of it. Oatts recalled that one of the Levies regarded throwing hand-grenades as effeminate. He preferred to stalk a Japanese soldier, let the lever go and then stuff it down his victim's neck; on one occasion he lost an arm but was not put off and regarded the incident as amusing.

The Levies' relationship with their seniors in 17th Division was less than cordial: the Divisional Staff tended to regard them as too unorthodox while the Levies thought the Division was too unenterprising.

One of Oatts's officers sent the GOC six Japanese heads which his men had removed, hoping the General would then show similar enterprise; he was promptly sent back to England for psychiatric treatment. None the less the 14th Army HQ was greatly impressed by the achievements of the Levies in harassing the Japanese and decided that Oatts should form two regular battalions. These then covered the British flank in the advance to the Irrawaddy.

After the war Oatts became administrator at Arbury Hall, Warwickshire (the Gothick showplace of the FitzRoy Newdegates, Viscounts Daventry); then ran the Victoria League in Edinburgh. He was a member of the Royal Company of Archers, the Queen's Body Guard for Scotland.

"Titus" Oatts had the personality and military skills to lead disparate groups successfully in battle; at the same time he was well aware of the bizarre contrasts around him.

Oatts published several books including *Proud Heritage*, a four-volume history of the Highland Light Infantry, which is far more readable than most regimental histories; one of the 14th/20th Hussars; another of the 3rd Carabiniers (now part of the Scots Dragoon Guards); and *Jungle in Arms*.

In earlier life Oatts had been an excellent horseman, good polo player, and a keen foxhunter and pig-sticker.

He married, in 1934, Cherry Morris, daughter of a former captain of the Warwickshire County Cricket Club. They had two sons and a daughter.

December 30 1992

MONIQUE "AGGIE" AGAZARIAN

MONIQUE "AGGIE" AGAZARIAN, who has died aged 72, flew Spitfire and Hurricane fighters – as well as more than 20 other varieties of RAF and Fleet Air Arm aircraft – during the Second World War.

"Aggie" was one of a small elite of intrepid women pilots to wear the wings and uniform of the Air Transport Auxiliary ferry organisation. One of her contemporaries was Amy Johnson, the pre-war record breaker, who died after baling out over the Thames estuary.

One of the few women taught to fly with the ATA – the majority held peacetime licences – Agazarian was pretty "green" when first confronted with a Spitfire. "I had been on leave," she recalled, "so when they asked me when I came back whether I had done my cockpit checks I thought they would not let me fly if I told the truth. So I said 'yes'.

"You had to be quick taking off in a Spitfire because they 'cooked' if they sat on the ground too long. So I just pointed it in the right direction and went."

Just after take-off, being unaccustomed to the cockpit layout, she caught her gauntlet in the prop control-lever and put it into course pitch. But she managed to recover "and had a glorious time".

"Spitfires really were delightful to fly," she enthused. "You just thought what you wanted to do and it did it. The first time I rolled I was quite nervous. But it turned over so sweetly. You really were part of the machine."

The 1st Lord Beaverbrook, then Minister of Aircraft Production, so valued "Aggie" and her fellow pilots that he gave them a pass, stating: "This pilot can authorise his or her own flights."

At the end of the war Agazarian interpreted this as permission for a low-level wing-tip "beat-up" of her mother's Knightsbridge home in a naval Seafire. That final fling typified Agazarian's irrepressible spirit. After resuming her studies on her return to civilian life, she went on to participate in a number of successful civil aviation business ventures.

The daughter of an Armenian-born businessman, Monique Agazarian was born in Surrey on July 17 1920.

When she was three her French mother bought a 1914–18 War Sopwith Pup for £5 at a Croydon auction and installed it at the bottom of the family garden.

The much-loved "toy" exerted a lasting influence on the Agazarian children. One brother, Noel, fought with 609 Squadron in the Battle of Britain and was credited with 11½ victories before he was killed in the Middle East in 1941. His Spitfire is displayed at the Imperial War Museum.

Another brother, Jack, was seconded from the RAF to the clandestine Special Operations Executive. Parachuted into France to help the Resistance, he was captured, tortured and executed. A third brother, Levon, flew fighters.

Young Monique was educated at the Convent of the Sacred Heart, Roehampton, before going to a Paris finishing school. Early in the war she helped nurse Sir Archibald McIndoe's "Guinea Pigs" at the Queen Victoria Hospital, East Grinstead. She was also attached to the RAF at Uxbridge.

Determined to fly like her brothers – despite being below the ATA's height requirement of 5ft 5in – she wangled her way through the medical, and learned to fly on Magisters.

When the ATA ferry organisation was stood down at the end of the war she ran a Malcolm Club at RAF Gütersloh in Germany and took a commercial B-licence.

Island Air Services, a passenger charter which also flew flowers from the Scilly Islands, employed her as office manager. Soon she was flying Proctor charters and joyrides from Croydon and the Scillies.

After the company acquired its first Dragon Rapide, she flew the Jersey route too. By 1948 she was managing director of Island Services' London operation. The next year she married Ray Rendall, a former RAF pilot whom she had recruited to fly for the firm. In that period she took IAS into joyriding, operating from Northolt and Heathrow. This proved a popular family treat and inspired some children to become pilots. Flights ranged from 10s to £1.15s for a view of London's dockland.

In 1950, by now chairman of Island Air Services (as the company had become) Agazarian launched weekend gambling jaunts to Deauville, extending the £4 return service to La Baule and Le Touquet. The same year she piloted the IAS Rapide G-ALB Pickles III in the King's Cup air race, but a port engine oil leak forced her to retire on the final leg.

Joyriding flourished at Heathrow until it was curtailed because of the ever-increasing amount of airline traffic. Towards the end of the 1950s she moved to Ramsgate Aerodrome in Kent, but it proved to be too distant from the market.

IAS was wound up and Agazarian briefly joined Air Links, before taking up residence in Lebanon. In 1973 she returned home and took a part-time job with Air Training Services, the first private company to operate a jet simulator.

When she took the business over in 1976 she worked out of the Piccadilly Hotel with the slogan "Fly Down Piccadilly". Later based at Wycombe Air Park, Booker, Buckinghamshire, she established a flight simulator and ground training centre between the Red Baron restaurant and control tower.

She continued to commute to Booker from Knightsbridge in her battered Peugeot ("Ben Hur") until she sold the business last October.

In 1988 she published *Instrument Flying and Background to the Instrument and IMC Ratings*.

Her marriage to Rendall was dissolved in 1973. They had three daughters.

March 7 1993

COMMANDER WARWICK "BRACES" BRACEGIRDLE

COMMANDER WARWICK "BRACES" BRACEGIRDLE, who has died aged 81, was a Royal Australian Navy gunnery officer with a record second to none; he won a DSC and Bar in the Second World War and a second Bar in the Korean War.

In January 1939 he joined the light cruiser *Amphion* which was renamed *Perth* and turned over to the Australians in June. He served in her in the Mediterranean, and in March 1941 took part in the action when three Italian heavy cruisers were sunk off Cape Matapan.

On the night of April 6 1941 in the harbour of Piraeus, Bracegirdle and another officer were rowing back to *Perth* in a skiff during a heavy German air raid when the ammunition ship *Clan Fraser* was hit and set on fire. There was an ammunition lighter alongside the ship and Bracegirdle and his companion risked their lives to tow the lighter some 50 yards clear before *Clan Fraser* disintegrated in an explosion which nearly killed them.

Perth went on to take part in the battle for Crete and in the subsequent evacuation of the army from the island in May when she was badly damaged by air attack. In

231

July *Perth* was in action against the Vichy French in Syria and her shooting resulted in a formidable shore battery being reported "off the map".

Throughout these hectic times Bracegirdle was quite unconcerned for his personal safety and his coolness when directing the ship armament when under fire was a great inspiration to his gun's crews. He was awarded the DSC.

After *Perth* returned to Australia late in 1941, Bracegirdle spent a year at the gunnery school at Flinders naval depot, and then joined the 8-inch-gun County-class cruiser HMAS *Shropshire* in December 1942. *Shropshire* sailed for the south-west Pacific, where she operated with the US 7th Fleet, supporting landings by General MacArthur's forces in New Britain, New Guinea and the Philippines.

In October 1944 *Shropshire* took part in the largest battle in naval history, the Battle of Leyte Gulf. In the early hours of the 25th, *Shropshire* joined a strong force of US battleships and cruisers lying in wait for Japanese ships off the northern entrance to the Surigao Strait.

Aiming by radar, *Shropshire* contributed 32 8-inch broadsides of rapid fire at a range of just under eight nautical miles in a brisk night action during which the Japanese flagship, the battleship *Yamashiro*, was sunk and a heavy cruiser badly damaged.

Shropshire went on to give gunfire support to the landings in Lingayen Gulf in January 1945. By then she had fired nearly 2,500 rounds of 8-inch shell since December 1943.

In the latter stages, the main danger was not Japanese ships but *kamikaze* suicide aircraft. Bracegirdle trained his gun crews to fire ahead of low-flying aircraft so that shell splashes deterred or even brought the aircraft down.

He also did a crisp trade with American ships, exchanging crates of wardroom whisky for heavier anti-aircraft guns. For all these operations Bracegirdle was awarded a Bar to his DSC and was twice mentioned in despatches.

Warwick Seymour Bracegirdle was born on December 22 1911 into a naval family. His father was Rear-Admiral Sir Leighton Bracegirdle, who was to serve as military secretary to the Duke of Gloucester, then Governor-General of Australia.

Young "Braces" was educated at Geelong Grammar School, Melbourne, before joining the Navy as a cadet at the Naval College, Jervis Bay, in 1925. He specialised in gunnery and commanded the winning Devonport field crew at Olympia in 1938.

After the war Bracegirdle passed the staff course at Greenwich, took command of the destroyer HMAS *Bataan* in September 1951 and served in the Korean War, carrying out patrols to blockade the west coast. As a unit commander, Bracegirdle provided effective gunfire to support United Nations operations in defence of friendly islands on the west coast.

For his Korean service he was awarded a second Bar to his DSC and appointed an officer of the American Legion of Merit.

His last two years were spent in London on the staff of the High Commissioner, before retiring in 1957.

"Braces" was the very best type of "Aussie" officer. His sense of humour and his bravery made him enormously popular in every wardroom and much loved by the sailors.

His naval career spawned anecdotes. When one sub-lieutenant (later an admiral), exhausted by watchkeeping in *Shropshire*, was seen to be nodding off at action stations, Braces switched on the loudspeaker full blast and bellowed: "God is watching you, Griffiths!"

And when one of *Bataan*'s sailors requested compassionate leave on the grounds that his home town was under flood water 6 feet deep, and his wife was only 5 feet 3 inches tall, Braces silently handed him an orange box and stamps to post it.

Bracegirdle was a different man when he left the Navy. Although he worked successfully for Morgan Crucible, Vospers and the Iranian Oil Co., he never had the same zest for civilian life.

But many of those who had served him kept in touch and often came from Australia to visit him. His house in England was a "pommy" outpost for the Royal Australian Navy.

He was married twice, and had two sons and a daughter by his first marriage.

March 23 1993

Digby Tatham-Warter

Digby Tatham-Warter, the former company commander, 2nd Battalion, The Parachute Regiment, who has died aged 75, was celebrated for leading a bayonet charge at Arnhem in September 1944, sporting an old bowler hat and a tattered umbrella.

During the long, bitter conflict Tatham-Warter strolled around nonchalantly during the heaviest fire. The padre (Fr. Egan) recalled that, while he was trying to make his way to visit some wounded in the cellars and had taken temporary shelter from enemy fire, Tatham-Warter came up to him, and said: "Don't worry about the bullets: I've got an umbrella."

Having escorted the padre under his brolly, Tatham-Warter continued visiting the men who were holding the perimeter defences. "That thing won't do you much good," commented one of his fellow officers, to which Tatham-Warter replied: "But what if it rains?"

By that stage in the battle all hope of being relieved by the arrival of 30th Corps had vanished. The Germans were pounding the beleaguered airborne forces with heavy artillery and Tiger tanks, so that most of the houses were burning and the area was littered with dead and wounded.

But German suggestions that the parachutists should surrender received a rude response. Tatham-Warter's umbrella became a symbol of defiance, as the British, although short of ammunition, food and water, stubbornly held on to the north end of the road bridge.

Arnhem was the furthest ahead of three bridges in Holland which the Allies needed to seize if they were going to outflank the Siegfried line. Securing the bridge by an airborne operation would enable 30th Corps to cross the Rhine and press on into Germany.

As the first V2 rocket had fallen in Britain earlier that month, speed in winning the land battle in Europe was essential. In the event, however, the parachutists were dropped unnecessarily far from the bridge, and the lightly armed Airborne Division was attacked by two German Panzer divisions whose presence in the area had not been realised: soldiers from one of them reached the bridge before the British parachutists.

Tatham-Warter and his men therefore had to fight

their way to the bridge, capture the north end, try to cross it and capture the other side. This they failed to do.

At one point the back of Tatham-Warter's trouserings was whipped out by blast, giving him a vaguely scarecrow-like appearance instead of his normally immaculate turnout. Eventually he was wounded (as was the padre), and consigned to a hospital occupied by the Germans.

Although his wound was not serious Tatham-Warter realised that he had a better chance of escape if he stayed with the stretcher cases. During the night, with his more severely wounded second-in-command (Captain A. M. Frank), he crawled out of the hospital window and reached "a very brave lone Dutch woman" who took them in and hid them. She spoke no English and was very frightened, but fed them and put them in touch with a neighbour who disguised them as house painters and sheltered them in a delivery van, from where they moved to a house.

Tatham-Warter then bicycled around the countryside, which was full of Germans, making contact with other Arnhem escapees (called evaders) and informing them of the rendezvous for an escape over the Rhine.

On one of these trips, he and his companion were overtaken by a German staff car, which skidded off the muddy road into a ditch. "As the officers seemed to be in an excitable state," he recalled, "we thought it wise to help push their car out and back on to the road. They were gracious enough to thank us for our help."

As jobbing painters, Tatham-Warter and Frank aroused no suspicions by their presence in the home of the Wildeboer family (who owned a paint factory), although the area abounded with Gestapo, Dutch SS and collaborators. Even when four Panzer soldiers were billeted on the Wildeboers, they merely nodded and greeted each other on their comings and goings.

Eventually, with the help of the Dutch Resistance, Tatham-Warter assembled an escape party of 150, which included shot-down airmen and even two Russians. Guided by the Dutch, they found their way through the German lines, often passing within a few yards of German sentries and outposts.

Tatham-Warter suspected that the Germans deliberately failed to hear them: 30th Corps had been sending over strong fighting patrols of American parachutists temporarily under their command, and the Germans had no stomach for another bruising encounter.

In spite of Tatham-Warter's stern admonitions, he recalled that his party sounded more like a herd of buffaloes than a secret escape party. Finally, they reached the river bank where they were ferried over by British sappers from 30th Corps and met by Hugh Fraser (then in the SAS) and Airey Neave, who had been organising their escape.

Tatham-Warter was awarded the DSO after the battle.

Allison Digby Tatham-Warter was born on May 26 1917 and educated at Wellington and Sandhurst. He was destined for the Indian Army but while on the statutory year of attachment to an English regiment in India – in this case the Oxford and Bucks Light Infantry – he liked it so much that he decided to stay on. He formally transferred to the regiment in 1938.

He had ample opportunity for pig-sticking: on one occasion he killed three wild boar while hunting alone.

The average weight of the boars was 150 lb and their height 32 in. He also took up polo – which he called "snobs' hockey" – with considerable success.

In 1939 he shot a tiger when on foot. With a few friends he had gone to the edge of the jungle to make arrangements for the reception of a tiger the next evening. As they were doing so, they suddenly noticed that one had arrived prematurely. They shinned up the nearest tree, accompanied by some equally prudent monkeys.

When the monkeys decided it was safe to descend the party followed, only to find that the tiger was once more with them. This time Tatham-Warter, who was nearest, was ready, but it was a close shave.

In 1942 the Oxford and Bucks became glider-borne. This was not exciting enough for Tatham-Warter, however, and in 1944 he joined the Parachute Regiment.

"He was lusting for action at that time," John Frost (later Major-General) recalled of Tatham-Warter, "having so far failed to get in the war. There was much of 'Prince Rupert' about Digby and he was worth a bet with anybody's money."

Tatham-Warter's striking appearance was particularly valuable when the British were fighting against impossible odds at Arnhem. For within the perimeter were soldiers from other detachments, signals, sappers and gunmen, who would not know him by sight as his own men would, but who could not fail to be inspired by his towering figure and unflagging spirit of resistance.

Brigadier (later General Sir Gerald) Lathbury recalled that Tatham-Warter took command of 2 Para "when the Colonel was seriously wounded and the second-in-command killed ... he did a magnificent job, moving around the district freely and was so cool that on one occasion he arrived at the door of a house simultaneously with two German soldiers – and allowed them to stand back to let him go in first."

In 1946 Tatham-Warter emigrated to Kenya where he bought and ran two large estates at Nanyuki. An ardent naturalist, he organised and accompanied high-level safaris and was an originator of the photographic safari. He also captained the Kenya Polo team (his handicap was six), and judged at horse shows (he had won the Saddle at Sandhurst). During the Mau Mau rebellion he raised a force of mounted police which operated with great success.

In later years Tatham-Warter took up carpentry and became highly skilled at inlaid work. Fishing and sailing were his other recreations.

In Richard Attenborough's controversial film about Arnhem, *A Bridge Too Far*, the character based on Tatham-Warter was played by Christopher Good.

In 1991 Dibgy Tatham-Warter published his own recollections, *Dutch Courage and "Pegasus"*, which described his escape after Arnhem and paid tribute to the Dutch civilians who had helped him. He often revisited them.

He married, in 1949, Jane Boyd; they had three daughters.

March 30 1993

JESS YATES

JESS YATES, who has died aged 74, was celebrated as the presenter of *Stars on Sunday*, a phenomenally popular

religious programme on British television in the early
1970s.

Yates, a cherubic figure known as "The Bishop",
would introduce the show seated at an electric organ –
on which he occasionally performed in a tremulous
manner – placed in front of a stained-glass window. He
was prone to make such observations as "We can't see
round the bend in the road, but God can."

Yates devised a restful formula of music not so much
sacred as saccharine, interspersed with Bible readings by
film stars and the occasional homily from a real-life
bishop – whose purple cassock would clash violently
with the scarlet leather armchairs. The show's *kitsch*
blend of sentimentality, celebrities and cosy escapism
attracted much ridicule.

Sean Day-Lewis of *The Daily Telegraph* remarked that
Stars on Sunday, "even when seen, can scarcely be
believed. Anna Neagle, regally clad, emerged confidently
from an extravagant mansion and read from a colossal
Bible arranged for her beside the drive; Gracie Fields
seemed overawed by the same surroundings; and Harry
Secombe arranged his features into a serious expression
to render a hymn accompanied by 100 choirboys with
candles at the ready."

Churchmen complained that the show "lacked religious content" and that Yates "painted a false picture of
religion". Yates responded by claiming the programme
was made "for older people who need to be comforted";
he could also cite the remarkably high ratings.

Yates – whose voice was likened by one critic to
"sweet and weak tea" – cultivated a pious image for his
appearances on *Stars on Sunday* and an air of sanctimony
pervaded his dealings with guests. All stars were vetted

for possible scandal and women were asked to appear "modestly dressed" in front of the cameras.

His own avuncular persona, however, proved unsustainable. In the summer of 1974 the *News of the World*, under the headline "THE BISHOP AND THE ACTRESS", revealed that Yates, "a married man" (in fact, he had been separated for some years), was carrying on a relationship with Anita Kay, a showgirl 30 years his junior who had recently "starred in Paul Raymond's nude revue *Pyjama Tops*".

Amid the ensuing furore Yates had to be smuggled from Yorkshire Television's studio in Leeds in the boot of a motor car. He ceased to present *Stars on Sunday* and was subsequently replaced as executive producer of the programme.

After Yates's contract with the television company expired the next year his attempts to resuscitate his career were not helped by continuing press interest in his personal life – fanned by the celebrity of his daughter, Paula, who married Bob Geldof.

Jess Yates was born in 1918 into a show business family; his mother booked stage acts. Yates joined the BBC on the production side in 1949. He was involved with such programmes as *Come Dancing*, *The Good Old Days* and the *Miss World* competition.

In 1958 he married Heller Toren, a former beauty queen and novelist. Their daughter, Paula, was born the next year.

Yates and his wife separated in 1965, and subsequently Mrs Yates and Paula moved to Majorca.

In 1969 Yates left the BBC and joined Yorkshire Television, where he eventually became head of children's programmes. Initially, he was asked to produce a series of six religious programmes for early evening viewing.

"I went for star names," Yates recalled, "because they would persuade people to watch." The first show had viewing figures of 600,000; at the end of the series viewing figures had risen to 7 million. Yates was asked to produce a further four programmes which led to a full 12 months' worth of *Stars on Sunday*; soon the audience was approaching 20 million.

Yates arranged for the stars to visit the Leeds studio to record their spots on videotape, then an innovation. "I'm a self-confessed despot," Yates said. "*Stars on Sunday* is the way I want it and the way I'm going to keep it."

Yates blamed his downfall on an unnamed colleague who had sneaked to the press. "Everybody knows", Yates declared, "there has been a personal vendetta on the part of a very prominent *artiste* to make sure I am removed from television for ever."

In 1977 Yates played the organ for a gala evening at the Odeon, Leicester Square; the featured number was "Here We Are Again". During the 1980s his engagements included seasons at a Scarborough theatre playing the organ and as an entertainments officer at a beach hotel in the West Indies.

Yates, who lived in North Wales, was also in demand as an after-dinner speaker, although he said that he disliked being introduced as Paula Yates's father: "I have a great yearning not to go to my grave as 'Bob Geldof's father-in-law'."

Yates's marriage was dissolved in 1975. He continued his relationship with Miss Kay, who wrote a book entitled *All We Did Was Fall In Love* (1975). But subsequently she married a younger man and moved to Australia.

In 1976 Yates made an appearance on the panel of the television talent show *New Faces* and later that year applied, unsuccessfully, for a position as an organist at a holiday camp.

April 12 1993

GEORGE IVES

GEORGE IVES, who has died at Aldergrove, British Columbia, aged 111, was the last surviving soldier of the Boer War.

Determined to surrender to old age only by inches, Ives retained vivid memories of his service in South Africa as a mounted infantryman – notably of chasing enemy commandos. The Boers never tarried for a pitched battle, and were generally content to shoot from the hills, killing more oxen than men. Nevertheless, Ives had a scar from a Boer bullet that had ricocheted off a rock to graze his cheek.

"My job was to get over there and kill Boers," Ives would recall in his soft Gloucestershire accent. "You went to war to kill someone, and they tried to kill you back."

Like most soldiers, he had mixed feelings about his service. He expressed little enthusiasm for the British cause, felt a deep sympathy for the enemy, and remembered uneasily his time guarding their womenfolk in ill-run concentration camps.

Ives was happier to remember the humanity displayed by both sides. On one occasion Christiaan de Wet, the great Boer general, was allowed to enter a British camp during a lull in the fighting to obtain medical supplies for his wounded men. He also remembered the ceaseless quest for beer.

The son of a coachman and a lady's maid, George Frederick Ives was born in France and taken to England to have his birth registered as November 17 1881, to ensure that he would not be called up for French military service. He was brought up largely in France, where his parents worked for the Tidmarsh family. He hoped to become a jockey until he grew too heavy.

Young George was working in his father's grocery shop in Bristol when news of the British defeats at Colenso, Magersfontein and Stormberg arrived in Black Week, December 1899.

In a burst of patriotism, he and thousands of others volunteered to join the Imperial Yeomanry. MPs, barristers, blacksmiths and butchers, few of them with any military experience, poured into half a dozen recruiting centres determined to do their duty.

Ives was one of the 123 who joined the 1st Imperial Yeomanry at Cheltenham. As mounted infantry, they had no sabres and were intended to match the fitness of the Boers' cavalry, but were usually employed in aid of other units. Even so, by their return home only 17 of the original volunteers remained.

Like most of his comrades, he was not inclined to become a settler on the veld after the war, despite government encouragement, but on his return to Britain he found widespread unemployment. Ives sent off for literature about emigration to the Dominions, and decided on his destination by the toss of a florin, with heads for Canada and tails for New Zealand.

It came up heads, and Ives joined a group of 2,000 colonists, including a large number of Boer War veterans, to open up a new wheat belt in the unpopulated Northwest Territories. Under the leadership of two Anglican clergymen, the party muddled its way west to found Lloydminster on what would become the Saskatchewan–Alberta border.

Ives and his father arrived in 1903 and purchased a quarter-section of 160 acres for $10 (£2). Under the preferential rules of purchase they had to break at least fifteen acres and build their own shack, made of logs with a sod roof. Their major problem was to find a well.

Ives proved a hard-working and methodical farmer, and at the outbreak of the First World War was surprised to be rejected for service because of a heart murmur.

In 1910 he felt prosperous enough to marry his wife of the next 76 years, Kay Nelson ("I used to call her Cayenne"); they had three sons and three daughters. But his wife disliked the hard life of the prairies, where the washing always froze on the line during the winter. So in 1919 they moved to White Rock, British Columbia, where Ives took a dairy farm until retiring at 60.

This proved merely an excuse to change jobs, and for the next 15 years he worked in a shipyard, building wooden scows, before retiring for the last time.

He and his wife continued to live in their house until 1984, when they moved to an old people's home. Ives proved a genial, if uncompromising, resident.

He pulled his chin up to a parallel bar by the arms until he was well past 100, and remained critical of his children's generation, complaining that youngsters in their eighties and nineties were apt to let themselves go.

After a story about him in the "Peterborough" column of *The Daily Telegraph* in 1992 he said that he would like to attend the Albert Hall service on Remembrance Day. Within a week he found himself brought over by a television producer. Afterwards he greatly enjoyed meeting Queen Elizabeth The Queen Mother, Lady Thatcher and John Major.

Right to the end Ives liked to talk about going down to the Legion for "a couple of pints". He maintained the ethical standards of his youth, and when a writer more than 60 years his junior, who was interviewing him, suggested that they retire to the quiet of his room, he was concerned for her reputation lest it became known she had been to a man's bedroom.

April 15 1993

LES DAWSON

LES DAWSON, who has died aged 62, exploited his corpulent figure and naturally doom-laden expression to create a television personality that was a *reductio ad absurdum* of the tradition of the "Northern comic", in the vein of Norman Evans or Robb Wilton.

Dawson's *forte* was the exaggeration of familiar music-hall jokes at the expense of the Wife: "I met her in the tunnel of love; she was digging it", and the Wife's Cooking: "I threw a bit to a bird the other day; it went into a corner and put a wing down its throat."

But it was the figure of the Mother-in-Law which –

despite the wealth of existing popular satire on the subject – he made his own, building a picture of a woman of unrivalled physical repulsiveness: "I'm not saying she's ugly, but every time she puts make-up on, the lipstick backs into the tube", with aggressive tendencies: "For all that, she does possess some things that men admire; like muscles and a duelling scar."

Dawson represented himself as the preferred target for his Mother-in-Law's boundless malevolence: "As soon as I heard the knock on the door I knew it was her because the mice were flinging themselves on their traps."

He gave new life to these clichés of northern comedy with his infectious love of word-play and language in general – he published several books, including two "straight" novels – and his keen sense of the absurd; some of his reflections carried strong echoes of the more off-beat American comedians, especially Woody Allen.

His range was, however, sufficiently broad to allow him to become one of the few solo stand-up comedians to achieve consistent success on television, in shows like *Sez Les, The Dawson Watch* and *The Les Dawson Show*, not to mention *Blankety-Blank*, the dire celebrity quiz show which he sent up remorselessly in his role as compère.

His ability to pull his chin over his nose (a privilege conferred upon him by a Mancunian youth who smashed Dawson's jaw during a fight in the early 1940s) proved irresistible to prime-time television audiences in the 1970s and 1980s.

Dawson's facility for identifying and mimicking the grotesque inspired characters like the frustrated Cosmo Smallpiece and – with the assistance of Roy Barraclough – Cissie and Ada. These were the matronly practitioners of "mimo-ing" – the Lancashire art, developed by mill-workers, of mouthing "unmentionable" vocabulary relating to reproduction or major surgery.

Dawson based the ladies on Norman Evans's "Over the Wall" sketch; he worked with Evans on the locally networked television show *Comedy Bandbox* in 1963. One of Cissie and Ada's most memorable performances was in a television commercial for cream cakes. Asked if he would like a slice, the Dawson character simpers: "Oh, just a little, chuck"; but on seeing the breadth of the proposed cut, he grabs the knife, snarling: "Not that *ruddy little!*"

Dawson began his career as a musical turn, slipping into comedy only on a particularly grim night in Hull. Having been pilloried throughout his performance at a working men's club, he took the stage for the second show – "well in the arms of Bacchus", as he later put it. So deep was the embrace that he was unable to provide himself with his customarily execrable piano accompaniment.

Dawson first astonished then delighted the audience with his gloomy, self-deprecating patter: "I'm not saying my act is bad, but the night variety died, they held my script for questioning."

His ham-fistedness at the keyboard and calculated air of despondency proved to be, if anything, more poignant in the face of adversity. His first national success, as a comic turn on the television show *Blackpool Night Out* in 1966, came in front of a highly unwelcoming audience: the oleaginous compère Dickie Henderson had watched several acts "die" before he introduced Les Dawson.

The comedian faced his predicament head-on: "I'm about as famous as Lord Godiva . . . if you're popular in

248

show business they give you a dressing-room on the ground floor. To give you some idea what they think of me, my room's full of falcon droppings and the mice have blackouts."

He left the stage to an ovation. In future, however ecstatic his reception, Dawson was to adopt the demeanour of a failure facing a hostile house.

Leslie Dawson was born on February 2 1931, in a "two-up-two-down" in a Collyhurst slum. He failed the entrance exam for North Manchester High School, and, his family having moved to the Blackley area, was sent instead to Moston Lane School.

His English teacher, Bill Hetherington, encouraged him to write; consequently it was with some regret that Dawson left school at 14 for the drapery department of the Co-Operative Society. He continued to nurse literary aspirations throughout his period of National Service in Germany in 1950: Dawson contributed stories to *The Soldier* magazine, and took a London University correspondence course in journalism.

Although he did eventually manage to gain employment on a local newspaper, he was sacked after a fortnight; Dawson's "serious" writing always had a tendency to be over-ornate. He later described how his 150-word obituary of an ex-deputy mayor was cut to read "Councillor X was buried yesterday."

Once demobbed, he travelled by train from Blackley to Paris, where he soon decided that he had not found his niche as a pianist in a brothel near the rue de la Goutte d'Or. On his return to Manchester a year later he found a job selling insurance.

Working as a salesman for Hoover in the early 1950s, he saw a poster inviting acts to apply to join Max

Wall's agency. Dawson passed the audition and moved to the capital though he maintained a traditionally northern view of London: "Poofs by the score, madmen and perverts; crooks, lesbian wrestlers and elderly matrons brimming with lust."

He was unfortunate enough to join Wall Enterprises at one of the many crisis points of its founder's career. Before Dawson was obliged to pack his bags and return to Manchester, however, Wall did manage to send him to the singing teacher Madam Styles Allen; he shared her waiting room with Julie Andrews.

In 1956, after spectacular success on Humberside, Dawson began to build up a solid following as a comic on the Manchester club circuit and to turn his intellectual frustration to his own advantage. He would greet audiences with a cry of: "Good evening, culture hunters," before launching into self-deflating patter in an arty vein.

His daytime concerns still centred around the vacuum cleaner, though his prospects with Hoover were dealt a fatal blow when an area manager spotted him in a show called *She Stoops to Concur*.

The management considered that Dawson's contribution — a rendition of "It's Witchcraft", delivered from a melée of naked women — was incompatible with his status as a salesman of domestic appliances.

Dawson married in 1960 and, with the support and guidance of his wife, Meg, gradually began to break into radio, in shows like *Midday Music Hall*.

An appearance on *Opportunity Knocks* in 1964 led to his triumph two years later on *Blackpool Night Out*. There followed guest appearances on shows like *The Golden Shot* and *Celebrity Squares* and then his own show.

In 1983 he launched one of his greatest successes, the Roly Polys. Dawson, with characteristic perversity, got the idea for an obese ladies' dance team while watching an emaciated *ensemble* rehearsing in Brighton. From the moment Dawson introduced them ("Let's hear it for *Les Femmes*"), Mighty Mo and her troupe were a resounding success.

His ability to overcome, even thrive on, tepid audiences and second-rate scripts made him an obvious choice to take over *Blankety-Blank*: he was host of the show from 1984 until his death.

Critical reaction to Dawson's literary *oeuvre* was more varied. *The Malady Lingers On* (1982) followed a path well trodden by Frank Muir and others with its puns on titles and proverbs; the sales were disappointing.

Hitler Was My Mother-In-Law (1982) suffered from the publisher's doomed attempt to woo the *literati* by publishing it first (against its author's wishes) under the title of *The Amy Pluckett Letters*. In a later work, a spoof detective novel, *Well Fared My Lovely*, a woman becomes convinced she is a vacuum cleaner: "She would lie for hours on the landing," Dawson wrote, "humming loudly with the cleaning hose rammed up her rectum. They took her to a mental institution where – although she still thought she was a vacuum cleaner – she started to pick up better."

Dawson got the idea for *A Time Before Genesis* while studying Buddhism on a visit to Hong Kong in 1976. His interest in fate and eastern religions was intensified by the loss of his first wife in 1986; her death from cancer devastated him.

Although he had served a traditional apprenticeship on the Northern club circuit of the 1950s and 1960s,

Dawson's humour had a degree of *largesse* not normally expected of a stand-up comic: he managed to maintain an "honest vulgarity" in an age when audiences were increasingly becoming attracted to comedians content to rely on the humour of obscenity or racial abuse.

As Arthur Marshall once said: "We could do with more like him."

Dawson is survived by his second wife, Tracy, and their infant daughter.

June 11 1993

GROUP CAPTAIN TOM GLEAVE

GROUP CAPTAIN TOM GLEAVE, who has died aged 84, was a gallant fighter pilot in the Battle of Britain, in which he was grievously burned.

Shot down in flames over Kent at the height of the battle in the summer of 1940, Gleave became one of the first "Guinea Pigs" – burns patients of Sir Archibald McIndoe, the RAF's celebrated wartime consultant in plastic surgery, at the Queen Victoria Hospital in East Grinstead.

Gleave had arrived there suffering from "standard Hurricane burns", to face, hands, arms and legs. McIndoe ("the Maestro" as Guinea Pigs called him) immediately set about growing him a new nose.

Gleave's seniority, as a regular Squadron Leader and "elderly" fighter pilot of 32, assured him the office of

252

Chief Guinea Pig for life. For more than half a century he inspired the club's fund-raising and welfare activities, ever mindful of the needs of surviving members as they entered old age.

The years of aftercare were the legacy of the spirit fostered in Ward 3, where McIndoe introduced a regime quite alien to the lie-to-attention, stand-by-your-beds attitude that had prevailed until then. Visitors to Ward 3 often retreated in horror – not because of the appalling nature of the Guinea Pigs' injuries, or the grotesque disfigurement of rhinoplasty patients growing new noses from other parts of their bodies, but at the discovery of beer barrels in the ward, and regular "grogging parties" at weekends.

A German cannon shell had ignited the right fuel-tank of Gleave's Hurricane as he attacked a formation of bombers over Kent; the fire engulfed him rapidly. He felt for the revolver which he wore in the cockpit as a last resort. His clothes were on fire, the skin of his hands and wrists blistering in white bubbles and the flames licking at his legs, but he rejected the option of suicide and struggled to escape, only to be thwarted by his oxygen tube, which refused to disconnect.

Clawing off the helmet to which it was attached, he opened the canopy. Then an explosion ejected him more suddenly and forcefully than he would have wished.

Having landed by parachute near the fighter station at Biggin Hill, Gleave was taken to Orpington Hospital. He came round from an emergency operation to find himself not in but under a bed. There was an air raid, and he could hear the noise of the bombs.

Shortly afterwards his wife arrived. Confronted by

her husband bandaged like a mummy with slits for his eyes (the lids were burnt) she asked him: "What on earth have you been doing with yourself?"

"I had a row with a German," replied Gleave. His answer later became the title of his short book about his wartime experience.

Thomas Percy Gleave was born on September 6 1908 and educated at Westminster High School and Liverpool Collegiate School. He joined the Sefton Tanning Company in 1924, and four years later earned a pilot's "A" licence at the Liverpool and Merseyside Flying Club. Later that year he went to Canada, where he worked for a tannery. On his return home in 1930 he was commissioned into the RAF.

Passed out as an "exceptional pilot" in 1931 – and subsequently as an "exceptional fighter pilot" – Gleave was soon a member of the RAF's aerobatic team. In 1933 he determined to enter the record books with a flight to Ceylon, but was obliged to crash-land his Spartan in mountainous Turkish terrain. The next year he qualified as a flying instructor. After several postings as an instructor, he joined Bomber Command on New Year's Day 1939.

When war broke out Gleave agitated for a fighter squadron, until eventually his wish was granted. He commanded 253, a Hurricane squadron, from June to August 1940, when he handed over to Squadron Leader H. M. Starr. After Starr was killed on August 31 Gleave resumed command.

Before Gleave was himself shot down his official score was "one confirmed and four probable": post-war investigation raised this to five Me109s on August 30 and a Ju88 on August 31.

Fighter Command's preferred policy during the Battle of Britain was for Spitfires to tackle the escorting 109s, while Hurricanes took on the bombers. For a Hurricane pilot to destroy a 109 was in itself an achievement, but to bag five in one day was astonishing.

The action in which Gleave shot down his 109s would have been sufficient, had confirmation been available, to rate him an official ace and at the least a DFC. Gleave was promoted wing commander while he was lying in bed at the Royal Victoria. Partially repaired by the Maestro, he was restored to non-operational flying in August 1941; a pale patch on his forehead indicated the provenance of his new nose.

Operationally fit by October, he was given brief command of the fighter station at Northolt before taking over Manston, the front-line airfield on the Kent coast. From there, on February 12 1942, he despatched six Swordfish biplane torpedo-bombers of the Fleet Air Arm's 825 Squadron on their ill-fated attempt to sink the battle-cruisers *Scharnhorst* and *Gneisenau* and the cruiser *Prinz Eugen* as they made their "Channel Dash". All six Swordfish were shot down in the Channel.

Convinced that circumstances had obliged him to send his men on a suicide mission, Gleave stood alone at the end of the runway and saluted each Swordfish as it took off.

Before leaving Manston in September 1942 Gleave pleaded for a long, wide runway of concrete or tarmac to save the crippled and short-of-fuel bombers which, having struggled across the Channel, were unable to reach their bases. Gleave's runway is still maintained for emergency military and civil landings.

Gleave next joined the planning staff of "Operation

Roundup" (later "Overlord"), the proposed invasion of Normandy. This entailed a promotion to Group Captain Air Plans, Allied Expeditionary Air Force. For his vital contribution to the invasion Gleave received the CBE and the United States Legion of Merit (later changed for the Bronze Star).

From October 1 1944 until July 15 1945 he was General Eisenhower's Head of Air Plans at Supreme Headquarters Allied Expeditionary Force. After VE Day Gleave returned to the "Sty" for further repairs. He later served as Senior Air Staff Officer, RAF Delegation to France, from 1945 to 1947.

Following further staff appointments at home he underwent more plastic surgery at East Grinstead, and was invalided out of the RAF in 1953. Thereafter Gleave joined the historical section of the Cabinet Office, where he was engaged on official histories of the Second World War. He spent more than 30 years on the task, mainly as a member of the Mediterranean and Middle East team.

He was elected a Fellow of the Royal Historical Society, and was air historian and deputy chairman of the Battle of Britain Fighter Association. He also served the Blond McIndoe Centre for Medical Research and the East Grinstead Trust.

Gleave was twice mentioned in despatches, received the French Légion d'honneur and Croix de Guerre, and was awarded the wings of the Polish and French air forces.

He married and had a son (who died in a canoeing accident in Canada) and a daughter.

June 14 1993

SERGEANT FRED KITE

SERGEANT FRED KITE, who has died aged 72, had the unique distinction of winning the Military Medal three times in the Second World War: all three were immediate awards.

The first occasion was in January 1943 when he was engaged in special reconnaissance duties, three miles west of Tarhuna, in what the citation described as "desperately difficult" conditions: "Sergeant Kite excelled himself", as the citation recorded. No hostile anti-tank gun, no field gun or machine-gun opened fire on the regimental front without Sergeant Kite reporting accurately the location to the Artillery observation posts.

As the resultant counter-battery fire neutralised the enemy guns Sergeant Kite pressed forward with his troop and engaged the hostile gun crews with small arms fire, causing much confusion and considerable casualties. On several occasions he became dangerously isolated. Nothing daunted, he continued his gallant and skilful actions time and time again.

His actions had much to do with the hurried and disorderly withdrawal of the enemy towards last light. His complete disregard of personal safety, his skilful leadership, and his good humour throughout were a fine example to all who watched him and listened to his wireless reports.

Kite's second MM was won in July 1944 for the actions near the village of Bras, Normandy: "At all times", noted the citation, "he displayed a very high standard of leadership and personal courage, and was an

excellent example to the remainder of the squadron."
When the squadron was held up by two enemy tanks
and two 88mm guns on the high ground at Bras, this
NCO, by clever use of the ground, pressed forward under
heavy tank fire and knocked out one Mark IV tank, one
Panther, and one of the 88mm guns, and held on to his
position under extremely trying circumstances. This
allowed the remainder of the squadron to get forward
into better positions.

The third MM came soon afterwards. On August 3
1944 at Le Grand Bonfait Kite was commanding one of
several tanks on the edge of an orchard, the duty of these
tanks being to support a company of infantry. This
position was strongly counter-attacked by enemy infantry and at least one Tiger and four Panther tanks. The
enclosed nature of the country enabled these tanks to
approach within the distance of 400 yards.

All the other tanks in the vicinity of Kite were hit
and set on fire but despite this he maintained his
position. He assisted in the correction of our own artillery fire, thus preventing the enemy infantry forming up
with his tanks for an attempt to advance on our position.

Kite kept his own tank in action and secured at least
five hits on enemy tanks at short range before his own
tank was hit and he himself was seriously wounded.

The citation stated that "Sgt Kite showed the greatest personal courage and his example of remaining in
action against odds that were much against him was an
inspiration to all. He undoubtedly helped to a considerable degree to beat off the attack on a feature of great
importance."

Montgomery's signature appeared on all three citations, first as GOC 8th Army, then as C-in-C 21st Army Group, and finally as a Field Marshal.

Frederick Kite was born in 1921 and as a young man was a promising hockey and football player; he had a trial for Port Vale before the outbreak of war ended any possibilities of a career as a professional footballer.

He joined the Royal Armoured Corps and was posted to the 3rd Royal Tank Regiment. In May 1940, when the German Panzers had broken through to the coast at Abbeville in the battle for France, 3 RTR were hastily despatched to Calais, on which two Panzer divisions were converging to take part in the defence of the town.

Sent to reconnoitre the situation at St Omer, they found it unoccupied but in flames. As they moved to occupy it they encountered the full weight of 1st Panzer Division and lost twelve tanks before withdrawing to Calais.

They were then ordered to send a squadron to test the road to Dunkirk and once again encountered 1st Panzer and lost more tanks. The remains of 3 RTR, mustering 21 light and medium tanks, were now confronting the combined strength of two German divisions.

Nevertheless – together with their comrades in the Rifle Brigade, the 60th Rifles, the Queen Victoria Rifles, the 1st Searchlight Regiment and some French troops – they put up such a spirited fight that they delayed the German advance to Dunkirk and undoubtedly helped to make the evacuation possible.

After escaping from Calais and returning home, Kite was soon sent overseas again, this time to Egypt in November 1940. He took part in Wavell's successful battles against the Italians in the desert, but was then involved in the disastrous ones against the Germans in Greece and Crete.

Kite escaped from Crete with a few other soldiers, in a Greek ship which they sailed themselves. Back in the desert he took part in more battles, including the July battle at Alamein.

After recovering from his wounds he returned to civilian life and became chief wages clerk in a factory.

A cheerful, modest, exceptionally brave man, "Buck" Kite might have had a successful professional career as a gamesplayer if he had not been wounded.

He married, in 1945, Elaine Cooper.

June 16 1993

VICTOR MADDERN

VICTOR MADDERN, the character actor who has died aged 67, had one of the most distinctive and eloquent faces in British cinema and television.

Although he was more inclined to scowl than smile, Maddern could deploy an astonishing array of expressions to characterise the heartfelt privations of the regular Cockney private soldier, the below-decks able seaman, the harassed petty crook or the average member of the British worker or – as in the case of *I'm All Right, Jack* – shirker.

Heavily lined, with a prominent jaw, brooding forehead, wary eyes and ruffled hair, the Maddern visage could express yeomanlike devotion and a disciplined respect for authority (particularly if Trevor Howard's old soldier was giving the orders) yet still indicate the presence of rumbling discontent, which on occasion broke out in unequivocal insubordination.

Not that Maddern's characters always lacked official authority. Promoted sergeant major in *Cockleshell Heroes* (1955), he licked a platoon of despised conscripts into shape. But generally he was more endearing as a grumbler than as a shouter.

Inevitably Maddern was typecast. But he was able to turn each trusty or dubious minion, whether in or out of uniform, jaunty or sly, into a lively and credible persona.

Maddern knew that a skilled and reliable character actor led a busy and varied life and he rarely sought leading parts, except occasionally in the theatre. As a result he remained almost constantly in work, acting in some 200 feature films.

A short, stocky figure, he was renowned for his forthright personality. During the filming of the television series *Dixon of Dock Green*, Maddern fluffed several lines while on camera.

Given the words "It's down at Dock Green nick" he came out with: "It's down at Dick Green Dock." Trying to correct himself he then said: "It's down at Dock Green Dick."

Exasperated, Maddern eventually cried out: "Who writes these bloody scripts? Can't I just say 'down at the nick'? Fuck Dock Green!'"

Born in Essex, on March 16 1926, Victor Jack Maddern joined the Merchant Navy at 15 and served in the Second World War from 1943 until medically discharged in 1946. He subsequently trained for the stage at RADA.

Maddern made his first screen appearance in *Seven*

Days To Noon (1950), playing a reluctant soldier obliged to shoot a psychotic scientist. In *Time Bomb* (1952) he found himself handcuffed to a trainload of high explosive, and in *Street of Shadows* (1953) – which had distinct echoes of Graham Greene's *Brighton Rock* – he played a dithering, friendless, small-time crook, fearful of both his own gang and Scotland Yard.

Maddern also made memorable appearances in *Private's Progress* (1959) and *I'm All Right, Jack* (1959), both acclaimed farces by the Boulting brothers. The latter remains a classic satire on the relationship between British industry and the trade unions.

Among his many other films were *Angels One Five, The Sea Shall Not Have Them, A Hill in Korea, Barnacle Bill* and *Carve Her Name With Pride*.

One of his earliest stage roles was Sam Weller in *The Trial of Mr Pickwick* (1952). As Helicon in Albert Camus's *Caligula* (1964) Maddern was singled out for critical praise, and in *My Darling Daisy* (1970) he brought a fine Cockney bravado and arrogance to his portrait of the notorious Frank Harris. He also did two stints in *The Mousetrap*, the West End's longest-running play.

Among his television roles were Private Gross in Denis Cannan's *Captain Carvallo*; a self-deluding, habitual criminal in the *Unknown Citizen*; and old Lampwick's son-in-law in *The Dick Emery Show*.

In addition to acting, Maddern ran a printing business and in 1991 opened a public speaking school. A lifelong Conservative voter, he offered special rates to Conservative MPs and constituency workers.

After a mailshot by Conservative Central Office he

reported a flood of interest for these cut-price "Victor Maddern Scholarships". "Politicians are like actors," he noted. "They have inferiority complexes."

In recent years Maddern devoted much of his time to charitable work.

He was married, and had four daughters.

June 24 1993

Sir Edward "Weary" Dunlop

SIR EDWARD "WEARY" DUNLOP, the Australian surgeon who has died in Melbourne aged 85, won his country's lasting admiration and affection for his conduct as a wartime prisoner of the Japanese.

Unlike some heroes, whose spectacular exploits are increasingly forgotten, "Weary" Dunlop found his reputation growing with the years, though he was the most unassuming of men. His courage and humanity amid cruel hardship appealed to new generations of Australians. For the lives he saved among fellow prisoners in Java, and later on the Burma–Thailand railway, they saw him as half-hero and half-saint.

It was not only his skills as a surgeon that counted, but his strength in standing between his patients and the Japanese, who tried to drive them out to work on the railway. He became their symbol of hope.

A strapping figure in days of peace – 6 feet 4 inches and 16 stone – Dunlop was savagely beaten by his captors and was twice readied for execution. Tied to a tree to be bayoneted, he heard the officer in charge count backwards from 30. The count stopped at one.

The same night he was again tied to the tree and again inexplicably spared. He concluded that perhaps the officer had come to respect his opinions.

Once, having failed to put lights out when the bugle sounded, he was stood for hours the next day in boiling sun while passing guards struck and kicked him at random. Told that he would be punished if he kept to his criminal ways, he lost his stoicism: "God Almighty," he yelled, "don't you think it punishment standing in this sun and being kicked and beaten by a pack of bandy-legged baboons?"

When this was translated the Japanese fell upon him with rifle butts, jeers, boots and sticks, until he was lying in the dust, ribs broken, scalp bleeding. He was then trussed up, leaning backwards with a large log between his thighs and knees.

Four hours later he was asked: "If we were so forgiving as to release you, would you have hard feelings against the guard?" He replied: "Hard feelings against what guard?"

This was enough to win release. As his circulation slowly returned he stood painfully to attention, bowed and said: "And now if you will excuse me I shall amputate the arm of the Dutchman who has been waiting all day."

"I was determined", he later wrote in his diary, "to show them that Australians were tough." He continued: "I steadied my tremulous hands, injected the brachial plexus and removed the totally paralysed, smashed-up and infected limb with the patient still on his rough stretcher. I patted his pale, sweating head and muttered some reassuring Dutch words to take my leave." He bowed to the Japanese guards and collapsed into bed.

Dunlop believed it was the duty of the strong to look after the weak, and the young after the old.

Ernest Edward Dunlop was born on July 12 1907 at Major Plains, North East Victoria. The younger of two boys, he was brought up on his parents' farm at Sheepwash Creek, near Stewarton, 120 miles north of Melbourne. At seven he was riding a horse five miles to school. Soon he thought nothing of walking barefoot across a frost-covered paddock or milking 20 cows.

Apprenticed at 15 to a country chemist, he qualified as a pharmacist in 1928, winning both the Pharmaceutical Society's gold medals. In 1934, determined to become a surgeon, Dunlop graduated with a first from Melbourne University, where he was given the absurd name of "Weary" (a tortured pun on Dunlop tyres). He was then commissioned as a captain in the Royal Australian Army Medical Corps.

In 1939 he was on the staff of the Postgraduate Medical School at Hammersmith, London, having qualified FRCS after a ten-week course at St Bartholomew's. When the Second World War broke out he was a specialist surgeon at St Mary's Hospital, Paddington.

Dunlop lived in a charmed circle led by Arthur Porritt (later Lord Porritt, Governor-General of New Zealand); he played poker at times with Alexander Fleming, and his friends included Jack Lovelock, the miler.

Dunlop himself was a first-rate athlete, having played rugby for the Barbarians and the British Commonwealth against a Combined Services side.

Enlisting in the Australian army in London, he served in the Middle East, Greece and Crete before sailing for the Pacific War. By now he was a lieutenant-colonel and CO of 2/2 Casualty Clearing Station. He landed in Java in February 1942 and was taken prisoner three weeks later.

Dunlop soon had his first taste of Japanese army ways. Commanding a hospital in Bandoeng, he was given 10 minutes' notice to shut it down and move on. He protested that patients were too sick to be moved, and when the Japanese threatened to bayonet the helpless, he stepped in front of the first, a blind soldier with a shattered face, amputated hands and broken leg. After a tense moment he was given one night to break up the hospital.

Dunlop was senior officer of a PoW camp in Bandoeng for three months before being sent on to the Burma–Thailand railway, there to carry out miracles of surgery without medical supplies, in squalor, stench and misery. The men were starved, wracked with dysentery, malaria, beriberi and tropical ulcers.

Needles and masks for anaesthesia were made from bamboo. Thread came from haversacks and parachute cord, a surgical snare from portions of a fork, hypodermic needle and wire. Operations were conducted under hurricane lamps.

A sense of humour and a light use of irony helped Dunlop through. His diary entry for April 10 1944 read: "Deaths: One. An amusing story of a geisha who came per barge for the pleasure of Commander Kukabu! It seems that on the way in she was apprehended by Ometz and was enjoyed by Ometz and three British other ranks for the sum of 15 ticals."

Dunlop kept his diaries in little notebooks and on scraps of paper, carefully hidden, and did not publish them until 1986.

Having spent the first year hating the Japanese beyond measure, he came to see them as a collection of good and bad, prisoners themselves of a ruthless and terrible system. After the war he worked for closer ties with Asian countries, including Japan. "Surely," he wrote, "some increased understanding should emerge from a tragic conflict in which, when all is said and done, Japanese losses vastly exceeded our own."

After the war Dunlop returned to surgery in Melbourne and a distinguished career. During the Vietnam War he took a surgical team to South Vietnam to work among civilians.

He was appointed a Companion of the Order of Australia in 1987, having been appointed OBE in 1947, CMG in 1965 and knighted in 1969.

He married, in 1945, Helen Ferguson, who died in 1990; they had two sons.

July 5 1993

ANNE CUMMING

ANNE CUMMING, who has died in London aged 75, was a sexual adventuress who wrote two erotic travelogues and in 1992 appeared topless in the *Sunday Sport* newspaper under the headline "Stunnagran!"

Cumming dressed conservatively and with style. But her conversation and behaviour were shocking. A fellow guest at a dinner party fainted when Cumming described to him in detail a sex-change operation she had attended in Casablanca.

Her candour was usually laced with wit. Asked why she had written her memoirs, she replied: "What can an old pensioner do to get by? Either take in laundry – or do your dirty washing in public."

Cumming said that she had slept with several hundred men. Her first memoir, *The Love Habit* (1977), detailed her exploits in the late 1960s and 1970s, which included a string of affairs with teenaged boys in New York. The *News of the World* bought the rights to the memoir and dubbed Cumming the "Randy Granny".

The Love Quest (1991), which chronicled Cumming's life from 1950 to 1965, was if anything more explicit. Cumming told how she blazed a trail through Europe and North Africa, and had one sexual encounter on horseback while galloping round the Sphinx.

She spent her first night in Rabat with a professional bicyclist: "All I can remember about him", she wrote, "was his remarkable muscle tone and his beautiful strong thighs . . . I like a man from the waist down."

Feeding such an appetite was hard work. Cumming recalled a night in Paris when she stood on the street dressed only in a mink coat and fluffy slippers, baring her body to passing men. No one stopped.

A granddaughter of Grimble Groves, a Conservative MP and brewery owner, Felicity Anne Cumming was born on December 14 1917 at Walton-on-Thames, Surrey. She spent much of her childhood on a farm in South Africa, but was educated at Horsely Towers, Kent, and at finishing schools in Germany and Switzerland.

She studied drama at the Old Vic and at Dartington Hall, where she met her first husband, Henry Lyon

Young. The marriage was dissolved in 1948, and the same year she married and divorced the novelist Richard Mason.

After 10 years' travel Cumming settled in Rome, where she lived for five years with the set designer Beni Montressor before deciding to devote herself to casual love affairs. She also became a respected publicist and dialogue coach in the burgeoning Italian film industry, working on films by Dino di Laurentiis and Federico Fellini, in whose *Roma* and *8½* she also appeared.

In 1979 she moved to New York, where she taught at the Michael Chekhov drama studio.

When Cumming was diagnosed HIV positive seven years ago she stopped sleeping with men, but continued to travel. In her last two years she visited Brazil, Oman, India and Russia.

Her final public appearance, earlier this year, was on a Channel 4 nude chat show, for which she wore only a pearl necklace and drop-earrings.

September 1 1993

NELL ALLGROVE

NELL ALLGROVE, who has died aged 83, endured extraordinary privations as an Australian nurse captured by the Japanese during the Second World War.

Born Ellen Mavis Hannah at Claremont, Perth, in 1910, she began her career as a pharmacist before switching to nursing. She trained at the Royal Alexandra Hospital, Adelaide.

At the end of 1939 she joined the Royal Australian

Army Nursing Corps and was sent to serve in Malaya. She was with the 2/4th Australian Casualty Clearing Station when the Japanese invaded Singapore in December 1941.

The hospitals, although swamped with casualties, were mostly destroyed and Mavis Hannah, with 64 other Australian nurses, was ordered to leave on February 12 1942. They joined the crowds seeking a place on the *Vyner Brooke*, which had seen better days as the property of the Rajah of Sarawak.

The ship, a dirty old tub, was obliged to run the gauntlet of Japanese spotter-planes along a route known as Bomb Alley. The nurses were hardly fortunate to gain a passage: the *Vyner Brooke* was bombed and sunk on St Valentine's Day.

Many passengers drowned, including 12 of the Australian nurses. Sister Hannah could not swim, but for two days and nights she clung to the side of a raft. When she finally landed on Banka Island she was immediately taken prisoner by the Japanese.

She spent the next three years in camps in Sumatra, where mere survival — on a diet of 2 oz of rice a day — required a formidable will. "If you couldn't laugh at the Japs," she recalled, "you'd had it." Although she earned many blows through her refusal to humble herself, she managed to find ways of getting her own back.

When ordered to carry water for the officers' baths, she said: "We never omitted to make our protest in it first, in a way that comes naturally."

When the Japanese "tried to make geisha girls of us" the Australians covered their uniforms with oil and dirt. A Japanese officer who had the temerity to tell Mavis Hannah that he loved her was promptly felled for his pains. Rather than lose face, he kept quiet about the episode.

Mavis Hannah was the only one of the eight sisters of 2/4th Casualty Clearing Station to leave the camp alive. Four were machine-gunned, two died of disease, one was drowned. Of the original 65, just 24 survived. Mavis Hannah weighed 4 stone 6 pounds when she was liberated.

In 1946 she married Joseph William Allgrove, a planter whose wife had died while he was a PoW on the Burma railway, and became known as Nell Allgrove.

In 1953 the Allgroves left the East and set up house at Dedham in Essex. Nell Allgrove campaigned tirelessly to gain adequate pensions from the Australian government for nurses who had been interned.

She also raised funds for Mencap and Lepra and was active in the Colchester branch of Queen Alexandra's Royal Army Nursing Corps Association. But she never forgot or forgave the past. Recently, after attending the Remembrance Day ceremonies at the Cenotaph, she unceremoniously turned some Japanese tourists out of a public house.

Earlier this year Nell Allgrove returned to Banka Island for the unveiling of a memorial to the nurses who had perished. But this time she was in a wheelchair, for the blows which the camp guards had inflicted had caused her spine to deteriorate.

Joseph Allgrove died in 1984; they had two sons and a daughter.

November 10 1993

LORD MILFORD

THE 2ND LORD MILFORD, who has died aged 91, was the only professed Communist in Parliament.

Although he contested the seat of Cirencester and Tewkesbury (later the constituency of his godson Nicholas Ridley) in the 1950 general election as a Communist candidate, the then Wogan Philipps gained only 423 votes and lost his deposit. But in 1962, on succeeding his father, the 1st Lord Milford, in the peerage, he chose to take his seat in the Lords.

In his maiden speech he called for the abolition of the Upper House. He condemned the Lords as "an undemocratic anachronism composed of the inheritors of wealth and privilege and bent on their protection, an indefensible obstacle to progressive legislation and the forward march of world socialism".

In his own case, however, he was not an "inheritor of wealth" as his father had disinherited him. The 1st Lord Milford, an ardent capitalist, had reputedly never spoken to his eldest son from the day he joined the party. In his will he avoided mentioning his heir by name; the trustees were instructed that "an avowed Communist or fellow traveller with the Communist Party" should forfeit all interest in his estate.

The new Lord Milford was heard in frosty silence by their lordships. It fell to the leader of the Labour peers, Earl Attlee, to offer the customary congratulations on a maiden speech. "There are many anomalies in this country," observed Lord Attlee. "One curious one is that the views of the Communist Party can only be heard in this House. That, of course, is an advantage of the hereditary principle."

Milford recalled that when he arrived at the House "all the people I had been with at Eton and Oxford welcomed me warmly. After my speech it never happened again and no one ever offered me a drink."

Undeterred, he continued to attend the Lords regularly. He liked to address the House on foreign affairs – American intervention in such countries as Vietnam and Nicaragua being a favourite topic – as well as social issues, education and the arts.

In one debate, when deploring the lack of interest in the arts in Britain, he shared his reminiscences of hearing a lunchtime poetry reading down a Chilean coal mine. "If you are talking in a pub here," he added, "and someone says 'What do you do mate?' and you say 'I am a poet', the conversation probably does not go on for long."

Milford hinted darkly that he gave his Lords' attendance allowance to the party funds. In reality, though, he was far from the militant firebrand some of his pronouncements might suggest; his romantic dream of a Communist utopia in Britain was very different from Stalin's brutal regime in the Soviet Union. Indeed he intensely disliked what he saw on his visits to Russia, but he blamed the application rather than the creed, and persisted in calling himself a Communist to the end.

Wogan Philipps was born on February 25 1902 into a remarkable family which produced a clutch of 20th-century peers. Several of the six sons of the Reverend Sir James Philipps, 12th Bt (the head of an ancient, if impoverished, Welsh dynasty which had inherited Picton

Castle in Pembrokeshire from the Wogans) became rich and influential through finance, shipping and other businesses, and three of them were made peers: Viscount St Davids, Lord Kylsant and Lord Milford. The career of Lord Kylsant, whose title died with him in 1937, ended unfortunately with a term of imprisonment which he suffered through infringing company law in what he felt to be the interests of his shareholders.

Lord Kylsant's youngest brother, Richard Philipps, chairman of the Court Line, Kia-Ora and other companies, was created a Baronet in 1919 and a peer, as Baron Milford, in 1939. He married Ethel Speke, a niece of the African explorer John Hanning Speke.

Wogan, their eldest son, was educated at Eton and Magdalen College, Oxford, and began life in a conventional enough manner. He attended debutante dances, drove lorries in the General Strike and joined the family shipping firm in the City of London.

"My family were all very rich businessmen, hunting, shooting and all that," he recalled. "They were all so tremendously anti-Semitic."

Surveying his brief career as a capitalist, he said: "I felt the resentment of the staff in the company when I joined. They must have felt 'Who's this little bugger?' During the General Strike I saw men lying about the street, down and out, and I began to wonder what it was all about."

In 1928 Philipps married the novelist Rosamond Lehmann and entered enthusiastically into Bohemian life. He joined the Labour party in the 1930s and during the Spanish Civil War served with the International Brigade as an ambulance driver. A contemporary recalled

274

that Philipps had "no supplies and just had sponges soaked in chloroform to calm the injured".

After being badly wounded himself, when a shell hit his ambulance, Philipps helped to organise shipping supplies and to assist refugees. Among the volunteers Philipps met out in Spain was the Communist Countess of Huntingdon (daughter of the Marchese Casati, of Palazzo Barberini, Rome), who was to become his second wife after his marriage to Rosamond Lehmann was dissolved in 1944. "We read a lot of Marxism together," he recalled. "We found we agreed on it."

Initially, however, he remained loyal to Labour and was elected to the Henley-on-Thames Rural District Council and selected as the party's prospective parliamentary candidate for the constituency in 1938.

During the Second World War Milford volunteered for service in the Merchant Navy but was rejected on medical grounds. Instead he worked as an agricultural labourer at a Government farm in Gloucestershire, and subsequently started his own small farm near Cirencester.

It was in the course of the war that Philipps joined the Communist party. His telephone was bugged by the local police; when he remonstrated, "Oh come on, Constable, get off the line!", a voice would reply: "Sorry, Sir."

Philipps was active in building up the National Union of Agricultural Workers in the county. He served on the union's local committee and represented the union on Cheltenham Trades Council for 15 years.

In 1946 he managed to win a seat for the Communists on Cirencester Rural District Council. "They were all Tories except me," he recalled, "and in the meetings notes were passed round about me, things like 'Doesn't he stink?'"

Three years later, after a concerted Conservative campaign, Philipps lost his seat on the council by a mere 14 votes.

Between political forays he carried on farming ("I introduced artificial insemination to Gloucestershire") until settling in Hampstead.

Wogan Philipps had a great love of the arts and was himself a painter of some distinction. He exhibited his oils in London, Milan and Cheltenham, and after succeeding to the peerage delighted in showing his canvases in the annual Parliamentarians Exhibition at Westminster.

These exhibits tended to have an egalitarian flavour. One was of a Tolpuddle Martyrs rally, another a semi-abstract showing two figures thrusting their arms skywards, celebrating *The Good News of the Fall of the Greek Junta*.

After the death of his second wife in 1953 he married thirdly, in 1954, Tamara, widow of William Rust, editor of the *Daily Worker*. He had a son and a daughter by his first marriage. The daughter, Sally, who died in 1958, married the poet P. J. Kavanagh – a union described in Kavanagh's acclaimed book, *The Perfect Stranger*.

The peerage now passes to Lord Milford's son, Hugo John Laurence Philipps, born 1929, a member of Lloyd's.

December 3 1993

IAN BOARD

IAN BOARD, who has died aged 64, was the proprietor of the Colony Room, a Soho drinking club favoured by Bohemians, artists, homosexuals and assorted loafers.

He inherited the club in 1979 from his patroness, the legendary Muriel Belcher, on whose birthday he died. Perched on a stool by the door, clad in tasteless leisurewear, his eyes protected by sunglasses, "Ida" (as he was known to his closest friends) would trade coarse badinage with his regulars. He had a kind side, though, and could be extremely courteous to visiting mothers, whom he immediately enlisted as allies against everyone else.

Board was an heroic smoker and drinker – until recently he would breakfast on brandy, and he once consumed a bottle of crème de menthe at a sitting – and if his drinking destroyed his youthful good looks it also shaped and nourished his magnificent nose.

A labourer's son, Ian David Archibald Board was born in Devon on December 16 1929. His mother died when he was four, and he was brought up by a woman who, as he recalled, had "been bunged in the pudding club" by his father.

"Boards are very randy," he declared. "They all have strings of children. I think I'm the only poof in the family." There were seven full Boards and one half Board.

Young Ian ran away to London at 16 and returned to Devon only twice in later life. He managed to avoid National Service because he was a bed-wetter ("an hereditary affliction," he explained, "which runs in cycles of seven years"), as well as a conscientious objector and a homosexual.

He became a *commis*-waiter at Le Jardin des Gourmets in Dean Street, and it was there that he met Muriel Belcher, who had run away with her mother from Birmingham at 16, after being slapped by her father for wearing lipstick.

Muriel fulfilled the role of "a queens' moll" at Le Jardin, which was frequented by the likes of Noël Coward. She took a liking to Ian, calling him "gel" from the start, and when she opened the Colony Room Club – so called because her life-long companion Carmel came from the colonies – he joined her as barman.

At first the Colony clientele were stockbrokers and City types, mostly "rich queens", but Muriel disapproved of any hanky-panky. Couples of either sex holding hands were told to "save it for the bedroom, dear".

One day Francis Bacon arrived, and he and Muriel immediately became friends. Bacon was on his uppers, and she gave him £10 per week to act as a "hostess", bringing people into the club.

By the 1950s the Colony had become the haunt of artists, writers and actors. The only unforgivable sin was to be boring. Some, like Dylan Thomas and Brendan Behan, failed the test.

Tom Driberg, Johnny Minton, Terence Rattigan, the Hermiones Baddeley and Gingold (*q.v.*), Frank Norman, James Robertson Justice, Lucian Freud, Joan Littlewood, George Melly and Craigie Aitchison were among the regulars.

In August Muriel, Bacon and Board used to holiday in the casino towns of the South of France. Bacon shunned the sun because it made his hair dye run. In the evenings, Ian and Muriel would watch him play roulette. It was in the days of currency restrictions, and they once found themselves stranded.

They decided to rob a rich acquaintance who was staying nearby. Board stood lookout while Bacon shinned up a lamppost. Then they went to the casino where Bacon gambled the loot. He began to win at the tables, but as he did so his face slowly turned a frightening black (he had run out of hair-dye and had used boot polish instead). Having won their fares and more besides, Bacon shinned up the lamppost and replaced the stolen money.

Beneath its tough exterior the Colony had a heart of gold, and every year the club gave a party for disabled children.

Now that Board has fallen off his perch by the door, regulars must look to its next occupant, Michael Wojas. As Board noted, "People say Soho isn't what it was. But Soho never was what it was."

June 29 1994

ROBIN COOK

ROBIN COOK, the novelist who has died aged 63, was a devotee of the low life and wrote chiefly about the milieu in which the upper and criminal classes meet.

He did so first under his own name in the 1960s, with such satires as *The Crust on Its Uppers*, and secondly as "Derek Raymond" in the 1980s, with a series of brutally explicit detective novels.

An Old Etonian, employed at various times as a pornographer, organiser of illegal gambling, money launderer, roofer, pig-slaughterer, mini-cab driver and agricultural labourer, Cook spent much of his early career among criminals. This gave him an original perspective on his upbringing. "The act of becoming a gentleman," he wrote in *The Legacy of the Stiff Upper Lip* (1966), "is one of murder . . . You can treat everyone badly if you have treated yourself badly, if you're not *there* any more."

Cook was fiercely dismissive of the genteel style of detective fiction perfected by Agatha Christie. "Who Killed Roger Ackroyd?" he would ask. "Who fucking cares?"

He complained that the details of homicide were often ignored by the "body in the library" school. His own work demonstrated a tolerance for the sordid which surpassed that of many of his readers. A publisher to whom he submitted his most outrageously nauseating book, *I Was Dora Suarez* (1984), claimed to have vomited when he read the manuscript.

Cook claimed that *I Was Dora Suarez* "struggles after the same message as Christ. *Suarez* was my atonement for 50 years' indifference to the miserable state of this world. It was a terrible journey through my own guilt."

In later years he was inclined to exaggerate his own criminal career, but his underworld connections were real enough. "My involvement", he explained, "was largely a protest against society. But in fact I was indirectly working for the Kray brothers. You see, I've always been ready to do anything – a weak character who'll always say yes. Because it's much easier to say yes than to say no. If you say no, it means you have to spend a lot of time arguing. If you say yes, you've already bought time and you can argue about it later."

Cook was jailed only once – in Spain, for voicing anti-Fascist opinions in a bar in the late 1950s. In the 1960s, as a subordinate of the notorious conman Charles de Silva, he was interviewed on several occasions by the police.

In the summer of 1960 Robin Cook's name was on the front pages of Sunday newspapers after he was taken in for questioning after the disappearance of a Rubens, a Renoir and works by 17th-century Dutch masters. These had been in Cook's possession but, according to the author, had been stolen from his flat.

"It was a scam," he confessed 30 years later. "The insurance company was in the sights – a company of which my father was, rather conveniently, a director." The paintings were never recovered.

"I have wandered between two very different worlds," Cook once said, "and I am a contradiction in terms. This is a very useful thing for a writer, because it means you can hold as many opinions as possible, all of them opposite."

Robert William Arthur Cook was born at Marylebone, London, in 1931. His father was chairman of a City textile firm and a director of the Royal Exchange insurance company.

He was educated at Eton, which he left after three years. "An absolute hot-bed of buggery," he recalled. "*Terrible* bloody place. They were trying to make you into a good all-rounder: a future banker; a cabinet minister; a bastard. The physical suffering was bad enough, the beatings. Worse was the mental torture. I have never worn an Old Etonian tie, except when out on a scam, in which case it can be quite handy. An Eton background is a terrific help, if you are into vice at all."

Having completed his National Service, Cook went to Spain, where he was involved in smuggling tape recorders and cars. After a period in North America he returned to England, broke, in 1960.

As a result of a chance encounter in Soho he began "fronting" for property companies run by Charles de Silva ("The Colonel"). "The villains needed people like me," Cook recalled, "because we were plausible and didn't have any form."

In the days before the 1961 Gaming Act he helped to run illegal gambling tables in Chelsea, and at one stage peddled pornography in Soho. "We had to pay protection to the police," he recalled. "Prominent public figures used to come in, trying to get something for nothing. Eventually we put a sign up saying: 'The following MPs will not be served'."

Although he became gaunt, almost cadaverous, in later life, Robin Cook was thin and dandyish in his prime. A friend from those days remembered him as "really very beautiful, but always dirty – never, never clean".

In the 1960s Cook published a number of novels based on his experience of Soho and Chelsea. *The Crust on Its Uppers*, his debut, lovingly chronicled the slang and mores of the London underworld. Like its successors it attracted a cult following but earned him little money.

Cook was not bothered by the lack of income or mainstream literary kudos. "I've watched people like Kingsley Amis struggling to get on the up-escalator while I had the down-escalator all to myself," he said. "I was moving downwards because that's where I wanted to be . . . I've no time for those who use writing as a means of social advancement."

In 1966 Cook moved to Italy, where he struggled to combine a literary career with wine-making. By the time he settled in France, in 1973, his muse seemed to have deserted him, and he earned his living as a farm labourer, living in a 15th-century tower in Aveyron in the Gorge du Tarn.

"I've always thought you can never see your own country properly unless you see it from another place," he argued. "It's like artillery, where you actually sight your gun backwards from the target you want to hit."

Cook was taken much more seriously as a writer in France than he ever was in Britain, and in 1991 he was made a Chevalier des Arts et des Lettres.

In the 1980s, still based in Aveyron, he began turning out such thrillers as *How the Dead Live* and *He Died With His Eyes Open*, which concerned the exploits of a maverick detective working for a unit called "Unexplained Deaths", who quotes liberally from *The Faerie Queen*. Cook called them his "Factory" novels (after the slang term for a police station).

He published his memoirs, *Hidden Files*, to considerable acclaim. One of his detective novels, *How the Dead Live*, was filmed by Claude Chabrol, and the rights to his "Factory" novels were bought by the BBC.

As well as his home in France, Cook maintained a flat at Willesden in London, and often revisited his old Soho haunts.

The instability of his professional life was reflected in his marital career. He married five times: Dora ("a terrible 63 days . . . I knew things were going wrong by day 20, when I put the shopping on the table and the table coughed"); Eugenie ("Fourteen months. A nice girl from Clerkenwell; I took a powder there"); Rose ("nine years with a year's sabbatical"); Fiona ("12 months"); and Agnès ("French. Fourteen months").

August 1 1994

DORIS SPEED

DORIS SPEED, the actress who has died aged 95, was celebrated for her superb portrayal of Annie Walker, the disdainful landlady of the Rovers Return in Granada Television's long-running drama serial, *Coronation Street*.

Annie Walker was created specifically for Doris Speed. She was said to have based her performance on the character of her own Aunt Bessie, who used to lead the Speed family in Christmas charades and had a withering look.

With her screen husband, the long-suffering Jack (Arthur Leslie), Speed appeared in the first episode of *Coronation Street* in 1960. She dominated the Rovers Return for the next 23 years, until illness forced her to leave the series.

Annie Walker struck a chord in the national psyche, as the embodiment of the genteel social climber, an icon of the proud petit-bourgeois tidiness which was subject to such virulent cultural attack in the 1960s. If there was a distinctly music-hall aspect to her character – and "the *Street*" is a television descendant of that tradition – Speed managed to bring an embattled dignity to her role, as well as affectionate satire.

Inclined to dress like the Queen, Annie Walker was ever mindful that she should be paid the respect she felt her due. Ever so "refained" – she preferred to see herself as an "Anne" – she looked down relentlessly on her common clientele. As aficionados of the *Street* knew well enough, though, Annie was the daughter of a mill clerk and had begun her career as a loom operative.

Annie did condescend to converse across the bar with the university-educated Kenneth Barlow, for whose ill-fated Silver Jubilee pageant in 1977 she took the role of Good Queen Bess. But she was extremely disgruntled when the unspeakably vulgar barmaid Bet Lynch was "highly commended" for her role as Britannia, while Good Queen Bess was ignored.

Annie was in her element as lady chairman of the local Licensed Victuallers' Association and enjoyed her finest moment when the widowed corner shop proprietor Councillor Alf Roberts invited her to act as his Lady Mayoress. Mrs Walker duly invested in a second-hand Rover and pressed the protesting potman Fred Gee into service as her chauffeur.

Doris Speed described Annie as "always a silly vain woman", but the character did not lack humanity. She proved a sympathetic "auntie" to the wayward slut Lucille Hewitt, for example, and a tolerant mother to her grasping son Billy, who finally wrested the tenancy from her in 1983. And with moist eyes she always cherished the memory of her husband, Jack.

Speed also said that Annie Walker "stood for everything I'm not", and despite playing the acidulous beldam for more than 20 years she had little in common with her. Speed admitted to a dislike of pubs and a lack of patience with Annie Walker's posturing.

Her colleagues on the *Street* used to describe the actress as "intellectual", "very politically minded" and "a keen socialist". She also developed a reputation for being easily distracted during filming.

"She hated handling props," recalled Jean Alexander (who played Hilda Ogden, Annie's put-upon drudge of a cleaner). "If she had to pour a cup of tea and speak at the same time she often used to 'dry'. Doris's famous stare into the middle distance was only to stop herself being put off by other actors."

In 1983 the tabloid press published details of Doris Speed's real age – she was over 80 but claimed to be still in her sixties. When she had joined the cast in 1960 she was already an old age pensioner, but insisted that she was in her early forties.

When the truth about her age was revealed Speed suffered severe depression. "It broke her spirit completely," recalled a friend, "she would never go back on the *Street* after that."

She eventually left the house she had shared with her mother for most of her life and entered an old people's home at Walshaw, Bury, where she remained until her death.

Doris Speed was born in Manchester on February 3 1899, the daughter of music-hall artistes George and Ada Speed. She made her stage debut at five in *The Royal Divorce*. "I toddled on in a velvet suit as the Infant Prince of Rome," she recalled.

She spent her early childhood touring with her parents: "I was at a different school every Monday, but I thought that was normal."

In 1915 she took a course in shorthand and typing

at a local technical college. Soon afer completing it she was offered a post with Guinness in Manchester, where she became a typist to support her parents' continued efforts on the stage.

She worked for Guinness for the next 40-odd years, becoming in her spare time an active member of the local amateur dramatics group, the highly regarded Un-Named Society. "Acting was all I ever wanted to do," she would recall.

After many years she established herself as an accomplished performer, and she began to receive offers of radio work in Manchester. In the late 1950s she appeared in a police series *Shadow Squad*, in an episode written by Tony Warren, and when Warren created *Coronation Street* for Granada he wrote the part of Annie Walker with Doris Speed in mind.

At first Speed twice turned down auditions for the *Street*. "I was in Bristol at the time," she remembered, "and it seemed such a long way to travel. In the end a friend persuaded me, and I took the milk train up to Manchester."

By this time Warren had already auditioned 24 actresses for the part, but had found none suitable. "I knew the part was mine as soon as I did the audition," Speed said. "It was just a feeling."

For the next 23 years she appeared twice weekly as the *doyenne* of pub landladies. "Annie Walker really was a dreadful snob," she admitted. "She used to complain because the corner shop didn't stock game soup."

When not rehearsing or filming, Speed spent her time playing bridge with other cast members and doing the *Guardian* crossword. "She played bridge like a professional," Jean Alexander remembered, "and went through crosswords like a knife through butter."

At home her preferred pastimes were reading theatrical biographies and watching the *Street*. "I study Annie to make sure that no silly mannerisms creep in," she said. "It's her I'm watching, not myself."

In 1977 Speed was appointed MBE and two years later received an award for "Outstanding Services to Television". She collapsed during filming in 1983 and was rushed to hospital suffering from stomach pains.

While recuperating at her home, Speed said that she had every intention of returning to the *Street* after her recovery, but continuing ill-health kept her at home.

During the next three years Speed's illness prevented her from returning to the programme. She became increasingly deaf and, with the loss of her hearing, reclusive.

In 1985 thieves broke into her house as she slept and ransacked the living-room. The shock of the robbery forced her into hospital, and she never returned to her home in Chorlton-cum-Hardy.

Three years later Annie Walker made her final appearance at the Rovers Return. Independent Television had asked Speed to take part in the 1988 Telethon and to pull a pint of beer for charity. She was filmed behind the bar looking frail but happy.

During the 1990 celebrations of *Coronation Street's* 30th anniversary, Doris Speed appeared on the television spectacular hosted by Cilla Black. When she entered, helped on stage by Miss Black, Speed received a standing ovation from the cast of the *Street*.

Although unsteady on her feet she managed to recount an anecdote about her mother. "She couldn't believe it when I told her they were going to pay me £50 a week," she said.

Miss Black, thinking that the story was over, started a round of applause, but Speed continued as if uninterrupted. "*'Fifty?'*" my mother said. "'You're never worth that!'"

She never married.

November 18 1994

JAMES WATTS

JAMES WATTS, the American neurosurgeon who has died aged 90, was, with his colleague the neurologist Walter Freeman, responsible for popularising the prefrontal lobotomy – one of the most contentious and macabre practices in the history of medicine.

The prefrontal lobotomy was an operation in which the leukos, or white fibres connecting the frontal lobes to the rest of the brain, were severed to relieve symptoms of anxiety in psychiatric patients. At first prescribed as an operation of last resort, it was soon being promoted as a remedy for all human sadness, and even a means for social control.

"Society can accommodate itself to the most humble labourer," observed Freeman, "but justifiably distrusts the thinker ... lobotomised patients make good citizens."

Ignaz Moniz had developed the leucotomy in Portugal

289

in the early 1930s, and in 1936 Freeman and Watts began practising the operation in Washington, renaming it the lobotomy.

A casual, softly spoken Southerner, Watts was then 32, nine years younger than Freeman, and the more circumspect of the two; he was also the qualified neuro-surgeon. Freeman was a Philadelphia-born doctor with a strongly Calvinist background, and a complex mixture of ambition, altruism and showmanship.

He believed in strong intervention for psychiatric disturbance, and later attempted to prove that Freudian analysts were suicidal depressives. Although a brilliant neurologist and neuropathologist, he had never qualified as a surgeon, and ostensibly needed Watts to perform the lobotomy under his guidance.

By the end of the year they had performed 20 lobotomies with Moniz's method, cutting holes in the top of the skull and inserting an instrument modelled on the apple corer. Later they modified the technique, making holes on either side of the head and using a steel probe with its end flattened rather like a butter knife; this was the prefrontal lobotomy.

After Freeman was caught operating, and repri-manded, he would sit in front of the patient, using his remarkable knowledge of the brain's geography to guide Watts's hands. To measure the brain Watts would insert a thin tube in one hole and feed it through the brain towards the hole on the other side. So accurate was he that he could pass the tube clean through and out the other side. "That's kind of fun," he said. "To be able to do that with that degree of accuracy is very good. And, of course, it always impressed."

Surgery was performed under local anaesthetic, and

the pair monitored the progress of the operation by engaging the subject in conversation, reckoning from the response how much matter had yet to be destroyed. The weird transcripts of the patients' failing utterances often pinpointed the moment at which some aspect of personality vanished.

Freeman, Watts recalled, was "a ham actor with a flair for the dramatic", and guests would be invited to watch operations in which Watts fiddled away inside the head while Freeman urged the subject to sing "God Bless America" or "Mary Had a Little Lamb". He might join in the chorus.

In one exchange, Freeman asked a patient, "What's going through your mind now?", to which came the reply, "A knife."

In 1942 Freeman and Watts used their considerable earnings to publish *Psychosurgery*. On the book's title page was a drawing of a swarm of black butterflies escaping from a trepanned skull, inspired by the French saying, *"J'ai les papillons noirs."*

"This work," the authors claimed, "reveals how personality can be cut to measure." The book sold out, with some copies reaching Europe.

But despite the growing enthusiasm, results were uneven. Patients often relapsed or became vegetables. Some died, either from bleeding during the operation or subsequent trauma. Others seemed to benefit, and lived long lives, although it was observed that the operation invariably dimmed some spark – that their spiritual lives perished.

One post-operative feature in male patients was an implacable drive for copulation. Freeman and Watts counselled concerned wives thus: "Her husband may have regressed to the caveman level, and she owes it to him to be responsive at the cavewoman level. It may not be agreeable at first, but she will soon find it exhilarating, if unconventional."

The majority of those lobotomised were women, and the operation perpetuated such 19th-century practices as ovariectomy and clitoridectomy, which were carried out on women diagnosed as hysterics.

By late 1945 traumatised war veterans were causing the asylums of America to overflow; nearly half the 1.5 million beds in public hospitals were occupied by psychiatric patients. Freeman wanted to work faster, and believed that if he developed a sufficiently simple technique he might operate independently of Watts.

Secretly he carried out a transorbital lobotomy. For this the patient was anaesthetised by ECT shocks; the eyelids were lifted and a sharp stiletto-like leuctome was hammered through the orbital bone to a depth of 2.5 inches, one incision through each eye socket.

The leucotome was then vigorously flexed. Freeman limited his post-operative advice to, "Wear a pair of sunglasses." The operation took 10 minutes and was first performed with an icepick taken from Freeman's kitchen drawer.

Watts thought the technique degrading and too freely administered. In 1946 he threatened to break off their association, and Freeman promised not to perform the operation in Washington. But in 1948 Watts caught Freeman performing transorbital lobotomies at their joint practice in the city.

"He asked me to hold the icepick," Watts recalled, "while he photographed the patient and the angle of the instrument. I said 'I'd rather not', and pointed out the

risks of transorbital lobotomy as an office procedure."
They could not be reconciled, and Watts walked out.

Freeman repeatedly traversed America promoting his
technique. Between 1945 and 1955, the peak years, at
least 40,000 Americans were lobotomised, many by
psychiatrists using the icepick. On occasion Freeman
himself would perform more than 20 in a day, developing a conveyor belt system, the sight of which caused
hardened soldiers to faint. One of his patients was the
actress Frances Farmer.

In the early 1960s the arrival of anti-depressants and
growing public suspicion brought about a rapid decline
in the use of the lobotomy. Before Freeman and Watts
split they performed at least 700 prefrontal lobotomies,
on patients as young as four. Watts had ethical doubts
about only one, a young female schizophrenic who loved
to play the harp.

"As I look back," he said, "I think I did it more to
help the mother than I did the patient, because the
patient was happy. Usually the voices call you bad
names, call you a pervert. They accuse you of all kinds
of bad deeds . . . every once in a while I used to think
about it and say, my gosh, did I do that for her comfort
or for the mother's? Maybe I did it for her mother's."

James Winston Watts was born at Lynchburg, Virginia, on January 19 1904, and educated at Virginia
Military Institute and Virginia University, where he
studied medicine. By 1930 he was a resident in neurosurgery at Chicago University, and two years later he
became a research fellow at Yale.

He published an influential paper in which he argued
that the large frontal lobes in humans were more
concerned with basic animal urges and functions than

previously thought, and that the mind did not function independently of the body – the frontal lobes could affect cardiac rate and kidney function. This brought him to the attention of Freeman.

The first patient they lobotomised was a 63-year-old woman who Freeman described as a "typically rigid, emotional, claustrophobic individual . . . a past master at bitching who really led her husband a dog's life". At the last minute she backed down, fearful that her head would have to be shaved. She was promised that her curls would be spared; this was a lie, but after the operation she no longer cared.

Patient 10 sued the duo for paralysis; Patient 18, an alcoholic lawyer suffering from paranoia, absconded from his bed after the operation, and was found drunk in a bar, the lobotomy having cured his paranoia but having left his addiction intact. Patient 20 had 18 cores made in her brain, and became the first fatality. Freeman remarked that he and Watts learned much more from their failures than their successes, because failures could be subjected to autopsy.

Freeman and Watts never lost their mutual respect. After their split Watts continued to live and work in Washington, practising privately and at the George Washington University hospital. He briefly experimented with the transorbital lobotomy, later forsaking it for more orthodox forms of neurosurgery. He retired in 1969.

Walter Freeman's personal life was always troubled. He once suffered from deep depression and a nervous breakdown, which left him with a lasting animosity towards the brain, and was later afflicted by diabetes and cancer. He died in 1972.

James Watts married, in 1931, Julia Harrison; they had two sons.

November 19 1994

JAMES FRERE

JAMES FRERE, who has died aged 74, was a picaresque and eccentric character on the fringes of the old establishment.

As Bluemantle Pursuivant of Arms and Chester Herald, he played an important ceremonial role in many great State occasions, and at the Coronation in 1953 was stationed closer to the throne than all but the Great Officers of State. He later claimed that he had stocked a nearby oak chest with cold duck, Perigord pie and black cherries in port wine, but could not gain access to them during the long ceremony.

At the Opening of Parliament the previous autumn the young herald had caught the eye of Cecil Beaton, who wrote in his diary: "The procession of the Heralds, in complete silence, brought vivid touches of scarlet, blue and gold. There was something quite haunting about one, a young man whose name I discovered to be Frere. His hair was sand-coloured, his complexion colourless, his eyes tired. With his pale, lovelorn face he seemed to be burnt out by some romantic passion. Nothing was left to him but to materialise – as he did – a perfect work of art, in his quartered tunic and sombre stockings, as he held the two Sceptres in pale ivory hands."

Frere's medieval looks, love of dressing up and taste

for ceremony were underlined by a somewhat contemptuous attitude. As Earl Marshal's press secretary during Coronation Year he frustrated reporters with his standard reply, "I really couldn't say"; and his haughty attitude to colleagues at the College of Arms and irresponsibility over money led to his resignation as Chester Herald in 1960.

He then turned to authorship. His first book, *The British Monarchy at Home* (1963), contained an unflattering portrait of the Queen and was attacked by *The Daily Telegraph* for its misuse of English.

It was followed the next year by *Now, the Duchesses*, written with the Duchess of Bedford, which described the lives of various ducal consorts. A third book, *Margaret Argyll and the Whigham Family*, was never written, though this title appeared against Frere's name in *Burke's Landed Gentry*.

James Arnold Frere was born on April 20 1920, the elder son of John Geoffrey Frere of Southern Rhodesia, scion of an East Anglian family. He was educated at Eton and Trinity College, Cambridge, and served as a lieutenant in the Intelligence Corps during the Second World War.

In 1948 Frere's extensive knowledge of heraldry led to his appointment as Bluemantle, and he was promoted Chester Herald in 1956.

Two years later he had the first of several brushes with the law when he was fined £5 for walking across a zebra crossing at Boston, Lincolnshire, against the express orders of the police constable on duty. Asked for his age and occupation the Chester Herald responded: "I'll see you damned first."

Frere's love of grandeur found expression in his

occupation – albeit short-lived – of various large country houses. In 1956 he acquired the 14th-century Assington Hall in Suffolk (along with the lordships of the manor of Assington, Shimplingfold, Levenya Stratton and Searles). His attempts to revive a feudal manorial court at the Hall – with himself in a purely ceremonial role – were thwarted when the house burned down the next year.

After his departure from the College of Arms in 1960 Frere moved briefly to the Villa Frere in Malta, palatial home of his great-great-great-uncle John Hookham Frere, a diplomatist.

Back in England a few months later he began a remarkable ramble through the English shires, living beyond his means in a series of unheated and unfurnished castles and stately ruins. In 1962 Frere's heraldic banner – featuring two lions' heads – fluttered briefly over Dacre Castle in Cumberland, which he had leased from the Hasells of Dalmain. Major "Teddy" Hasell later pronounced his tenant to be "a man of straw".

Frere moved on to Mynde Park in Herefordshire, an enormous rambling house belonging to the Twiston-Davies family. In 1964 Frere resurfaced at Orleigh Court, Buckland Brewer, Devon, which was described in Sir Nikolaus Pevsner's *Buildings of Britain* as "in a bad state of repair and recently rather slummified".

A few years later he moved to Doddington Hall, Somerset, a house described by Pevsner as "a ruin", and in 1975 he was found at Stogursey Castle in the same county, a stately pile said to have been destroyed in the Middle Ages.

Frere caused considerable interest among his rural neighbours, walking the country lanes dressed in belted tweeds and occasionally casting an approving glance at the flag flying over his current country seat.

His love of ceremony also drew him into the Roman Catholic Church, and he was appointed a Knight of Malta in 1959.

Eight years later, he left the Church and resigned his knighthood, but other more obscure titles and positions were soon acquired.

Frere's bulging and ever-changing entry in *Who's Who* pronounced him to be, among other things, a Liveryman of the Worshipful Company of Scriveners, Marchese de le Unión, a Knight Grand Cross of the Supreme Military Order of the Temple of Jerusalem and a Knight Grand Cross of the Military Order of the Collar of St Agatha of Paterno.

In later years Frere lived more happily in a cottage at Llanymynoch, Powys.

He was unmarried.

December 8 1994

FANNY CRADOCK

FANNY CRADOCK, the irascible *grande dame* of the kitchen who has died aged 85, rejoiced in her singular combination of *haute couture* and *haute cuisine*.

In her various television series in the 1950s and 1960s Mrs Cradock eschewed aprons and appeared in Hartnell ballgowns while roaring gravel-throated orders – "More *wine*, Johnnie! More *butter*! Don't *stint*" – at her forbearing companion, a kindly looking cove sporting a monocle.

She also wrote children's fiction and romantic novels, and was a prolific journalist – principally for *The Daily Telegraph*. With the late Johnnie Cradock (her third husband) she wrote articles about restaurants, food and wine under the pseudonym "Bon Viveur".

It was easy to make fun of Fanny Cradock and the much-put-upon Johnnie – she was, for instance, guyed as "Fanny Haddock", the husky-voiced harridan in the wireless comedy shows *Beyond Our Ken* and *Round the Horne* – but she did much to awaken British regard for cooking after the war and to improve the standards of commercial catering.

Her aim was to make good cookery easy and fun for the post-war generation of housewives, who had grown up during the years of food shortages. But she was dedicated to classical cookery, and refused to cut corners.

She was particularly proud of the fact that in 1956, before an audience of 6,500 *Daily Telegraph* readers in the Royal Albert Hall, Queen Elizabeth The Queen Mother said that she believed the Cradocks had been largely responsible for the improvement in British catering.

The Cook's Book and *The Sociable Cook's Book*, which the Cradocks wrote for the *Telegraph* at the request of readers, were both extremely popular.

Yet latterly Mrs Cradock became as celebrated for her bad temper as for her cooking. "I have always been extremely rude," she boasted, "and I have always got exactly what I wanted."

Her broadcasting career finally came to an end in 1987 when she was sacked by the BBC for attacking the mild-mannered presenter Pamela Armstrong in front of a studio audience. "Nobody, but *nobody* goes on my set!"

she shouted at the bemused Miss Armstrong. "I've never seen such a *bloody shambles* in all my life!"

The BBC discontinued her spot on the show. "It's obvious she's not feeling too well," a spokesman said; "we think it better if she doesn't appear."

She was born Phyllis Pechey in the Channel Islands on February 26 1909. Her father, Archibald Pechey (alias Valentine or Mark Cross), was a butterfly collector and a writer of novels, pantomimes and plays; his greatest success in the theatre was the Aldwych farce *Tons of Money* (1922). Fanny's mother, Bijou, was an actress and a singer.

At the age of one, the infant Fanny was given to her grandmother ("the Belle of Leicester") as "a birthday present", and remained with her until she was 10. She later claimed to have learnt almost everything about food and wine from grandmother.

"All the food was pink," she recalled of one of their elegant *soirées*, "pink mousse on pink glass plates chilled in pink ice into which pink moss rosebuds had been frozen."

Away from the table, young Fanny spent her early childhood dressmaking and communing with the dead: "I was on intimate terms with the court of Louis XIV," she recalled.

She was sent to board at the Downs, which she described as "the hell pit", "prison" and "that awful hole". At 15 she was expelled for encouraging other girls to contact "the spirit world".

Although her parents wanted to send her to a finishing school Fanny was determined to stay with her grandmother. She earned her keep by cooking dinner each evening: "They insisted I was in evening dress and in my place by the time the fish was served," she claimed. "To save time I wore my Schiaparelli beaded frock and slave bangles in the kitchen – that's how I learned to cook in ballgowns."

At 17 she eloped with her first husband to Brighton, but he died a few months later in an accident, leaving Fanny a pregnant widow. After her father went bankrupt in 1928 she was reduced to earning a living by washing up at a Roman Catholic canteen.

She pawned some clothes in order to place an advertisement for a dressmaking service in a local newsagent's window. Another source of income was demonstrating a Swiss roll mix, and selling vacuum cleaners door-to-door.

She made a second marriage, though it is not mentioned in her highly unreliable memoirs, *Something's Burning*.

In 1939 she met Johnnie Cradock, an amiable Old Harrovian, and began an association which lasted until his death in 1987; they did not marry until 1977.

Initially they lived in a house which was celebrated for both its ghosts and its hospitality. "Our cooking used to amaze our friends," Fanny Cradock recalled. "They thought we had black market supplies from Fortnum's."

Locally available food would be ingeniously disguised: "Bracken shoots were asparagus and I used liquid paraffin for my pastry. We caught and cooked sparrows from the garden and often ate baked hedgehogs (rather like frog's legs)."

While Johnnie Cradock served in the Army during the Second World War, Fanny spent her time writing novels. She had some success with such bodice-rippers as *The Lormes of Castle Rising* and *Storm Over Castle Rising*, under the name Frances Dale.

After the war she turned to cookery writing, publishing *The Practical Cook* (1949) and *The Ambitious Cook* (1950).

Fanny Cradock also wrote a "Hair and Beauty" column for *The Daily Telegraph* (as Elsa Frances); a cookery column for the *Daily Mail* (as Frances Dale); a series of articles on the lost city of Atlantis (as Philip Essex); and two more columns for *The Daily Telegraph* (as Nan Sortain and Bon Viveur).

Mrs Cradock liked to savour the memory of numerous "run-ins" with hoteliers, restaurateurs and members of the public. She recalled one *contretemps* with some youths outside a hotel who refused to move their car: "I went in kicking low. I can still remember how exhilarating was the slosh of handbag on fleshy nose." The youths fled.

In 1954 the Cradocks toured Britain lecturing on cookery for the Brains Trust. Two years later they gave the first live televised cookery demonstration.

Before the show Mrs Cradock was so nervous that she had to leave the set, run to the nearest church and pray for 20 minutes before she could face the cameras. Johnnie Cradock's encouragement was more prosaic. He froze and was pushed on to the set by a technician who whispered: "Get a move on, you silly sod, you're on."

Fanny Cradock went to enormous lengths in the service of television. She dieted rigorously and even had plastic surgery on her nose when technicians told her it was "too big" and was "casting shadows over the food".

As the years advanced she became increasingly eccentric and temperamental. In 1964 she was charged with careless driving, and fined £5; the arresting officer described her as "abusive and excited".

When he asked her to move her Rolls-Royce (parked across the stream of traffic) she called him a "uniformed delinquent" and told him to wait while she finished her conversation. When he insisted she move her car, she reversed into the car behind.

"You told me to back up," she said in court. "I was just doing as I was told."

In 1968 the Cradocks published a plan to produce a "second Fanny and Johnnie". The couple searched for two teenagers: "We want to groom them so that in the future they can continue to educate people towards decent standards of *cuisine*," announced Mrs Cradock.

Later that year a film crew visited *chez* Cradock, where they found that one cupboard contained 60 whole-sale-sized packets of cornflakes, and another was packed with cases of sardines.

Mrs Cradock claimed that the cornflakes were eaten entirely by her "houseboy" – "sometimes as many as three packets at a time".

She ate the sardines herself. Her speciality was a dish called "Dog's Dinner": mashed sardines and boiled egg, squashed on to brown bread.

By the 1970s her memory for detail – always some-what variable – seemed to be failing. When, in 1977, she finally married Johnnie Cradock at a register office there was confusion over both her age and her name.

Mrs Cradock claimed she was 55, even though her elder son was then 50 and her second son 48. She thought her family name was de Peche rather than Pechey, and, when pressed, claimed it was Valentine.

In 1983 Mrs Cradock was again prosecuted for dangerous driving. She had swerved across her lane (perhaps following her grandmother's advice to chauffeurs to "stick to the middle of the road") and caused a collision. When the other driver tried to talk to her she shouted, "How dare you hit my car!" and drove off.

The other driver followed her for 15 miles, "honking and signalling". He finally overtook her and stood in front of the car, waving her down. Mrs Cradock proceeded to run him over. In court she told the judge that the other driver's "threatening behaviour" had made her afraid to stop.

Country neighbours of the Cradocks used to complain of Mrs Cradock's erratic behaviour, especially of her distressing tendency "to lash out with her walking stick at those who got in her way".

In 1987 Mrs Cradock went missing for seven days during a court case involving jewellery stolen from her home. She eventually appeared, claiming that the police search had not been very thorough: "I was at home all the time."

The Cradocks received numerous gastronomic awards, including the Grand Mousquetaire d'Armagnac, and were appointed Chevalier et Grande Dame de la Tripiere d'Or.

December 29 1994

SIR NICHOLAS FAIRBAIRN

SIR NICHOLAS FAIRBAIRN, the Conservative MP for Perth and Kinross who has died aged 61, brought a dash of roguish colour to the House of Commons.

Many found him too much of a good thing, but

behind the frivolous façade, the rather petulant expression and the ridiculous clothes (Fairbairn prided himself on designing and making his own outfits, usually in tartan), there was a serious lawyer and a courageous politician.

Fairbairn made his name as a defence counsel at the Scottish Bar, where his most dramatic case was as defence counsel to Patrick Meehan, charged with murder. He pursued the case long after losing it, and seven years later his judgement and tenacity were vindicated when the conviction was quashed and Meehan was granted a Royal Pardon.

There was a measure of outrage among the Scottish legal establishment when the maverick Fairbairn was appointed Solicitor-General for Scotland in 1979; and no little gloating when he was dismissed by Margaret Thatcher in 1982 after a Commons row over his decision not to prosecute in an alleged rape case. Fairbairn, who subscribed to the theory that women often say "no" to sex when they mean "yes", once called women who made rape allegations "tauntresses".

Sex and alcohol played a large part in "Nicky" Fairbairn's life, the influence of the latter often provoking ribaldry from the Opposition benches and embarrassment on his own. He once riveted the House with an account of how Mrs Thatcher had rebuffed the amorous advances of a well-known Scottish drunk (thought by some to be himself) with the cutting observation: "You are not up to it!"

Fairbairn's own erotic career included an incident when one of his girlfriends, Pamela Milne, was reported to have tried to hang herself from a lamppost outside his

London house after discovering he was to marry another woman (whose husband had cited Fairbairn as co-respondent).

The anguished Miss Milne later claimed that Fairbairn had begged her to be "the Mistress of Fordell" (his castle in Scotland), and given her an engagement ring. "Sometimes he would ring saying how much he loved me," she recalled. "Other times he would shout demanding his ring back, because he was broke."

Fairbairn's own account of his relationships tended to be more romantic. He recalled that his attraction to women had begun at the age of eight when he became infatuated with his prep-school matron. "Any relationship I have with a woman is essentially sensuous and romantic rather than lustful," he explained. "I go to great lengths to please. I design clothes for the woman I am in love with, write poems and paint pictures for her, send flowers and adorn her with jewels."

Fairbairn thought harems and polygamy preferable to monogamy and fidelity, and deprecated what he saw as a lack of style in women MPs (excepting the Speaker, Miss Betty Boothroyd). "They lack fragrance on the whole," he said. "They're definitely not desert island material . . . They all look as though they are from the 5th Kiev Stalinist machine-gun parade."

He was once admonished by the BBC for choosing as his luxury on the radio programme *Desert Island Discs* a photograph of Mrs Khrushchev, whose ugliness he thought would prevent him from fantasising about sex.

The lamppost episode occurred while Fairbairn was in the Government and led to speculation that he might have to resign. Mrs Thatcher and Willie Whitelaw interviewed him and, according to Fairbairn, proved understanding and sympathetic. But when the storm broke over the alleged rape case he was peremptorily sacked.

During the campaign for the 1992 general election Fairbairn embarrassed his party by warning of the dangers of uncontrolled immigration: "Under Labour," he said, "the country would be swamped with immigrants of every colour and race." Other Tories were quick to distance themselves from this outburst, over which Fairbairn was typically unrepentant.

The furore did not seem to damage him in the eyes of his constituency, which returned him with an increased majority, but in April 1994 Fairbairn announced that he would not stand at the next election. "My sole reason for entering politics was to destroy socialism," he said. "I never thought I'd see it in my day, but all over the world the dragon seems to be dead and my motivation is gone."

Nicholas Hardwick Fairbairn was born in Edinburgh on Christmas Eve 1933, the son of a distinguished psychiatrist who was convinced of the necessity of frequent involuntary releases of tension through sneezing and orgasm. As an adult Fairbairn would claim to have been permanently scarred by his parents' incessant quarrelling.

Educated at Loretto and Edinburgh University, he was called to the Scottish Bar in 1957; he took Silk 15 years later.

With not wholly unwarranted bombast – for he really was a man of parts – Fairbairn described his occupations as "author, forester, painter, poet, TV and radio broadcaster, journalist, dress designer, landscape gardener, *bon viveur*, raconteur and wit".

He made his entry into politics as the Conservative candidate for Central Edinburgh at the 1964 general election; he again fought that seat with no success in 1966. But in 1974 he succeeded Sir Alec Douglas-Home at Kinross and Perthshire West (later renamed Perth and Kinross).

For all his exhibitionist posturing, Fairbairn was an effective champion of the arts. As a council member of the Edinburgh Festival and chairman of the Traverse Theatre and of the Scottish Society for the Defence of Literature and the Arts, he proved a doughty opponent of the puritanical city fathers. He was also an effective chairman of Scottish Heritage.

In the 1960s and early 1970s he was director of Ledlanet Nights, an enjoyable if somewhat chaotic attempt to create a sort of Scots Glyndebourne at the Kinross-shire pile of his quondam political opponent, the publisher John Calder.

Another of Fairbairn's favourite, if unlikely, causes was birth control: he was a member of the council of World Population Crisis and chairman of the Edinburgh Brook Advisory Centre.

He was knighted in 1988. After 1960 (when he purchased Fordell, a ruined Fifeshire castle, for £100) he had adopted the feudal style of "Baron of Fordell", and it gave him great pleasure to be addressed as such. He did much of the restoration work on the castle himself.

His memoirs (*A Life is Too Short*) were notable chiefly for their bizarre and recondite vocabulary. Each year, in an effort to amuse, Fairbairn would list different recreations in *Who's Who*. His most celebrated entry read: "making love, ends meet and people laugh". The latest

– "languishing and sandwiching" – suggests a sad falling off.

He married first, in 1962, Elizabeth Mackay, elder daughter of the 13th Lord Reay; they had four daughters (one of whom died in infancy) and a son (who also died in infancy). The marriage was dissolved in 1979 and in 1983 he married Suzanne Mary Wheeler.

February 20 1995

VIVIAN STANSHALL

VIVIAN STANSHALL, who has died aged 52, was a picaresque musician, satirist and all-round eccentric.

Like Peter Cook, Stanshall was a godfather of the irreverent and surrealist comedy later popularised by *Monty Python's Flying Circus*. He could declaim like John Betjeman and play the ukulele like George Formby, but listed his chief influences as "Ivor Novello, Noël Coward and Little Richard".

Stanshall's heyday was the mid-1960s, when as the singer of the Bonzo Dog Doo-Dah Band he brought his anarchic humour to a wide audience, hitting the charts in 1968 with "I'm the Urban Spaceman" – perhaps the only top-ten single ever to feature a hosepipe solo.

Roger Ruskin Spear (who performed on saxophone and with exploding sculptures) recalled the early days of the band: "The Bonzos started from the throw-outs of various jazz bands. We were all thrown out for playing too loudly and too badly, and we ended up playing together."

To begin with the Bonzos concentrated exclusively on novelty foxtrots, covering old 78s, but after going electric in 1966 they branched out into rococo parodies of more mainstream pop. The Bonzos owed much in spirit to the work of Spike Jones, but the group's unique appeal was largely the result of Stanshall's eclectic tastes and his considerable talent as a mimic. He was capable of unsettlingly accurate impersonations of Coward, Elvis Presley and Jack Buchanan, among others.

With songs such as "Cool Britannia", "Can Blue Men Sing the Whites (or Are They Hypo-crites)" and "My Pink Half of the Drainpipe" – and a truly wild stage act – the Bonzos came to the attention of Paul McCartney, who cast Stanshall in the Beatles' television film *Magical Mystery Tour* (1967).

After the Bonzos split up in 1970 Stanshall enjoyed a brief renaissance introducing the instruments on Mike Oldfield's hugely successful *Tubular Bells* ("Grand p*ia*no," he intoned, "mandol*in*, two slightly dis*tort*ed guitars").

In the 1970s and 1980s he found himself increasingly unable to cope with the pressures of popular success. As with Spike Milligan, his zany talent masked deep depression.

The highpoint of Stanshall's later career was the cult film *Sir Henry at Rawlinson's End* (1980), which starred Trevor Howard as Stanshall's bizarre alter ego Sir Henry ("If I had all the money I've spent on drink," ran a typical line of Sir Henry's, "I'd spend it on drink").

But Stanshall never lost the respect of his many devoted admirers, who included James Cameron, John Cleese, Jack de Manio and Stephen Fry.

Stanshall always devoted much of his energy to

practical jokes. In the 1970s he was frequently joined in these by his best friend Keith Moon, the drummer of The Who, whose riches and recklessness allowed Stanshall to indulge his quirky sense of humour on a wider stage. Stanshall had particularly fond recollections of his "trouser testings".

Though the routine was not so formalised as to preclude improvisation, in its purest form the prank consisted of Stanshall's entering a West End tailor's and asking to see "the strongest pair of trousers in the shop". Despite the apparent implausibility of such a request, most shopkeepers were, as he remembered, "only too eager" to provide him with a garment in what they considered their most durable fabric. Stanshall would then enlist the assistance of a bystander (Moon), and together they would "test" the garment so thoroughly that it would disintegrate, leaving each of them holding a leg.

The tailor's cries of anger and surprise were, Stanshall recalled, the cue for the second accomplice – a one-legged man, hired from a theatrical agency – to come into the shop and exclaim: "Just the job! Wrap them separately!"

Vivian Stanshall was born on March 21 1942 and grew up in north London. On leaving school he spent a year in the Merchant Navy earning the money to send himself to art school. In later years he would recall heroic drinking sessions with Melanesians in the New Hebrides.

In 1962 he enrolled at the Central London School of Art, where he met Rodney Slater, "Legs" Larry Smith and Neil Innes (who would become the core group of the Bonzos). They began to perform in the evenings in such south London pubs as the Tiger's Head, Catford. Stanshall spent his free time studying for an A level in Ancient Greek at the Camden Working Men's Institute.

The band's growing popularity – particularly in the United States – led to overwork and high living. Consequently Stanshall resorted for many years to alcohol and tranquillisers.

In the 1970s he made a number of increasingly crazed solo records and developed his skills as a broadcaster, conducting exercise classes for old jokes and sometimes deploying freshly minted ones. At a chemist's shop near Broadcasting House, for instance, where he was seeking one of his innumerable prescriptions, he once heard a man in front of him say: "I'm going on holiday and I need an insect repellant." The chemist gave him a tube of something called *Wasp-eze*.

Fascinated, Stanshall approached the counter and said, "As a matter of fact, I'm just off to Africa, and I'm a bit worried about being pestered by big game." He then demanded an aerosol spray called *Repel-ephant*, and a tube of *Rhin-no*!

All this was incorporated into his wireless routine the next day, which began with a mock advertisement: "Hi! Having pachyderm problems?"

Barred from the set of *Sir Henry at Rawlinson's End*, for which he had written the script, Stanshall retreated to a converted First World War Irish navy patrol boat at Chertsey, where he remained for nearly two years, unable to work and so stricken by anxiety attacks that he could barely pluck up the courage to go out and collect his post.

After drying out at Weston-super-Mare in 1986, Stanshall recovered sufficiently to complete two new episodes of *Sir Henry* for BBC Radio. He also had an unsuccessful comic opera, *Stinkfoot*, produced at the Bloomsbury in 1988 (a project financed by Stephen Fry and Pete Townshend).

Stanshall's main source of income was from voice-overs for advertisements. In 1992 he did a total of three hours' paid work. But after he appeared on Jools Holland's New Year's television show in 1993, Bella Freud, the fashion designer, declared that 1994 would be "the year of Vivian Stanshall as spiritual leader".

It proved to be the year of Vivian Stanshall as promoter of Ruddles Ale – in a series of television commericals which he wrote and performed, and which, uniquely for an advertisement for alcohol, featured scenes of spectacular drunkenness.

Recently he divided his time between a bedsitting-room in Muswell Hill and his mother's bungalow at Leigh-on-Sea in Essex, which was not entirely to his taste: "I have to endure the floral carpet, the floral upholstery and the floral wallpaper."

Last year in a Wimpy bar in Leigh-on-Sea he was set upon by a gang of youths whom he had lectured on the inadvisability of ethnic cleansing. "A fight took place. I acquitted myself. My eyes blazed. My fists were clenched . . . then out came the Stanley knives. They cut me all over, ruined a perfectly good shirt. The encounter ended when one party ran away. I will leave it to you to decide which one it was. Little did they know with whom they were tangling: Vivian Stanshall, star of a beer ad."

March 7 1995

ODETTE HALLOWES, GC

ODETTE HALLOWES, who has died aged 82, was tortured by the Germans while working for Special Operations Executive (SOE) during the Second World War, and was subsequently awarded the George Cross.

In November 1942 Odette Sansom (as she then was) landed by boat in the South of France, with instructions to help to establish a Resistance circuit at Auxerre. When that plan was abandoned she acted for several months as a courier for the Resistance circuit based at Cannes, which was operated by Captain Peter Churchill. In February 1943 the group was forced to relocate to the mountains surrounding Annecy, where they arranged arms drops for the *Maquis*.

After a brief spell in London, Churchill parachuted back into France on April 15; the next night the Resistance circuit was betrayed, and Churchill and Sansom were captured. The traitor was believed to be a young French double agent, who, it is thought, was killed in a gunfight with members of the Resistance in the rue de Rivoli, Paris.

On the way to a prison at Fresnes, Churchill and Sansom were able to confer, and in order to protect each other agreed to pretend to be married. Sansom also pretended that Churchill was a relation of the Prime Minister, a claim which probably helped to ensure their survival. She stuck to her story through some 14 subsequent interrogations.

Her citation for the George Cross read: "She drew Gestapo attention from her commanding officer and on to herself, saying that he had only come to France on her insistence. She took full responsibility and agreed that it should be herself and not her commanding officer who should be shot. By this action she caused the Gestapo to cease paying attention to her commanding officer after only two interrogations."

The Gestapo were determined to locate a wireless operator and another British officer, whose whereabouts they were (correctly) convinced were known to Sansom. "The Gestapo tortured her most brutally to make her give away this information," continued the citation. "They seared her back with a red hot iron and when that failed pulled out all her toe nails ... [she] refused to speak and by her bravery and determination she not only saved the lives of the two officers but also enabled them to carry out their most valuable work."

She was condemned to death and in May 1944 was taken to Germany, along with six other women agents; three were executed at Dachau concentration camp and three at Natzweiler.

Sansom was held at Ravensbrück, where she was first placed in a cell 10 feet by 6 feet, with no light, only straw for bedding and water for sustenance. Later she was moved to a cell overlooking the camp crematorium. She saw women being dragged to their deaths behind the crematorium's iron doors and heard the screams of victims of the beatings constantly administered in the adjacent cell. Her evidence was later used in the trial of 16 of the camp's guards.

In April 1945 she was unexpectedly released, and found her way to the advancing Allies.

The daughter of a French bank manager who was killed in the First World War, Odette Marie Celine

Brailly was born at Amiens, France, on April 26 1912. She was educated privately and at the Convent of Ste Thérèse, Amiens.

She was a quiet, withdrawn child, who cared for horses and for music. At eight she went almost blind, and it took several years for her to regain her sight completely. She later said that the experience helped her to cope with her incarceration in Ravensbrück.

In 1931 she married Roy Sansom, an Englishman and old friend of her family, and the next year they moved to Britain.

In the spring of 1942 Mrs Sansom heard a BBC broadcast in which the War Office requested photographs and postcards showing the European coastline. She sent off some family snapshots of her brother playing on the beach at Boulogne. It turned out that the War Office had arranged the broadcast to contact potential agents, and she was soon recruited to SOE.

At the end of her training she was assessed as enthusiastic, though "impulsive and hasty in her judgements ... Her main asset is her patriotism. Her main weakness is her complete unwillingness to admit she could ever be wrong."

Though Colonel Maurice Buckmaster (*q.v.*), the head of SOE's "F" Section, was not impressed by this assessment, he saw Sansom's stubbornness as a potential asset. In September 1942 she said goodbye to her children, and handed over to SOE a great bundle of letters to be posted to her family at intervals. Buckmaster gave her two farewell presents – a silver powder compact and a poison pill.

On her return to England in 1945 Sansom was

deeply traumatised. She was presented with the George Cross by King George VI in November 1946.

The next year she married Captain Peter Churchill. The marriage was dissolved in 1953 and in 1956 she married Geoffey Hallowes.

She was the subject of a biography, and of a film, *Odette* (1950), directed by Herbert Wilcox and starring Anna Neagle in the title role.

In the 1960s there was a certain amount of controversy aroused by the official history *SOE in France*, which questioned the effectiveness of the organisation's operations. But Hallowes's reputation remained unsullied.

She was appointed MBE in 1945 and awarded the Légion d'honneur in 1950. She was vice-president of the Women's Transport Services (FANY), a regular attender at FANY reunions and a stalwart of Forces charities.

On one occasion her medals were stolen by a burglar; but such was her popularity that they were soon returned, along with an abject letter of apology.

She and Roy Sansom had three daughters.

March 17 1995

KENNY EVERETT

KENNY EVERETT, who has died aged 50, was a disc jockey and television comedian with a disconcerting line in coarsely satiric comic sketches in what one of his characters, Cupid Stunt, would have insisted were "all in the best *pahssible* taste!"

"Cuddly Ken", as he liked to be known, first came

to public attention in the 1960s, when his manic broadcasts for pirate radio won him a large following among adolescents. Snapped up by BBC Radio 1, Everett pioneered the role of disc jockey as popular entertainer, with nonsensical jingles, scatological extemporisations and wild lunges at figures of authority.

Nervous and unconfident in company, he found that the seclusion of the radio studio allowed him to escape from his own neuroses into a world of fantastic invention. "Radio is a good place to work," he said, "if you are not really a jolly person, but want to appear to be one."

Among Everett's favourite creations was the Captain Kremmen series – a cross between *Dan Dare* and *The Goons*, which began life on Capital Radio. Everett as the skinny hero did battle with the Enemies of the Universe (the Krells, a species of man-eating blancmange).

From the late 1970s Everett was much in evidence on television. Diminutive and bearded, with receding hair and wildly rotating eyes, he presided over an hysterical melange of music and fustian lampoon, laden with innuendo. His zenith in this line came with *The Kenny Everett Video Show* and *The Kenny Everett Television Show*.

Everett created a gallery of memorable grotesques, the foremost of which were Sid Snot (a filthy Hell's Angel), Mr Angry of Mayfair, Marcel Wave (a fastidious French hairdresser), the Thora Hird-inspired Verity Treacle and the pneumatic American starlet Cupid Stunt, for whom Everett coined the celebrated catchphrase about taste, as "she" crossed her legs with an extravagant lack of discretion. There was also a bearded baby, who used to say: "When I grow up I'm going to be Kenny Everett – pathetic, isn't it?"

Everett introduced to television the dance group Hot Gossip, who writhed athletically in scanty leather; he indulged his fascination for lavatories; addressed royalty as "Your Royal Aubergineness"; and terrified his producers when he offered viewers Ferraris as prizes, failing to mention that they were Dinky toys.

In 1970 Everett was sacked by the BBC for making a jibe about Mary Peyton, the wife of the then Minister of Transport, after she had taken her driving test – "She only passed because she slipped him a fiver – I know these people."

The BBC took him back, but in 1984 he made another unfortunate joke, albeit one handed him on a piece of paper by his producer. "When England was an empire," he gurgled, "we had an emperor, when we were a kingdom, we had a king, and now we are a country, we've got Margaret Thatcher."

This was characteristically inconsistent of Everett, as in the previous year he had "come out" as a Tory at a Young Conservatives' rally attended by the Prime Minister, at which he jovially yelled (to the embarrassment of the assembled faithful): "Let's bomb Russia! Let's kick away Michael Foot's stick!"

In 1985 Everett came out as a homosexual, declaring that since his sexual predilection had twice led him to attempt drug overdoses he found it impossible to accept the label "gay". He was upset by the hostile reaction of his fans.

By the late 1980s Everett's critics were arguing that his insinuating humour failed to conceal a dwindling comic inspiration. Everett was hurt: "I'm so thin-skinned, I'm completely raw."

In 1989 Everett vowed never again to dress up as Sid Snot or Marcel Wave, and returned to the isolation of the radio studio. It was announced that he was suffering from an Aids-related illness, but he maintained his sense of humour.

"I see death in my own philosophical way," he remarked. "I can't imagine I was nowhere before this. I'd like to come back living in Italy or Spain or somewhere. As long as I don't come back bald or in Bosnia, I don't mind."

The son of a tugboatman, Kenny Everett was born Maurice Cole into a working-class family of Liverpool Roman Catholics on Christmas Day 1944; he was educated at St Bede's Secondary Modern and St Peter Claver College. A spindly, sensitive child, he recalled his school-days with distaste: "Most kids thought the best way to get on top was to punch someone in the mouth – usually me."

After leaving school, he had a brief flirtation with the priesthood and spent a year at a missionary college. "I'm no longer Catholic," he later said. "I'm freelance." His first job was "scraping gunk off sausage-roll trays" in a Liverpool bakery, before moving on to an advertising agency and to the advertising department of the *Journal of Commerce*.

Having acquired an ability to impersonate every-thing from the Goons to the opening of the airlocks in *Journey into Space*, he bought two tape recorders and began to make his own programmes, interspersing music with bouts of silliness.

He changed his name to Kenny Everett, and in

1964 became a disc jockey for Radio Luxembourg; before long he moved to the pirate ship Radio London, where he teamed up with Dave Cash for *Kenny and Cash on London*.

When the Government cracked down on the pirate stations Everett switched to Radio 1. Sacked from the BBC for the second time, he joined the new Capital Radio, where he was reunited with Cash.

In 1968 Granada Television teamed him up with the practical joker Jonathan Routh and the Australian academic Germaine Greer for *Nice Time*, on which massed ventriloquists' dummies sang "Congratulations". Subsequent television successes included *The Kenny Everett Explosion*, *Making Whoopee*, *Ev*, *The Kenny Everett Video Show* and *The Kenny Everett Television Show*. He even hosted a religious quiz show – one of his many attempts to create a more orthodox act.

In 1991 he played the "wacky" Billiard Marker in his first West End musical, *The Hunting of the Snark*, a short-lived show by Mike Batt (best known for his songs for *The Wombles of Wimbledon*) based on Lewis Carroll's epic nonsense poem.

For 12 years Everett was married to a spiritualist known as Crystal Clear. When they parted his wife revealed that the main obstacle to nuptial bliss had not been Everett's homosexuality but his profound depressions. "Even the plumber would leave our house feeling depressed after talking to Ev," she wrote. She further described him as "a little boy whose hobby is polishing the bathroom taps"; when they split up she found him a flat with three bathrooms.

After his divorce Everett moved in with his friend Nikolai Grishanovich (a computer analyst and former

Red Army soldier) and Grishanovich's wife. "I'm not a homosexual," he would say, planting a kiss on Grishanovich's cheek, "just helping out."

The menage was later augmented by the arrival of a Spanish waiter: "There's nothing worse than only having one husband," explained Everett.

Grishanovich died in 1993. Latterly Everett lived alone in a flat he kept obsessively tidy, even vacuuming the plastic grass on the balcony.

Everett was fond of animals, and at one stage had a chihuahua–Yorkshire terrier cross, two cats, a parrot and several horses. His companion in his last years was a cat called Pussy Cat.

By way of recreation, Everett enjoyed needlework.

April 5 1995

LANA TURNER

LANA TURNER, the film actress who has died in Los Angeles aged 75, packed as much melodrama into her life off-screen as into her sizzling appearances before the camera.

"My life has been a series of emergencies," Turner once observed, and indeed her career would have done credit to a Hollywood scriptwriter. Her father was murdered when she was nine, and she was partly brought up by unloving foster parents before she wooed and won the American public.

It was in fact Turner's tight-fitting sweaters which first suggested her dramatic potential – it was as "The Sweater Girl" that she became a pin-up in the Second

World War. Though she was said to change her costumes more often than the expression on her face, the young Turner always had a compelling mixture of sexiness and ordinariness.

Cheap showgirls, sleazy adulteresses, murderous wives, alcoholic actresses and neurotic mothers were her stock in trade. The most enduring of her films is perhaps *The Postman Always Rings Twice* (1946), in which she and John Garfield whip up an overpowering sexual chemistry as she incites him to murder her husband.

"You won't find anything cheap around here," Turner told Garfield.

"The harder the wind blows, the hotter it gets," Garfield returned. Still tighter than the dialogue was the white "hot pants" suit Turner wore.

Turner was also striking in *The Bad and the Beautiful* (1952), playing an alcoholic film star opposite Kirk Douglas's megalomaniac producer. And in 1957 she was nominated for an Oscar when she took on the role of a neurotic mother in *Peyton Place*.

Off the screen, she worked her way through seven marriages, as well as engaging in widely publicised affairs with Frank Sinatra, Tyrone Power and Howard Hawkes. "When I was a playgirl, honey," Turner remembered at the end of her life, "I played."

In 1958 there was a sensation when Turner's current lover, a gangster called Johnny Stompanato, was stabbed to death with a carving knife by her 15-year-old daughter Cheryl.

Cynics observed that mother and daughter had previously communicated chiefly through the pages of fan magazines; it seemed that Turner had been unaware that her fourth husband, Lex Barker (Johnny Weissmuller's successor as Tarzan), was regularly raping Cheryl, then barely a teenager.

At the coroner's inquest Turner explained how Stompanato had been killed. "We had a violent argument," she told the court, "and he went to the closet where he had a jacket and a shirt on a hanger. He came to me like he was going to strangle me with the jacket. I said, 'Don't ever touch me again. I want you to get out.' I went to the door, and, as I opened it my daughter was standing there. She came in, and everything happened so fast I thought she had hit him in the stomach. I never saw a blade."

The court found that the killing was a justifiable homicide, in that Cheryl had acted to protect her mother's life. Years later mother and daughter came to refer to this episode as "the paragraph", since neither of their names was ever mentioned without a reference to the case.

Turner's ardent love letters to Stompanato, read out in court, did her image no harm. In 1959 she made a fortune from her percentage of the profits of Douglas Sirke's *Imitation of Life*, the plot of which centred on an actress's troubles with her daughter.

By this time the ordinariness which she projected in her earlier films had long since been exchanged for contrived sophistication and glamour. The actress and her legend had achieved a perfect symbiosis.

A mine foreman's daughter, Julia Jean Mildred Frances Turner was born at Wallace, Idaho, on February 8 1920. Her parents moved to California, where they separated, and her father was killed by thieves. Years of poverty followed, though there was some attempt to educate the girl at a convent in San Francisco and at Hollywood High School.

According to the legend, at the age of 15 Turner was playing truant from school and sipping soda at Schwab's drugstore on Sunset Boulevard when she was observed by the editor of the *Hollywood Reporter*, who passed on his discovery to the director Mervyn LeRoy.

In no time Turner was under contract to Warner Brothers, and after a bit part in *A Star Is Born* (1937) made a distinct impression with her provocative walk in *They Won't Forget Her*. Later she would pass on the secrets of this perambulation to her daughter: "Pretend there's a nickel stuck between your buttocks and you have to hold it there for dear life so it won't fall out."

Moving on to MGM with LeRoy – Jack Warner held she would never amount to anything and willingly let her go – Turner appeared in several more minor roles before making a breakthrough in *Ziegfeld Girl* (1941) with Judy Garland, Hedy Lamarr and James Stewart. In the part of an ill-fated showgirl, she lightened her hair to a golden blonde, sat in a bubble bath wearing diamond and emerald jewellery and walked on a mink coat flung on to the floor.

Turner's next success was in a western, *Honky Tonk*. "Clark Gable kisses Lana Turner and It's Screen History", announced the posters, and certainly when Gable knocked down her door on their wedding night, she did not look displeased.

Her subsequent ventures with Gable – in *Somewhere I'll Find You*, *Homecoming* and *Betrayed* – were less memorable. Back in 1942 *Johnny Eager* featured another much touted pairing, with Turner as a society girl being pursued by Robert Taylor's gangster. The publicists hit upon the formula "T-N-T" – for Taylor and Turner.

By now Turner was the GIs' favourite, a popularity relentlessly exploited in such vehicles as *Slightly Dangerous*, *Marriage is a Private Affair*, *Keep Your Powder Dry* and a remake of *Grand Hotel*.

In the box office hit *Green Dolphin Street* Turner braved an earthquake, a tidal wave, a native uprising and childbirth; in *Cass Timberlane* she lured Spencer Tracy's judge into marriage against his better judgement; and in *The Three Musketeers* she essayed Milady de Winter, sounding, according to the *New Yorker*, "like a drive-in waitress exchanging quips with hotrodders".

In 1960 in league with Anthony Quinn she killed another husband in *Portrait in Black*. The next year she had a less fulfilling role opposite Bob Hope in *Bachelor in Paradise*. Her performance in *Madame X* (1966) pleased her fans more than the critics. Latterly film roles became scarce, and Turner herself described *Persecution* (1974), a British horror film, as "a bomb".

She turned to television and in 1969 appeared with George Hamilton in a series called *The Survivors*. She bravely took to the stage, touring in *Forty Carats* in 1971 and four years later performing in a production of *The Pleasure of His Company* in Chicago. In 1981 she briefly returned to television in *Falcon's Crest*. Her last films were *Bittersweet Love* (1976) and *Witches' Brew* (1978, released 1985).

In latter years Turner developed a horror of explicit sex on screen. "Thank God I was never asked to do nude scenes," she said in 1983. "I watch some of the things they do today and even when they kiss – the mouths opening before they get together, the tongues lashing in and out, the bodies grinding – it's all so different from the beautiful kisses we had from our lovely leading men. It offends me, it's ugly. I turn my eyes away."

In 1981 the National Film Society presented Turner with an Artistry in Cinema award. Her autobiography, *Lana . . . The Truth*, was published in 1982.

Lana Turner married first, in 1940 (dissolved 1941), the bandleader Artie Shaw; secondly, in 1942, Steven Crane. It was subsequently discovered that Crane was already married, and another, legal, wedding took place in 1943, prior to the divorce in 1944. Cheryl, Turner's only child, was born of this union.

Turner married thirdly, in 1948 (dissolved 1952), Henry "Bob" Topping; fourthly, in 1953 (dissolved 1957), Lex Barker; fifthly, in 1962 (dissolved 1962), Fred May; sixthly, in 1965 (dissolved 1969), Robert Eaton; and seventhly, in 1969 (dissolved 1972), Ronald Dante.

"I used to lean on men," Turner reflected after the end of her last marriage. "But whenever a crisis happened, they fell apart, and suddenly I became the strong one. I am not ashamed to say that I have no desire to marry again."

July 1 1995

BAPSY MARCHIONESS
OF WINCHESTER

BAPSY MARCHIONESS OF WINCHESTER, who has died in India aged 93, became the third wife of the 16th Marquess of Winchester in 1952, when he was in his 90th year, and spent much of the next decade engaged in public squabbles with her husband's friend Eve Fleming.

An enthusiastic self-publicist, Lady Winchester was prone to circulating documents extolling her own virtues. One described her as "a great and gracious lady . . . an unofficial ambassador for India . . . recognised for her beauty and grace . . . for her wealth and fabulous jewels". Another listed the many heads of state who had received her, including Calvin Coolidge, the King of Afghanistan, King Farouk of Egypt and Emperor Haile Selassie.

Lady Winchester ensured that even her marital disputes were widely broadcast. While she was wintering in India in 1953 her husband went to Nassau to visit Eve Fleming, the mother of Ian Fleming. Lady Winchester followed him, and stalked the pair, rather in the manner of the native lady, forever staring, in Somerset Maugham's short story "The Force of Circumstance".

According to Ivar Bryce, a neighbour, "There was almost always an overweight Indian lady clad in a dingy sari, pacing the main road . . . occasionally pausing to raise and shake her fist towards the main house."

She wrote vitriolic letters to her husband: "May a

viper's fangs be forever around your throat," she raged, "and may you stew in the pit of your own juice."

Lady Winchester claimed that Eve Fleming had made Lord Winchester a prisoner, and forced him to stay in courier rooms at hotels while she took comfortable suites. When Bapsy Winchester saw her rival press the Marquess's left thigh in 1954 she sued her for enticement. The litigation continued in various forms over the next four years, and in 1957 the case came before Mr Justice Devlin at the High Court in London.

Lady Winchester proved a temperamental witness, sometimes talking ceaselessly, at other times stubbornly mute. When in communicative mood she claimed that her husband had at first worshipped the ground she walked on, and then "murdered" her. At one point the judge became so exasperated that he threatened her with a night in prison.

Lady Winchester's counsel told the court that his client had been portrayed as "a sort of mixture of Jezebel, Sapphira and Mrs Malaprop". In fact, he said, she was "a wronged woman distraught . . . like Dido – with a willow in her hand upon the wild sea banks and wafting her love to come again to Carthage".

The court found against Mrs Fleming, but to Lady Winchester's fury the verdict was later reversed in the Appeal Court. Lord Winchester and Mrs Fleming retired to Monte Carlo, with Lady Winchester still in pursuit. He died in 1962, just short of his 100th birthday.

Bapsybanoo Pavry was born at Bahrat, India, in 1902, the daughter of Khurshedji Erachji Pavry, whom she claimed was High Priest of the Parsees in Bombay; Lord Winchester maintained that his father-in-law was merely the priest of a fire temple.

Young Bapsy was educated at Columbia University, New York, and in 1928 was presented at court to King George V. In 1930 she published a book, *Heroines of Ancient Iran*, for which she was awarded the Iranian Order of Merit twenty-five years later. In 1947 she was a delegate at the Unesco Paris Peace Conference.

When she married in 1952 she circulated a document claiming that she was the first non-European ever to become a marchioness.

Her husband was by no means the most distinguished in his line. William Paulet, created Marquess of Winchester in 1551, had been Lord President of the Council under Henry VIII, and served as Lord Treasurer under Edward VI, Mary and Elizabeth. "By truth," Elizabeth said of him, "if my Lord Treasurer was a young man, I could find it in my heart to have him as a husband before any man in England." He was still in office when he died, in his late eighties, in 1572. He had built Basing House, near Basingstoke, which the 5th Marquess held for Charles I during a prolonged siege.

The younger son of the 14th Marquess, who was born in 1801, Montagu Paulet succeeded as 16th Marquess in 1899, when his elder brother was killed in the South African War. "Monty" Winchester's first two wives died in 1924 and 1949 respectively, without children.

When he died in 1962 the marquessate passed to a kinsman. From then on Lady Winchester divided her time between London and Bombay, escorted by her brother Dasturzada, Dr Jal Pavry. In London the pair lived at the Mayfair Hotel, and doggedly solicited invitations to public functions. When her brother died in

330

1985 Lady Winchester put out a statement that she had "received messages of sympathy from all over the world".

She was a member of the Council of World Alliance for International Peace through Religion, and in 1989 made an endowment to Oxford University, in memory of herself and her brother, for the study of international relations and human rights.

Lady Winchester wrote hundreds of letters to celebrated figures, and usually received replies from their secretaries. But her extensive archives, presented to the City of Winchester between 1974 and 1995, did include such triumphs as Christmas cards from King Olav of Norway, a reproduction portrait of herself by Augustus John, and photocopies of thank-you letters from George Bernard Shaw.

September 9 1995

BARBARA SKELTON

BARBARA SKELTON, who has died aged 79, published three works of fiction and two striking volumes of autobiography, remarkable chiefly for the light they shed on her career as a *femme fatale*.

Her memoirs, *Tears Before Bedtime* (1987) and *Weep No More* (1989), rarely erred on the side of discretion. In particular she penned an hilariously funny portrait of Cyril Connolly, her first husband who divorced her on grounds of her adultery with the publisher George Weidenfeld.

She then married Weidenfeld, who in turn divorced

her on grounds of adultery with Cyril Connolly. Finally she was briefly the fifth of the millionaire physicist Derek Jackson's six wives.

Skelton enjoyed love affairs with King Farouk of Egypt; the painters Felix Topolski and Michael Wishart; Alan Ross, founder of the *London Magazine*; and Bob Silvers, founder of the *New York Review of Books*. The cast also included a Metropolitan policeman – "sex is a great leveller," she reflected.

Anthony Powell admired the "peculiarly incisive malignity" of Skelton's memoirs. It has even been suggested that she might have afforded certain characteristics for the lethal Pamela Flitton, who drives men to their death in Powell's *A Dance to the Music of Time*.

However irresistible others found her feline sex appeal, Skelton herself was dismissive of her beauty – "bun-faced, with slanting sludge-coloured eyes". She was also distinctly unappreciative of conventional male good looks.

Rather, she liked to dwell in detail on her lovers' physical shortcomings – on Connolly's elephantine torso and Chinese coolie legs, or on Weidenfeld's hands and pallor intruding "like flaws or speckles in an otherwise perfect photograph".

Skelton's conversation was as sharp and funny as her writing. She enjoyed sharing the fruits of her wide reading; and however sullen and sulky she might appear, good humour would instantly return in the company of anyone who could make her laugh.

The daughter of an Army officer and a Gaiety Girl of Scandinavian origin, Barbara Skelton was born in 1916.

She was a passionate and uncontrollable child, on one occasion running at her mother with a carving knife in a jealous rage. Fascinated from an early age by the havoc-wreaking possibilities of passion, she was expelled from her convent school when a bundle of love letters was found in her desk.

The letters, written by herself and addressed to herself, showed a degree of moral corruption which the nuns were unable to countenance. Her education thus ended, Miss Skelton was given a job as a model at a Knightsbridge dress-shop.

Her patron, a rich friend of her father's, quickly established his protégée as his mistress, and Barbara Skelton was launched on her career of petulant promiscuity.

Cocktails and tangos at the Savoy soon palled and were followed by a brief sojourn with a paternal military uncle in India, where she broke the heart of a poetic and peace-loving soldier. An attempted elopement resulted indirectly in the death of her admirer.

She returned to London and an erratic modelling career, which included a spell working for Schiaparelli.

During the first years of the Second World War she set up house with an unsurprisingly unattractive Free Frenchman – "a balding stocky man with a pale reptilian face". Recruited to the Foreign Office by Donald Maclean, she was posted to Egypt as a cypher clerk at the embassy.

Friendship with King Farouk flourished after a chance encounter at a restaurant, much to the disquiet of her Foreign Office superiors, who transferred her to Athens. She was to renew her acquaintance with Farouk some years later, when she joined him at Monte Carlo. He whipped her with a dressing-gown cord, providing material for her first novel, *A Young Girl's Touch* (1956), in which the heroine is beaten in similar fashion by King Yo-yo.

After the war Skelton lived a hectic and Bohemian social life in London, consorting with, among others, Peter Quennell (whom she nicknamed "The Bastard") and the film maker John Sutro. In 1969 Skelton's novel *A Love Match* was withdrawn when Sutro and his wife threatened to sue her for libel.

Skelton's acquisition of a red Sunbeam Talbot convertible resulted – according to Nancy Mitford – in the captivation of Cyril Connolly. They were married in 1950, and for the next four years lived together in her cottage in Kent.

In her memoirs Skelton describes Connolly lying abed morning after morning sucking the sheet and crying out in an ectoplasmic voice, "I wish I was dead," or more simply, "Poor Cyril."

Rage seems to have presided over the ill-starred marriage from the very beginning. When Skelton one day asked her husband what he had all over his face (it was in fact red wine), he furiously replied: "*Hate!*"

Visits to other people's houses were invariably disastrous. "Do come back when you're less cross," suggested one hostess. Nevertheless Skelton retained a residual affection for Connolly: "He had such enormous charm and intelligence," she wrote, "and he never bored me."

Her affair with George Weidenfeld began with the tortured permission of Connolly. "I am simply obsessed with him sexually," she noted of her new admirer. "I no longer remark on his hands or his toenails. And I have told him that he must grow some new black hair on his back. I have even threatened to smear him with bone lotion to further the process."

A Young Girl's Touch was dedicated to Connolly and published by Weidenfeld; and in 1956 Skelton divorced the first and married the second. "A feeling of utter despair followed the ceremony," she recorded. During the honeymoon she chanted "Until Death Us Do Part" at her husband through clenched teeth.

Weidenfeld's attempts to make her behave like a smooth social hostess – "Gush, *gush*," he would whisper to her at dinner-parties – were to no avail. She continued to play with Connolly, and in time the publisher sued for divorce.

Skelton's marriage to Weidenfeld and her affair with Connolly both ended in 1961. She then embarked on a series of liaisons with younger men, and took up with Kenneth Tynan, who maintained that "sex means smack and beautiful means bottom and always will".

Subsequently, Skelton lived for some years in New York, where she worked variously as a dental nurse, secretary and elderly lady's companion. She also wrote a book of short stories, *Born Losers* (1965), about the sex war in New York.

Of her third foray into matrimony in 1966 Barbara Skelton observed: "A marriage can be founded on many things . . . It was not for love that I married Professor Jackson." The union, dominated by Skelton's menagerie of small violent mammals, was of brief duration.

Skelton then went to live in a farmhouse in Provence, where for more than a decade she shared the favours of the French journalist Bernard Frank with Françoise Sagan. Cyril Connolly visited her there shortly before his death, and spent an afternoon rummaging through her papers. "You certainly were a sexpot in your day," he concluded.

In 1993 Skelton returned to Britain, where she divided her time between a flat in the King's Road and a cottage in Worcestershire. Her affection was chiefly bestowed on two cats – her "pussers", as she called them.

January 29 1996

SIR FRANK WHITTLE

AIR COMMODORE SIR FRANK WHITTLE, who has died in America aged 89, was the greatest aero-engineer of the century.

Whittle ensured that Britain was the first to enter the jet age when, on May 15 1941, the jet-propelled Gloster-Whittle E 28/39 flew successfully from Cranwell. During 10 hours of flying over the next few days, the experimental aircraft – flown by the test pilot Gerry Sayer – achieved a top speed of 370 mph at 25,000 feet. This was faster than the Spitfire, or any other conventional propeller-driven machine.

Although this was a moment of triumph for Whittle, it was tinged with some bitterness, for he had had to overcome years of obstruction from the authorities. He felt, with justification, that if he had been taken seriously earlier, Britain would have been able to develop jets before the Second World War broke out.

He had been granted a patent for the first turbo-jet engine in October 1932, but the Air Ministry's indifference had caused a long delay in realising his ideas. Thus it gave Whittle particular satisfaction when, days after the E 28/39's maiden flight, Sir Archibald Sinclair, the Air Minister, and a gathering of officials stood stunned as Sayer put it through its paces over Cranwell.

As John Golley noted in his biography: "Whittle – who had been the first man to get a turbo-jet running – had thrust Britain forward into the Jet Age and stood the aviation industry on its head."

Whittle's engineering genius led to the creation of several other aircraft: the RAF's Gloster Meteor, which saw action during the latter stages of the Second World War; the de Havilland Comet, the world's first passenger jet, and Concorde.

Frank Whittle was born on June 1 1907, in the Earlsdon district of Coventry, the son of a foreman in a machine tool factory.

When Frank was four his father, a skilful mechanic who spent Sundays at a drawing board, gave him a toy aeroplane with a clockwork propeller and suspended it from a gas mantle. During the First World War Frank's interest in aeroplanes grew when he saw aircraft being built at the local Standard works, and was excited when an aeroplane force-landed near his home.

In 1916 the family moved to Leamington Spa, where Frank's father had bought the Leamington Valve and Piston Ring Company, which comprised a few lathes and other tools, and a single cylinder gas engine. Frank became familiar with machine tools and did piece work for his father.

Frank won a scholarship to Leamington College, but had to leave when his father's business faltered. Instead he spent hours in the local library, learning about steam and gas turbines.

In January 1923, having passed the entrance examination, Whittle reported at RAF Halton as an aircraft apprentice. He lasted two days: 5 feet tall and with a small chest measurement, he failed the medical.

Six months later, after subjecting himself to an intense physical training programme supported by a special diet, he was rejected again. Undeterred, he applied using a different first name, passed the written examination again and was ordered to Cranwell where he was accepted.

In 1926, strongly recommended by his commanding officer, he passed a flying medical and was awarded one of five coveted cadetships at the RAF College. The cadetship meant that he would now train as a pilot. In his second term he went solo in an Avro 504N biplane after eight hours' instruction.

Whittle graduated to Bristol fighters and, after a temporary loss of confidence due to blacking out in a tight loop, developed into something of a daredevil. He was punished for hedge-hopping. But he shone in science subjects and in 1928 wrote a revolutionary thesis entitled *Future Developments in Aircraft Design*.

The paper discussed the possibilities of rocket propulsion and of gas turbines driving propellers, stopping short of proposing the use of the gas turbine for jet propulsion. However, Whittle launched his quest for a power plant capable of providing high speed at very high altitude.

In the summer of 1928 he passed out second and received the Andy Fellowes Memorial Prize for Aeronautical Sciences. He was rated "Exceptional to Above Average" as a pilot on Siskin operational fighters – but red-inked into his logbook were warnings about overconfidence, an inclination to perform to the gallery and low flying.

At the end of August 1928, Pilot Officer Whittle joined No 111, an operational fighter squadron equipped with Siskins and based at Hornchurch, and was then posted to the Central Flying School, Wittering, for a flying instructor's course. In his spare time he conceived a gas turbine to produce a propelling jet, rather than driving a propeller. A sympathetic instructor, Flying Officer Pat Johnson, who had been a patent agent in civilian life, arranged an interview with the commandant.

This led to a call from the Air Ministry and an introduction to Dr A. A. Griffith at the ministry's South Kensington laboratory. Griffith was interested in gas turbines for driving propellers, and scorned Whittle's proposals. The Air Ministry told Whittle that successful development of his scheme was considered impracticable. Whittle nevertheless took out his jet patent, and qualified as a flying instructor.

Johnson, still convinced by Whittle's ideas, set up a meeting at British Thomson-Houston, near Rugby, with the company's chief turbine engineer. While not questioning the validity of Whittle's invention, BTH baulked at the prospect of spending £60,000 on development.

At the end of 1930 Whittle was posted to test float-planes at the Marine Aircraft Experimental Establishment at Felixstowe. On leave he publicised his jet engine proposal, unsuccessfully. But a friend from Cranwell days, Rolf Dudley-Williams, was based at Felixstowe with a flying-boat squadron, and his efforts on Whittle's behalf soon bore fruit.

In the summer of 1932 Whittle was sent on an engineering course at RAF Henlow. He did so well that he was permitted to take a two-year engineering course as a member of Peterhouse, Cambridge, where in 1936 he took first-class honours in the Mechanical Sciences Tripos.

While he was at Cambridge his jet engine patent lapsed; the Air Ministry refused to pay the £5 renewal fee. But he had an inquiry from Dudley-Williams, who was by then a partner with another former RAF pilot, named Tinling, in General Enterprises Ltd.

The two men undertook to cover the expenses of further patents, to raise money, and to act as Whittle's agents. In the New Year of 1936 an agreement was signed between Dudley-Williams and Tinling, Whittle, the president of the Air Council, and O. T. Falk & Partners, a firm of City bankers.

A company, Power Jets, was incorporated and Whittle received permission from the Air Ministry to serve as honorary chief engineer and technical consultant for five years, providing there was no conflict with his official duties. It was as well, because in July, turbo-jet experiments began at Junkers and Heinkel in Germany; at this stage, Whittle's ideas were not subject to the Official Secrets Act. It was a relief when the He 178, after some promise, was scrapped.

Whittle, seeking somewhere to develop his design on modest Power Jets capital, returned to BTH at Rugby and the company contracted to build a "WU" (Whittle Unit), his first experimental jet engine. He tried to persuade companies to develop the specialised materials he needed.

First attempts to run Whittle's jet at Rugby in April

1937 caused alarm as it raced out of control and BTH hands bolted for cover. Money was needed for further development, but this was scarce. An Air Ministry contract provided a paltry £1,900.

In 1938 BTH moved the test-bed to its Ladywood works at Lutterworth where, in September, the engine, reconstructed for the third time, was assembled. A further £6,000 was pledged by the Air Ministry and engine tests resumed in December.

With the outbreak of war in September 1939, the project gained a further lease of life. The Air Ministry commissioned a more powerful W 2 from Power Jets, and asked the Gloster Aircraft Company for an experimental aeroplane, specified as E 28/39.

With finances more secure, Whittle faced a new threat. Relations with BTH, never easy, deteriorated as the company took the view that the jet engine would not compare favourably with conventional power plants. Whittle was further bedevilled by the politics of possible participation by the Rover motor-car company.

In the event, the Government cut the ground from under Whittle's feet in early 1940, bypassing Power Jets and offering shared production and development contracts direct to BTH and Rover. Power Jets was demoted to the level of a research organisation.

Then the Air Ministry, eager to obtain an operational jet fighter, sidestepped Whittle, ignoring the E 28/39 and authorising Gloster to press ahead with a twin-engined jet interceptor specified as F 9/40. This was to become the Meteor. In 1941 the ministry's Director of Engine Production was to agree to Rover alterations to Whittle's design behind his back.

But fortunately, on July 9, Lord Beaverbrook, the

Minister of Aircraft Production, personally assured Whittle that the jet fighter would go ahead. Whittle was relieved by the reprieve, but agonised over the difficulties of, literally, getting his engine off the ground. He smoked and drank heavily, and the elbowing-out by BTH and Rover further depressed him.

But the events of April and May 1941, when he saw his E 28 test-bed aeroplane flying successfully at Cranwell, lifted his gloom. When Johnson, who had long encouraged Whittle, patted him on the back and said, "Frank, it flies," he replied: "Well, that was what it was bloody well designed to do, wasn't it?"

Details of Whittle's inventions were made available both in Britain and America. Rolls-Royce, de Havilland and Metropolitan-Vickers became involved. In June 1942, Whittle was flown to Boston to help General Electric to overcome problems. It built the engine under licence in America with the astonishing result that Bell Aircraft's experimental Airacomet flew in the autumn of 1942, beating the Meteor into the skies by five months.

On his return home, Whittle arrived at Power Jets' new factory at Whetstone and was astonished by its size after so many years of parsimony, although in practice it could not provide the capacity that would be needed.

Rolls-Royce stepped in and took over work on the W 2B engine, which in 1943 cleared the way for Whittle to plan improvements which would evolve as later mark numbers. Then, with Rolls-Royce in almost total control of Power Jets, Whittle lost touch for three months while attending the RAF Staff College.

Fearing that private industry would harvest the pioneering work of Power Jets for nothing, he suggested it should be nationalised. By the time Whittle had come to regret this proposal, he was taken up on it by Sir Stafford Cripps, the Minister of Aircraft Production. Cripps imposed a price of £135,563 10s, and renamed the company Power Jets (Research & Development). Whittle received nothing, having earlier handed over his shares worth £47,000 to the ministry.

But six months later Whittle was promoted Air Commodore and had the satisfaction of knowing that Meteors of 616 Squadron were shooting down V1 flying bombs.

In 1946 Whittle accepted a post as technical adviser on Engine Production and Design (Air) to the Controller (Air) at the Ministry of Supply. In 1948 he retired from the RAF on medical grounds.

Soon after, he was awarded an ex-gratia sum of £100,000 by the Royal Commission on Awards to Inventors, and he was knighted. In 1986 he was appointed a member of the Order of Merit.

Whittle settled in America in 1976, and was a member of the Faculty of the Naval Academy, Annapolis, Maryland. He published *Jet* (1953) and *Gas Turbine Aero-Thermodynamics* (1981).

Frank Whittle married in 1930, Dorothy Mary Lee; they had two sons. The marriage was dissolved in 1976 and that year he married Hazel Hall.

August 10 1996

TINY TIM

TINY TIM, the American pop singer who has died aged 62, specialised in horrendous falsetto vocalisations of sentimental songs, and cultivated an appearance of utter ghastliness to match.

His greatest success, in 1968, was a version of "Tiptoe Through the Tulips" which had first been recorded 39 years before. Critics wrote of the surreal awfulness of the performance. But for a year or two Tiny Tim was a weird enough phenomenon to compel attention, even in the heyday of hippiedom.

Although he washed obsessively, no one would have guessed it by looking at him. Tiny Tim's frizzy hair tumbled down over his shoulders, framing the gigantic nose which dominated his face. One critic who saw him on stage was reminded of a 16-stone floor mop; another remarked that he teetered about like a pregnant gazelle.

Off-stage, Tiny Tim clutched a shopping bag which contained his ukulele and his cosmetics. Long before the heavy metal bands of the 1970s, he was affecting white make-up – which he was still wearing when the 1970s bands were being resurrected for nostalgic fans.

In a way he was always consistent. "As a singer only one thing stands between him and success," it was observed, "complete and utter failure."

Tiny Tim was born Herbert Buckingham Khaury in New York on April 12 1930, the son of a Roman Catholic Lebanese father and a Polish Jewish mother. He was never a handsome boy, and his looks were not improved when, on a school outing, he slipped and broke his nose on a cannon that had once belonged to George Washington.

As a young man he gained some notoriety in the homosexual clubs of Greenwich Village with his cracked falsetto renderings of classic songs. "Why d'you gotta sing like a fairy?" his mother demanded.

Khaury adopted a number of pseudonyms in those early days: Larry Love, Darry Dover, Emmett Swink, Rollie Dell, Julian Foxglove and Winifred Lee. His idiosyncratic interpretations of "Be My Baby" and "Sonny Boy" attracted notice, and in 1968 he appeared as Tiny Tim in the film *You Are What You Eat*, which celebrated the more radical manifestations of black power and flower power.

Taken up by Reprise Records, he made an album called *God Bless Tiny Tim*, which included his unforgettable reworking of "Tiptoe Through the Tulips". As a single this number made the Top Twenty for six weeks, though it never went higher than No 17. That year, 1968, he made an appearance at the Royal Albert Hall.

A reviewer of that concert, while noting Tiny Tim's gift for summoning up the half-forgotten songs and gestures of such crooners as Rudy Vallee and Al Jolson, found that he seemed to love his audience rather more than they loved him. In America a critic likened him to "a haunted house, inhabited by ghostly song-and-dance men".

No one was ever quite sure how serious Tiny Tim was trying to be. "I am really a vampire of songs," he reflected, "and vampires suck blood. When I sing 'Great Balls of Fire' I enter the body of Elvis Presley for a moment."

Aside from music, Tiny Tim presented himself as a Biblical fundamentalist: "I found Christ in 1953," he would say. He also supported America's involvement in Vietnam. "Even in the days of King David," he explained, "there were religious wars and people had to fight."

At the end of 1969, Tiny Tim was married before a television audience of millions on the *Johnny Carson*

345

Show. His bride, Vicki Budinger, had stood in line to meet him in a Philadelphia store. The couple promised to be "sweet, gentle, kind, patient, not puffed up, charitable, slow to anger and swift to forgive".

But Tiny Tim refused to kiss his betrothed until the knot had been tied. "I am a weak person and if I kiss a girl it might lead to the ultimate. I can't allow that to happen until I marry." After the wedding, he announced that he and Miss Vicki would sleep in separate rooms for three days, "as dictated by the Scriptures".

It later transpired that he had interpreted the Scriptures with even more rigour than he professed. "Nothing happened to us sexually for six months," Miss Vicki vouchsafed. They had a daughter, Tulip, in 1971, but separated in 1972 and, against Tiny Tim's wishes ("I'm a 'Till Death Do Us Part' man"), divorced. "I blame Women's Lib," he said. "They're getting women further and further into men's domain."

Meanwhile Tiny Tim had appeared at the Isle of Wight Pop Festival in 1970 leading a crowd of 250,000 in a rendering of "Land of Hope and Glory". Two months later, though, at Batley Variety Club in Yorkshire, a former Coldstream guardsman decided to "shut him up" for "running England down" and knocked the microphone out of his hand. Deeply affronted, Tiny Tim cancelled the rest of his tour and returned to America.

By that time his career was entering steep decline – though only the year before he had been earning $50,000 a week at Caesar's Palace, Las Vegas. In 1975 he was back in Greenwich Village, living in the spare room of his mother's apartment. "Why d'you gotta look like a nut?" she remonstrated.

In the next two decades Tiny Tim's only notable achievement was to set a world record for non-stop singing: in 1988, at Brighton, he clocked in at three hours 11 minutes.

He married a second time, and this time divorced without resistance. But for nearly 30 years, unknown to Tiny Tim, a fan had been waiting for her chance. "When I was a girl," Sue Gardner explained, "all my friends liked the Rolling Stones and Jimi Hendrix. I thought they were out of their minds. When Tiny came on he sang songs that were happy and wholesome, and nice for children. I loved him even then. I always wanted to meet him but I never knew how to find him."

In 1995 she finally obtained his number through a newspaper, and telephoned on impulse. They were married shortly afterwards. Tiny Tim wore a purple suit and serenaded the guests with "Sweet Sue".

Subsequently, a new record, "Girl", was sufficiently well received to inspire hopes of a tour. "I've made 27 comebacks already," Tiny Tim said in 1996, "maybe this will be my year." But his heart was playing up, and when his doctor ordered him to cut down to one glass a day, he acquired a bigger glass.

In September he collapsed on stage after suffering a heart attack at a ukulele festival in western Massachusetts.

December 2 1996

RONNIE SCOTT

RONNIE SCOTT, the tenor saxophonist who has died aged 69, gave his name to one of the world's great jazz clubs.

He was a sardonic master of ceremonies at Ronnie Scott's, habitually affecting to regard the audience as completely inert or worse. A typical welcome would be: "You're a great crowd tonight. Stone dead, but great. You should have been here last Tuesday. Somebody should have been here last Tuesday. A fellow rang up and asked, 'When does the show start?' and we said, 'When can you get here?'"

Though it induced groans, Scott's patter became an essential part of a night at Ronnie Scott's. Sometimes there would even be requests for particular jokes.

The club in Frith Street, with its whitewashed walls, gingham-covered tables, slow service and indifferent food, hardly changed over the years. But it continued to feature the best jazz. Scott was proud of presenting Sonny Rollins and Count Basie, Sarah Vaughan, Ella Fitzgerald and Carmen McCrae.

What Scott expected from jazz was "melody, I like to hear a guy make up tunes as he plays. To me that is the whole idea, the instant composition, with all the things that go with it, like warmth and feeling and time."

Ronnie Scott's was opened in 1959, in partnership with a fellow saxophone-player, Pete King, in a cellar in Gerrard Street, Soho. Scott had visited New York in the 1940s, been bowled over by bebop, and wanted to emulate the jazz clubs of 52nd Street, in particular the Three Deuces. But he always claimed that he started a club "so that I could guarantee myself somewhere to play".

At first the club promised to provide four nights of British jazz a week. Pete King soon gave up playing to concentrate on managing the club. It was through his tenacity, according to Scott, that Zoot Sims agreed to play for four weeks in 1961. This booking set the club's tone and established its reputation.

Since they were musicians themselves, Scott and King knew how to maintain good relations with other jazz-men, even the more temperamental. Within three years they had brought to the club a top-class roll, who "through no coincidence at all," Scott said, "all happened to be tenor saxophonists". These included Dexter Gordon, Al Cohn, Stan Getz and Sonny Rollins.

The club moved to its present site in Frith Street in 1965. It now had to attract twice as many customers to cover overheads, but Scott did not compromise its standards. In 1967 he booked the Buddy Rich band and the innovative tenor saxophonist Coleman Hawkins. Though he might sign up novelty acts such as Cheech and Chong or The Scaffold, Scott's ideas were usually imaginative. He once paired the classical guitarist John Williams and the jazz guitarist Barney Kessel; he even persuaded Jimi Hendrix to play, in the last week of his life.

In the late 1960s financial success did not come easily. Scott and King would regularly meet on Sunday mornings to decide whether they could afford to open on Monday.

Scott always regarded himself in the first place as a performer: "I think of myself as a saxophone player.

Having a club is very nice but it is really incidental to what I want to do."

Ronnie Scott was born on January 28 1927 in Aldgate, east London. His father, Joseph Schatt, was a Russian immigrant and as Jock Scott played the saxophone in Jack Hylton's dance band. When Ronnie was four his parents divorced; his mother remarried when he was eight. In the meantime Ronnie went to the Jews' Infant School, Aldgate, then to an elementary school in Stamford Hill.

Though the boy had had little contact with his father he was determined to follow in his footsteps and become a musician. He bought himself a cornet for five shillings, and then a soprano saxophone. He was given lessons by Jack Lewis, a dance-band player.

On leaving school aged 15, Ronnie Scott found a job in the Keith Prowse music shop. He would spend his spare time playing informally with other musicians in wartime bottle clubs. In 1944 he joined the Johnny Claes band and 18 months later found a place for a time with Ted Heath's band.

By taking a series of jobs on transatlantic liners Scott was able to experience American jazz at first hand. He was highly impressed by the bebop of Gillespie, Parker and Powell.

In 1948 Scott joined Club Eleven, Britain's first jazz club, which began in Great Windmill Street and moved to Carnaby Street. In 1950 the premises were raided for drugs. At the ensuing trial the magistrate asked in passing, "What is bebop?" A helpful constable supplied the answer: "A queer form of modern dancing – a negro jive."

In the 1950s Scott played with a number of ensembles including the Jack Parnell band, with Pete King, and a nine-piece co-operative with Benny Green, Jimmy Deuchars and Victor Feldman. They would often try out their latest ideas on surprised audiences at dance halls who were expecting easy listening.

After a failed attempt to form a big band, Scott joined Tubby Hayes in 1957 to form the Jazz Couriers. Scott, exhibiting the influence of Coleman Hawkins, was able to produce a large tone with an aggressive attack to it. The Couriers split up in 1959. During the years that he was running his own club, Scott would usually play with a quartet.

Among the albums that Scott recorded were *The Night is Scott and You're so Swingable* (1965), *Great Scott* (1979) and *Never Pat a Burning Dog* (1990).

Scott's autobiography, *Some of My Best Friends are Blues*, written with Michael Hennessy, was published in 1979. A biography by John Fordham (1989) took its title from one of Scott's customary exhortations to his audience: *Let's Join Hands and Contact the Living*.

Scott was appointed OBE in 1981.

Ronnie Scott never married; he had two children.

December 26 1996

JOLIE GABOR

JOLIE GABOR, the mother of Magda, Zsa Zsa and Eva, who has died aged 97, was always determined that her daughters should achieve celebrity.

"You will be rich, famous and married to kings," she told them – and to that end insisted that they should master every possible accomplishment. "I wanted them not just to skate," she said, "but to skate like Sonja Henie; and I wanted them to play the piano so magnificently that a Rubinstein would be green with envy."

No talent was too arcane to be overlooked. "When will you be able to do that?" she demanded after taking her daughters to watch a fire-eater at a circus. This maternal solicitude bore fruit; if none of the girls married kings, they all became show-business personalities, with the keenest instinct for publicity.

No doubt there was an element of frustrated ambition in Jolie Gabor's hopes for her daughters. Born Jolie Tillemans into a prosperous merchant family in Budapest, she wanted to be an actress, only to have her dreams dashed when, at 17, she was married off to Vilmos Gabor, a former cavalry officer who owned a jewellery business.

"In the back of my mind I had the idea to get a divorce six months later," she remembered. "But like a fool I fell pregnant and had a daughter. Then I had another daughter and another. And all the time I wanted sons." Six months stretched out to 22 years.

Jolie Gabor finally divorced her husband in 1939, and escaped to America with no possessions beyond $100 in cash, a sable coat and a 30-carat diamond. Fortunately her daughter Zsa Zsa had preceded her to New York and married the hotel tycoon Conrad Hilton within three weeks of stepping off the boat. "Her heart is so big," Jolie observed, "I believe she would have married Connie Hilton just for my sake."

Subsidised by Zsa Zsa, Jolie Gabor started a small jewellery shop on Madison Avenue. Soon it was a big jewellery shop. "When you look as beautiful as my daughters, you don't struggle," Jolie Gabor reflected. "The best combination in the world is brains and looks. And also to know how to enjoy yourself."

She cast a benevolent eye over her daughters' copious matrimonial adventures, reserving a special affection for the actor George Sanders, who married both Magda and Zsa Zsa. "You know, Jolie," Sanders wrote to her, "I think marriage is for very simple people, not for great artists like us."

Zsa Zsa, however, cast a colder eye on her third husband. "Ven I vas married to George Sanders, ve vere both in love with him. I fell out of love vith him, but he didn't."

In 1957 Jolie Gabor married Count Edmond de Siegethy, who had escaped from Hungary in 1956. He arrived in New York with only $27 and proceeded to spend $20 on flowers for Jolie.

"Any man who could be so generous had to be special," she concluded, "so I married him."

The match, she noted proudly, took the matrimonial score of herself and her daughters to 13; eventually the daughters would notch up 19 marriages on their own account.

It hardly boded well for Jolie's marriage to de Siegethy that, at a family reunion in Vienna in 1958, she told Vilmos Gabor that he had always been her *real* husband. Nevertheless her second marriage endured. "You see, my darling," she explained to a journalist in 1973, "he insists every day that I take 14 vitamin pills, and that I use only the best lotions on my face. The Hungarians worship beauty."

Jolie Gabor expressed outrage at suggestions that her daughters married for money. Zsa Zsa, for example, never

took any alimony. And Eva (who died in 1995) concluded that men were a necessary evil: "Sex", she said "is
very good for pimples."

Jolie Gabor loved parties and was always ready to
pawn a diamond to pay for champagne.

"Life's a gamble," she held, "you must know how to
play it." She spoke of her daughters with pride, yet she
knew what was due to herself: "I too am a success."

April 3 1997

"Bunny" Roger

NEIL ROGER, who has died aged 85, was universally
known as "Bunny" because, so he claimed, when his
nurse first set eyes upon him she exclaimed that he
looked like "a dear little rabbit".

The rabbit turned into a bird of exceedingly rare
plumage. Couturier, art collector, *flâneur*, wit and exotic,
Roger's creation was himself. In the years after the
Second World War his delicately perambulating figure
became one of the minor sights of London. For passers-
by he seemed something between a reincarnation of Beau
Brummell and a *fin-de-siècle* apparition from the pen of
Aubrey Beardsley.

This consummately dandified image would appear
round the corner of a Mayfair street dressed from head to
toe in flared, pinch-waisted Edwardian apparel of exquisite cut and of the palest shades – cerulean blue, lilac,
shell pink, lavender – the whole ensemble topped by a
curly-brimmed bowler and a high, stiff collar with

jewelled tie-pin. The effect was to draw admiring glances or perhaps mutterings of disapproval.

In his passion for dressing-up he expressed a streak of bravado. But he had invented for himself a style which fitted him as perfectly as his wasp-waisted jackets. He wore it defiantly, a challenge to all comers.

Roger was also one of the most inventive party-givers of his age. To this he devoted the same fastidious sense of style and dedication as he brought to his own appearance.

His series of New Year's fancy dress parties, given from the 1950s in his house in Knightsbridge, had themes such as *Sunset Boulevard* and *Quo Vadis* (when two Christians were rather unsuccessfully put to the torch in a damp London garden). They attracted many of the more adventurous spirits of the Bohemian *beau monde*, as well as providing copy for rapt write-ups in society glossies and scandalised disapproval in the popular Sunday press.

Roger's final sequence of parties, given at his last house in Addison Road, near Holland Park, had the themes of Diamond, Amethyst and Flame to celebrate his 60th, 70th and 80th birthdays. They were included in *Harper's & Queen*'s list of the most memorable balls of the half-century. The Amethyst Ball had Roger at 70 still dancing in the early morning summer sunshine.

His last great party, on the theme of Hades, saw him appearing through flame and smoke in a sparkling creation of scarlet sequins to preside over 400 variously demonised guests. Characteristically at the time of his death he was planning the next party to celebrate his 90th. It was to be called the Haunted Ballroom.

Neil Munroe Roger was born on June 9 1911 in London, the second of three sons of a self-made Aberdonian industrial magnate, Alexander Roger, whose chief business was in cable and telephones. Alexander Roger was knighted in 1916 for his war work, and returned to public service in the Second World War as a government adviser.

It would be hard to conceive a starker contrast between father and son. When his father asked him what he would like as a present if he was chosen for his school's first XV, Roger replied: "A *doll's house*, please, Father."

He was educated at Loretto, Edinburgh, where he was miserable, and at Balliol College, Oxford, where he read history under the sharp eye of F. F. ("Sligger") Urquhart but mostly devoted himself to the pastimes of the late Twenties: popular music, dancing and developing his stock in trade as a winningly exotic personality.

After leaving Balliol without a degree, Roger attended the Ruskin with a view to becoming a dress designer. In 1937 he inaugurated his first London showroom in Great Newport Street with a grand Society opening.

One quality he did inherit from his father was fortitude, and it was this which saw him through a strenuous war in the Rifle Brigade in which, during the Italian campaign, he saw much active service. Typically, he claimed to have advanced through enemy lines with a chiffon scarf flying as he brandished a copy of *Vogue*. He also said that being in no man's land at least gave him a chance to repair his make-up.

After the war he again set up as a designer, in Bruton Street. From there he moved to create his own *couture* department at Fortnum & Mason's. There he sold pretty, much-pleated dresses in filmy materials for women of a certain age, most of them his friends.

After leaving Fortnum's Roger established himself at the fashion house of his friend Hardy Amies, in which he was an investor. He continued for nearly two decades to make charmingly suitable outfits for his well-bred, well-heeled customers.

For his friends, Roger's party-giving was not only a demonstration of his love for dressing-up and the diversions of make-believe, but also of his generosity. Whether he was holding house parties on a grand scale at his Highland estate or giving dinners and small summer garden parties in Addison Road, each entertainment was brought to a fine edge of perfection.

Beneath the cultivated epicene exterior lay a stalwart friend, a man with no illusions or false sentiment, who was possessed by a stoic tough-mindedness. Few who knew him well failed to recognise that the gossip and gossamer of the surface disguised a character of formidable strength.

Erudite and formidably well read (he had latterly developed a passion for ecclesiastical history), Roger could also name every small-part actor of an MGM comedy of the 1930s.

In his last years he had begun to live a somewhat Proustian existence, largely alone in his London house of 26 rooms filled with paintings by Delvaux, Burra, Derain and Sutherland and his eclectic and ornate collection of old furniture.

He still, however, punctuated his routine with Christmas and summer visits to Dundonnell, his romantic seat in the north-west of Ross and Cromarty. Here

was a place for roaring log fires and the dancing of
Scottish reels in which, well into his ninth decade, he
was an indefatigable participant.

May 1 1997

SIR JOHN JUNOR

SIR JOHN JUNOR, who has died aged 78, was editor of
the *Sunday Express* for 32 years, from 1954 to 1986, and
one of the last survivors of the Fleet Street generation
that came to prominence under Lord Beaverbrook.

There is room for debate about Junor's success as an
editor, for the circulation of the *Sunday Express* actually
halved (from 4 million to 2 million) under his leadership.
But as a columnist on that paper from 1973 to 1989 he
won a keen following for the blunt manner in which he
wrote what so many readers thought, but would never
have dared to say quite so forcefully themselves. His
pieces, and especially the abusive passages, profited from
being read out aloud in Junor's rich Scottish tones.

He dismissed homosexuals as "poofs", "powderpuffs"
and "pansies", and expressed the view that Aids was the
punishment ordained by God for sodomy. In particular
he anathematised those "who flaunt their homosexualism
and try to subvert and convert other people to it. These
are the people I have an utter hatred for, because I think
they are spreading filth."

Other categories which aroused his wrath included
Anglican bishops – "trendy old women"; the Irish –
"wouldn't you rather", he demanded after the Brighton

358

bombing, "admit to being a pig than to being Irish?";
the Press Council – "po-faced, pompous, pin-striped,
humourless twits"; and the Greenham Common women
– "sluts".

Taxed with racism, Junor would point out that the
President of Gambia was a friend. But he did not disdain
general principles: "Never trust a bearded man," he
would tell subordinates, or "Only poofs drink white
wine." Concerned by the rising crime statistics, he
wanted to hear more of "the whack of birch on bare
backsides".

Particular *bêtes noires* were Lord Denning – an "unctuous old humbug"; Lord Attenborough – "ancient,
affected, side-whiskered trendy"; the Archbishop of Canterbury, Dr Runcie – "a pathetic old man" who deserved
"a kick up the backside"; and the Bishop of Durham –
"a vain old fool", "a really nasty piece of work, an evil
man", whose ordination had provoked the Almighty into
hurling a thunderbolt at York Minster.

Viscount Whitelaw "would not be two-faced if there
were a third one available"; Neil Kinnock was "a weak,
wet Welsh windbag"; and President George Bush
appeared as "a neutered old tabby". Further down the
hierarchy, Jonathan Dimbleby featured as "a bumptious
little twerp", while Sara Keays was excoriated as a
"vicious, vindictive, scheming bitch".

"Pass the sick bag, Alice" was the stock conclusion
to these reflections on the passing scene. Alternatively,
"Aren't there times when you truly feel like pulling the
duvet over your head and turning your face towards the
wall?"

By contrast, erring heterosexual men, such as Cecil

Parkinson, conspicuously failed to provoke his disapproval. Junor appeared to find comfort in the reflection that, according to the Church of Scotland, "marriage is a contract, not a sacrament". He himself had a keen eye for the other sex – although, in the words of a friend, he was not so much a lover as a plunderer of women.

On the positive side, Junor believed that Britain was "the greatest nation in the world", though he also nursed a surprising weakness for the French. Mrs Thatcher, the Princess of Wales and Selina Scott all aroused his passionate enthusiasm. Mrs Thatcher reciprocated by knighting him in 1981, writing a foreword to *The Best of JJ* (1981), and turning up at a dinner party to celebrate his 25 years as editor.

"The moralist of the suburbs", as Junor was called, also found room in his column for inside political gossip, dollops of romantic slush and occasional maudlin reflections on the wonder of bird life ("the miracle of the swallows"), the sufferings of animals ("those poor, dumb reckless creatures") and the cuteness of children ("little mites"). But it was rage that drove him. Aware of this, he always carried a tape recorder so that he could catch his fury on the wing. The style that resulted was once described as that of a Rotarian on Ecstasy.

Junor's greatest strength as a columnist was that his contempt for the chattering classes was even more intense than theirs for him, so that he never cared a scrap about provoking their disdain. Nor did he make cowardly calculations of self-interest. No good journalist, he used to say, should ever go anywhere without his resignation in his pocket.

He was the last journalist to be summoned before the Bar of the House of Commons, as a result of an article he wrote in the *Sunday Express* in 1956, which charged MPs with doing very well out of their supplementary petrol allowances at a time when the rest of the country was severely rationed. He acquitted himself before the House with dignity, offering a statement that was half apology, half defiance.

Junor liked to dwell on Auchtermuchty, a small town in Fife, as the repository of the Calvinist virtues which he upheld against the depradations of modern life. But it was observed that the closest he usually permitted himself to come to this paradise was to drive through it on his way to the Royal and Ancient at St Andrews.

For all the theoretical glories of his native Scotland, Junor lived in England – in Surrey – and remained there even after leaving the editorship of the *Sunday Express*. The Scots, he decided towards the end of his life, had become "a bunch of whingeing third-raters".

Yet though Junor enjoyed the good life and the best restaurants, he never forgot his humble origins, or the fact that the majority of his readers did not enjoy the salaries and expenses of Fleet Street. He himself never ceased to count the pennies. "Now tell me something," he asked a journalist who had told him the cost of lunch at a restaurant, "does that figure include vegetables?"

John Donald Brown Junor was born in a Glasgow tenement on January 15 1919. His father was foreman in a steel roofing works, but it was his mother, a fanatical whist player, who was the dynamo of the family. She pushed her three sons to work hard, so that John and his brothers (one became a schoolmaster, the other a doctor) all went from state school to university.

Junor read English Literature at Glasgow University, where he became President of the Liberal Club and discovered a talent for public speaking. In the summer vacation of 1938 Lady Glen-Coats, prospective Liberal candidate for Orkney and Shetland, invited Junor to tour her constituency and to speak on her behalf. For this he received a cheque for £30, and an insight into a way of life beyond the tenements of Glasgow.

In 1939, after graduation, Junor acted as private secretary to Lady Glen-Coats (receiving £4 a week and his car). They visited Berlin together just before the Führer marched into Poland.

Junor joined the Navy as a midshipman (RNR), serving in the armed merchant cruiser *Canton*, a converted P&O liner. Later he transferred to the Fleet Air Arm.

His training revealed that he was by no means a natural pilot. Yet he survived a critical moment when his aircraft's directional instruments failed in pitch darkness. There was nothing to do but to pray, "my mouth quite dry". Salvation duly arrived in the shape of another plane, which guided him in to land. "I came to the conclusion," Junor said, "that someone up there had decided I had some purpose still to serve in life."

"I was a devout coward," he admitted. Relief from the hazardous business of taking off and landing on aircraft carriers came when he was appointed editor of *Flight Deck*, the Fleet Air Arm magazine.

In 1945 Junor was demobbed as a lieutenant, but not before he had fought Kincardine and West Aberdeenshire for the Liberals at the general election of that year, losing to the Tories by only 642 votes. He went on to unsuccessful contests at East Edinburgh in 1948 and Dundee West in 1951.

Meanwhile he had been working in London for an

Australian newspaper and news agency, and in 1947 had joined the *Daily Express* as a reporter under Arthur Christiansen. In 1951 he was still undecided over a political or a journalistic career. "If it is politics," Beaverbrook told him, "you will reach the highest echelon. But if it is journalism, I will put on your head a golden crown."

Junor chose the golden crown. He was Crossbencher on the *Sunday Express*, and then assistant editor of the *Daily Express*. In 1953 he moved to the *Evening Standard* as deputy editor, and the next year became editor of the *Sunday Express*. But though he served his master well he was never guilty of the sycophancy which distinguished so many Beaverbrook acolytes, including many on the Left.

Junor claimed in his memoirs, *Listening for a Midnight Tram* (1990), that he ran the *Sunday Express* very much according to his own lights. "I had always been totally unreasonable," he wrote. "I had never once taken on the staff anyone I didn't personally like. I always took the simplistic view that if I didn't like him then other members of the *Sunday Express* staff might not like him either."

He would take the trouble to call his writers to tell them that their work was "piss poor". But as Michael "Inspector" Watts recalled, "the one thing we used to dread from him above all was praise – oh *God* it was awful. Because you knew that after praise, within a week or fortnight, would come the lash." Nevertheless, Junor was always good company, and could be kind as well as irascible.

In 1963, unable to stomach the thought of supporting Harold Macmillan at the forthcoming election, Junor resigned. Before he had worked out his six months' notice, however, Macmillan was struck down with prostate trouble and left office. Junor returned to a post that had been eagerly coveted by Arthur Brittenden and Derek Marks.

But under his leadership the *Sunday Express* notably failed to move with the times. Well into the 1980s the paper was still fighting the Second World War, with tales of military derring-do illustrated by line drawings. There were also contemptuous references to artists and "long-haired" pop stars, and advertisements that seemed to concentrate heavily on garden sheds.

Junor's own column, though, retained its punch and popularity, and he continued with it after he gave up the editorship in 1986.

In 1990, outraged that Lord Stevens of Ludgate should have appointed a new editor without consulting him, Junor took his column to the *Mail on Sunday*. He always stressed the importance of insisting on one's own worth. "If you can walk over a man once," he believed, "you can walk over him as often as you like." His column lost none of its force in its new habitat.

Junor married, in 1942, Pamela Welsh; they had a son and a daughter, both of whom became journalists.

May 5 1997

ANDREW FOUNTAINE

ANDREW FOUNTAINE, squire of Narford in Norfolk, who has died aged 78, was from 1957 President of the National Labour Party ("National because we love our country, Labour because we love our people"); later, in 1967, he helped to form the National Front.

Fountaine was obsessed by the notion that miscegenation constituted a threat to the British race. "If it is Fascist to try and stop that," he declared, "then Fascism is a bloody good thing." Among those he deemed racially alien were all Americans, and Italians south of Rome.

The National Labour Party soon amalgamated with the White Defence League to form the British National Party. In 1962 Fountaine organised an Aryan camp on his Norfolk estate, where he raised the symbolic sun-wheel of "pure Northern Europeans".

But for all his speechifying in Stepney and Notting Hill, Fountaine's call went unheeded. In 1967 he merged the British National Party with the League of Empire Loyalists to form the National Front. "Hitler had some first-class ideas," he told the press.

In March 1968 Fountaine became the first National Front candidate to contest a parliamentary seat when he stood in a by-election at Acton. His concern over alien immigrants "living one third off prostitution, one third off National Assistance, and one third off Red gold" won him 1,400 votes.

Soon afterwards, though, he was expelled from the Front by A. K. Chesterton (cousin of G. K. and head of the Empire Loyalists), who accused him of having issued a "ludicrous" directive on the action to be taken in the case of civil war. After that, Fountaine kept his distance from politics for some years.

In 1976 another row in the National Front gave him the chance to make a comeback, as deputy chairman to the leader, John Tyndall. He stood for Coventry North-West in a by-election, but recorded only 986 votes.

The advent of Mrs Thatcher brought no joy to Fountaine, who considered that she was presiding over "the greatest bunch of traitors in history". By contrast, he explained, the ethos of the National Front was based on "love of our country".

Love, however, was not in evidence among his colleagues. After another ignominious defeat at Norwich South in the 1979 general election, Fountaine took it upon himself to suspend Martin Webster, one of the Front's leading figures. Tyndall retaliated by expelling Fountaine, who reacted by forming the National Front Constitutional Movement.

That was Fountaine's last political throw. After 1981 he largely abandoned his efforts to save the British race and concentrated instead on planting trees on his estate.

Andrew Douglas Algernon Maclean Fountaine was born on December 7 1918, into a family established in Norfolk since medieval times. The family seat of Narford Hall was begun by Sir Andrew Fountaine of the Royal Mint in the 1690s and is notable for the painted decoration by Giovanni Antonio Pellegrini; the house was substantially enlarged in the 1860s to the designs of William Burn. Young Andrew's father, Vice-Admiral Charles Fountaine, was naval ADC to King George V. The boy was sent to Stowe; his hopes of passing through Dartmouth Naval College, however, were undermined by glandular fever.

At 17 he drove an ambulance for the Abyssinians, who were under attack from Mussolini – "though now I see that I was on the wrong side". The error was corrected when he fought for Franco in the Spanish Civil War.

He was an undergraduate at Magdalene College,

Cambridge, and in 1938 became a Fellow of the Chemical Society.

On the outbreak of the Second World War, Fountaine managed to get into the Navy by persuading a friend who resembled him to undergo the medical examination on his behalf. He rose from Ordinary Seaman to Lieutenant-Commander, as a gunnery officer on the aircraft carrier *Indefatigable* in the Pacific. He was wounded in a kamikaze attack off Japan, and later saw the flash of the atomic bomb which was dropped – unnecessarily, as he thought – on Nagasaki.

In 1946, on his father's death, Fountaine became master of the family estate. The next year, he made his mark at the Conservative party conference, where he introduced a resolution "finally to root out the ever-increasing subversive foreign influence within our own country and the Dominions overseas".

The Tory rank and file cheered lustily before being quelled by Quintin Hogg. In 1948 Fountaine again delighted the party conference when he described the Labour administration as "a group of conscientious objectors, national traitors, semi-alien mongrels and hermaphrodite Communists".

He was adopted as Conservative candidate for Chorley, in Lancashire. When the National Union refused to endorse him, he stood as an Independent Conservative in the general election of 1950, and failed by only 361 votes to capture the seat from Labour. Soon afterwards he announced his plans to launch a nationalist movement.

Fountaine also made determined efforts to contact Harold Macmillan. "Used to ring him up at his home," Fountaine recalled, "and he'd pick up the receiver, and as soon as he heard it was me, pretend he was the butler."

In 1959 Fountaine (who had been elected to serve on Norfolk County Council in 1951) stood for Norwich South as an Independent Nationalist, declaring that "the man who can gain the allegiance of the Teddy Boys can make himself ruler of England". He failed, though, to gain the allegiance of his own mother, a New Zealander, who vociferously opposed his candidature.

Away from politics, Fountaine enjoyed racing around the country in his Mercedes sports car.

Fountaine married first, in 1949, Anne Senior; they had a son and daughter. He is survived by his second wife Rosemary, with whom he had a son.

September 25 1997

THE REVEREND PETER GAMBLE

THE REVEREND PETER GAMBLE, who has died aged 77, was a colourful priest-schoolmaster who admitted in retirement that his homosexuality had been the mainspring of his personal life.

His brief experiment in running an Anglo-American school in Oxfordshire in the 1960s ended disastrously through a combination of drug-taking by pupils and financial insolvency. He was obliged to spend the last years of his teaching career at Harrow School.

Earlier he had been chaplain and housemaster at Milton Abbey, which he left after a row with the headmaster. This was followed by eight years as chaplain and tutor at Millfield, where his brother, Brian, was also a teacher.

His gifts as a teacher were considerable, as was his appreciation of beautiful boys. Though his autobiography *The More We Are Together* (1993), subtitled "Memoirs of a Wayward Life", indicates he often sailed close to the wind in his relationships with boys, the physical element was limited and never created scandal.

The Anglo-American school project, whose blameless patrons included Sir John Gielgud, Dame Rebecca West, Douglas Fairbanks Jnr, Sir George Thomson and T. E. Utley, was never sufficiently thought through and always lacked adequate financial backing. It was unfortunate for Gamble and those associated with him that when it started in 1967 the extent of the developing drugs problem among older schoolchildren was not widely recognised and there was little experience of dealing with it.

Gamble took a very tough line. During the first year of the school's life four of its 42 pupils (all in the 16–18 age range) were expelled and another two suspended. A member of the teaching staff was dismissed for spending a weekend with a girl pupil. Matters were further complicated when Sir John Tilley, in whose home the school was housed, accused Gamble of being too rigid, and gave him notice to leave the house at the end of the academic year.

New premises were soon found at Barcote Manor, on the Berkshire–Oxfordshire border, and a bank loan financed the purchase. A language school for foreigners wishing to learn English was also established at Carfax, Oxford, enabling Gamble to continue to use an Oxford address. For a time all was well. Pupils came from America and other parts of the world, as well as from Britain, and the regime was unfashionably strict. Academic results were encouraging.

But by 1970 the drugs squad was making inquiries about the extra-curricular activities of some pupils, and Gamble once again employed draconian measures – expelling four pupils, easing out another six, and placing four more on strict probation. This was reassuring to the parents of the innocent, but reduced the school roll to a point where the enterprise was barely viable financially.

September 1971 saw another fall in enrolment and the school went into voluntary liquidation. Gamble, with the then Bishop of Portsmouth, John Phillips, making kindly noises at his side, met the angry creditors who accused him of gross irresponsibility. But eventually Barcote Manor was sold at a favourable price and all were paid in full.

Several months passed before the erstwhile headmaster joined the teaching staff at Harrow, where he was given responsibility for A-level English and Latin. "There were", he later recorded, "many good-looking boys amid my pupils, but it was for Alec that I fell."

Peter John Gamble was born in Streatham Hill, in south London, in 1920. He attended two local private schools and left when he was 16 without any academic qualifications. His first job was in Fleet Street as an office boy with a monthly magazine, *The Review*.

Before long he was not only making the tea but also writing some of the book reviews. This was not enough to satisfy the proprietor, who soon dispensed with his services. He then joined *Readers' News*, the organ of the

Readers' Union, and after a spell of answering readers' letters he became deputy editor.

In 1940, however, the Readers' Union moved out of London to avoid the wartime bombing and it was decided that the deputy editor's services were no longer required. This left him with a number of problems besides that of immediate employment. He had joined the Peace Pledge Union and was totally opposed to the war, and he had also had some dealings with the British Union of Fascists, which made him the subject of a police investigation.

Having cleared himself of Nazi sympathies – "I only wrote a letter to Hitler" – and registered as a conscientious objector, he was taken on as a teacher at a boys' private school in Wimbledon. His teaching skills at this stage were undeveloped but he got on well with the boys and fell in love with Julien from Belgium. Their close relationship ended when Julien was old enough to join the Belgian Navy.

Gamble himself moved on to Belvedere Lodge School at Esher, Surrey, but his contribution to the educational life of the nation was not deemed essential and, on appearing before a Conscientious Objectors' Board, he was ordered to join the Westminster Civil Defence, then struggling with the Blitz.

The importance of this task failed to inspire him and he contrived during his off-duty hours to return to the Readers' Union as head of editorial. This brought him into contact with a number of leading figures in London, with time to spare for patronage of the capital's private clubs for homosexuals.

All this came to a sudden end when he was posted

to east Devon to join a regional Civil Defence column then engaged in the relief of bomb-torn Plymouth. Dissatisfied with his lot, Gamble went absent without leave and when traced was sentenced to a month in Exeter prison.

On his release he declined to wear Civil Defence uniform and was jailed for another month. An attempt to make him serve with hard labour was thwarted when his lawyer discovered that such a sentence could not be imposed on a conscientious objector.

By this time the Civil Defence authorities believed they could manage without him and he was sent to work in a coalmine at Bolsover in Derbyshire. This occupied him for just over a year, and then a local tribunal, having decided that he had done his best in the circumstances, released him from the colliery in September 1945 in order to teach at Kingsholme School.

After a good start with English and Latin, Gamble found himself in trouble with the headmaster for kissing a boy. Although this was smoothed over, he left soon after for another preparatory school – Waltons at Banstead. While there he discovered that his war service entitled him to a government further education grant and he secured admission to St Catherine's Society to read English.

Accommodation in the university and the city being severely limited, he lodged at Ripon Hall, the Church of England's liberal modernist theological college, and while there was encouraged to seek Holy Orders. His protestation that he knew no theology and believed very little of the Christian faith was swept aside and, after acceptance by a Church selection conference and a few months at another theological college, he was ordained by the ultra-modernist Bishop of Birmingham, E. W. Barnes, to a curacy at Erdington.

This occupied him from 1952 to 1954 and, finding no vacancies for school chaplains, he went to Paris as assistant chaplain at the Embassy Church. This involved conducting services at Anglican centres in Belgium, Holland and France. After just over a year he returned to England to resume his chequered career in education and renew his contacts with the homosexual clubs of Soho.

That he was not cut out for parochial ministry was demonstrated when, following his retirement from Harrow, he filled in as a curate. A Remembrance Day sermon in which he condemned the western powers' reliance on nuclear weapons led to a protest meeting of assorted colonels and other members of the congregation in the churchyard after the service. Other sermons on theological matters were no less controversial.

October 3 1997

ANTON LAVEY

ANTON LAVEY, the founder and high priest of the Church of Satan, who has died in San Francisco aged 67, had begun his career in the circus, putting his head into the jaws of a lion; when the beast removed a chunk of his neck, however, he decided to look for alternative employment.

Later he would look back fondly on the sleaze that he had encountered during those years. Anton Szandor LaVey was born in Chicago in April 1930, of a parentage he preferred to keep anonymous. Without his circus experiences in California, he felt, he might never have developed his taste for theatrical display or formulated a sufficiently debased view of human nature. Moreover his talents as an organist – he had accompanied the circus acts – helped to turn his thoughts in the direction of a church.

First, though, he gained further experience of human depravity as a photographer with the San Francisco Police Department. When they put him in charge of answering calls about supposed supernatural happenings, the pieces of his life fell into place.

In April 1966, on Walpurgisnacht, when evil is supposed to hold sway over the world, he shaved his head, declared himself a prelate in the House of Satan, and established his headquarters in a former brothel in the suburbs of San Francisco. He developed elaborate rituals for black mass, advocating the use of buxom nude girls as servers, thoughtfully allowing, however, that clothed women might be used should nakedness prove impracticable.

Claiming to be exploring "an untapped grey area between psychiatry and religion", he expressed a distaste for the mindless hippy radicalism of the 1960s. His *Satanist's Bible* (1967) proposed a sub-Nietzschean philosophy, wherein might equals right, and immediate self-gratification constitutes the chief duty of man.

"Be simply animal man," *The Satanist's Bible* instructs, "hate your enemies, and if someone smites you, smash him." Against this ideal he set the weak – "those who arrange their lives so that they are full of bitterness and animosity and self-rebuke, very often transferred to others".

"What we advocate", LaVey elaborated in 1970, "is what most Americans practise, whether they call it Satanism or not. We are the new establishment. We are for law and order, for the stability of society. We are the new conservatives."

The West coast of America proved fruitful of disciples, some of them celebrities. Sammy Davis Jr declared his interest, and so, LaVey claimed, did Marilyn Monroe. But the cult's most prominent champion was Jayne Mansfield.

This alarmed Sam Brody, her lover and lawyer, who vigorously resisted LaVey's influence. When Jayne Mansfield and Brody were killed in a car crash in 1967 – the actress reportedly being partially decapitated – LaVey let it be known that at the time of the accident he had been cutting out her photograph and had accidentally snipped off the top of her head.

In 1968 his movement received a fillip from the film *Rosemary's Baby*. "It did for Satanism what *Birth of a Nation* did for the Ku Klux Klan," LaVey exulted. He himself featured in one brief scene as the Devil – though it hardly advanced his claims as Satan's high priest that he had to be heavily made up for the role.

The Church of Satan gained a place in the San Francisco *Yellow Pages*, and – after LaVey had acted as chaplain at a military funeral – was officially recognised by the US armed forces.

But the murders perpetrated by Charles Manson and his followers in August 1969 suggested that such a movement might be rather more dangerous than a sick joke. Years later Susie Atkins, one of Manson's knife-wielding groupies, blamed LaVey for her descent into depravity and murder.

LaVey insisted that Manson's gang were drugged freaks, too weakly vile to qualify as Satanists. But his movement never recovered from the horror of Manson's crime, and gradually dwindled into insignificance.

Early in the 1990s LaVey was driven to bankruptcy by a fight over alimony with his wife Diane, whom he had married in 1962 and who had been associated with his work as high priestess.

Undaunted, he kept up the bad work, prophesying in *The Devil's Notebook* that the world was on the brink of a second wave of Satanism, characterised by a growing misanthropy and an increasing desire for isolation. At other times, however, he would refer to his Church as "simply a living".

LaVey left orders that he should be buried under the epitaph "I only regret the times that I was too nice". His daughter Karla, another high priestess, explained that he had died at the end of October, but that the news had been held over for fear of upsetting his supporters during Hallowe'en.

"If there *is* an after-life," LaVey had held, "it will depend on the vitality and lust for life of the individual before he dies, and on nothing more than that."

November 11 1997

"Big Daddy"

"Big Daddy", the fighting name of Shirley Crabtree, who has died aged 64, was the star attraction of the professional wrestling circuit during its televised heyday in the 1960s and 1970s.

Weighing in at 28 stone and clad in spangled top hat and overburdened leotard, Big Daddy was a portly avenging angel in a comic-book world of heroes in white trunks and villains in black masks.

At its peak, wrestling drew Saturday afternoon audiences of 10 million, attracted not so much by the finer points of the hammerlock and Boston Crab as by its unvarying rituals. These began with the commentator Kent Walton's transatlantic tones of welcome – "Greetings, grapple fans" – and climaxed with the entry of Big Daddy into the ring, usually to save a small wrestler from the attentions of his *bête noir*, Giant Haystacks.

His arrival was accompanied by chants of "*Ea-sy, ea-sy*" from stout matrons in the crowd, in manner the spiritual descendants of the *tricoteuses* who sat by the guillotine.

For Big Daddy's vast belly easily held opponents at bay before he despatched them with his speciality – the "splashdown". This was a manoeuvre in which he mounted the ropes, leapt on top of his stupefied opponent, and squashed him flat to the canvas.

These antics brought Big Daddy notable fans, among them The Queen, whose interest in the sport was first recorded in Richard Crossman's *Diaries*, and Margaret Thatcher, who found the wrestler a useful topic of conversation in Africa, where he was a household name.

The *persona* of Big Daddy was the creation of Shirley Crabtree's brother, Max, and only came relatively late in the wrestler's career. The name was taken from that of the character played by Burl Ives in the film of *Cat On A Hot Tin Roof*.

Max Crabtree was one of the sport's main promoters, and the revelation in the mid-1980s that the result of many of the bouts was predetermined, while no surprise to those who had seen the unathletic carriage of Big Daddy, dented its popularity.

Some in the profession blamed the Crabtree brothers for making the sport too predictable, and its image was further damaged when Mal Kirk, a similarly large wrestler, died of a heart attack in 1987 while fighting Big Daddy.

A year later ITV stopped showing wrestling deeming audience taste to have changed. The sport has never recovered its lustre.

Shirley Crabtree was born in Halifax in 1933, though as he strove to prolong his career his real age became as uncertain as the true colour of the blond hair he sported. He was named after his father, who had in turn been called after the eponymous heroine of Charlotte Brontë's novel by his mother, a 22-stone music-hall actress. She admired the character so much that she chose her baby's name before knowing its sex.

Shirley senior became a rugby league player for Halifax and later worked as a circus strongman. He believed that poverty could only be resisted by the tough, and taught his three boys to wrestle from an early age. This came in useful in the playground of Battinson Road Primary School where such skills were needed to fend off jokes about Shirley Temple.

When young Shirley was seven, his father left their mother, who subsequently brought up the boys, working in a brickyard for the half wages paid to women. Shirley particularly disliked Christmas, as the presents dispensed to him by well-meaning charities were invariably dolls and girls' annuals.

He left school at 14 and worked as a doffer in a

cotton mill, replacing empty bobbins with full ones. Two years later he left to join Bradford Northern rugby league club, but his aggressiveness led to numerous suspensions for foul play and he became a lifeguard at Blackpool instead.

Crabtree began his wrestling career as a middle-weight, weighing in at a mere 16 stone and fighting as "The Blond Adonis" and "Mr Universe". His two brothers often appeared on the same bill, until Max, who had the best technique, became a promoter, and Brian after breaking his leg turned to refereeing.

By the early 1960s Shirley Crabtree had realised that it was the larger wrestlers who gained the biggest following, and he began to boost his weight with a concentrated diet of steak, eggs and cream cakes. His size made him a considerable attraction on the circuit, but he was still cast in the mould of villain, most notably as "The Battling Guardsman", a role created for him by his brother.

Crabtree had briefly served in the Coldstream Guards, and would enter the ring wearing a bearskin, to the sound of Joseph Locke singing "The Soldier's Dream". It was not until 1975 that the Big Daddy character was created, with his first leotard being made from the chintz covers of his wife's sofa.

He was twice married and had six children.

December 3 1997

DOROTHY SQUIRES

DOROTHY SQUIRES, the singer who has died aged 83, so relentlesly followed the return journey from riches back to rags that at times her life seemed a ridiculous parody.

It was not that she was without some responsibility for her eventual misery. She had pathologically jealous feelings of love and hatred for her former husband, the film actor Roger Moore. Having tasted fame as a star selling millions of records, she was later made bankrupt, evicted from her home and eventually declared a vexatious litigant. She was repeatedly arrested for offences related to her drinking, including assault and dangerous driving.

Her behaviour became increasingly eccentric. She once placed a full-page advertisement for a concert in *The Stage*; it included several appeals to God ("If vengeance be thine . . .") and enjoined everyone planning to attend the concert to "have bums on seats by seven-thirty sharp, in honour of Her Britannic Majesty Queen Elizabeth II". But none of the Royal Family was attending the concert.

She was born Edna May Squires on March 25 1915 in a travelling van parked in a field at Pontyberem, Carmarthenshire. She always referred to herself as "Nenna". She was brought up at Dafen, near Llanelli, found a job at a local tinplate factory and toyed with nursing, but decided instead to be a singer.

"I was 16½ when I auditioned for Billy Reid," she would recall. Reid was 22 years older, and married "to a dead ringer for Myrna Loy", but neither fact proved an obstacle to Miss Squires's affair with the bandleader. "Extreme youth was my only excuse for breaking up that marriage," she later said. "Besides, his wife had been away on holiday for eight months."

They formed an act called The Composer and His Voice, which toured the variety halls, with Miss Squires singing and Reid at the piano. She moved in with him and they caused a scandal by living "as man and wife". During the years the couple were together, she made her wireless debut on *Variety Bandbox*, singing ballads with The Billy Reid Accordion Band.

The couple scored hits with Reid's songs "Gypsy" and "I'm Walking Behind You". With the proceeds, Miss Squires bought a house and Reid bought the Llanelli Theatre. Despite Dorothy Squires's initial success, it seemed that Reid's songs sold better in the United States if American artists recorded cover versions.

The Ink Spots sold a million with "Gypsy", and Eddie Fisher's version of "I'm Walking Behind You" was a No 1 in 1953. To her enormous chagrin, Dorothy Squires never made it as big as she expected.

Her break-up with Reid has been described as a "catalogue of tears and fisticuffs". In the seemingly endless court cases that followed, Reid claimed he had contributed a large amount to the cost of her house and Miss Squires claimed that she had invested in his theatre. She also claimed that Reid beat her in public and that he was so jealous he had to follow her.

The couple finally parted after a scene in the Llanelli Theatre bar in 1950. Miss Squires's father tried to separate the arguing pair and was slapped in the face for his pains. During the court case, Dorothy Squires was asked by a barrister if she liked Reid, and answered: "Well, would *you* like him?"

Dorothy Squires met Roger Moore in 1952. Moore was then a struggling actor who made a living as a male model, advertising chunky knitwear, Brylcreem and Macleans toothpaste. He was 25 (12 years younger than she) and married to a skater, Doorn van Steyn. These difficulties had little effect on Miss Squires and she and Moore began an affair. Moore left the Streatham council flat he shared with Doorn, and moved into Squires's mansion. Moore was eventually divorced, and married Miss Squires in 1953.

The Moores entertained regularly at her suburban spread, St Michael's Mount – so regularly that she tried to have it registered as a club. The application was turned down, to the relief of the neighbours, who complained about the noise.

Dorothy Squires often found herself at odds with the press and the BBC. As early as 1953 she was accusing the Corporation of nepotism and claiming the press hounded her.

She and Moore travelled to America in 1954, he to make his first Hollywood film, and she to seek publicity. However, after the film, he became more widely known in America than his wife. "By God!" she exclaimed. "In England I wouldn't be Mrs Roger Bloody-Moore."

In 1956, when Roger Moore was appearing in the television series *Ivanhoe*, the couple wrote a song to go with it. It was intended to be sung by a baritone over each episode's opening titles, but on the day of the recording, it proved impossible to find a male singer. Dorothy Squires volunteered to sing, saying: "I'll give it all the balls I've got!" The song was never used.

Moore became increasingly successful in America, but Miss Squires found that she was no more popular than when she had first arrived. She did manage cabaret bookings but often lost her temper if the audience wanted to dance.

Though Dorothy Squires made it into the British hit parade in 1961 with "Say It With Flowers" (accompanied by the toothy nine-fingered pianist, Russ Conway, late of the Merchant Navy), by then her marriage had started to collapse. Moore occasionally spent the night sleeping outside the house rather than face Miss Squires indoors.

Although Dorothy Squires had always been a "social drinker", her consumption grew rapidly when the press began to concentrate on her marital problems. One night Moore had to stop her "ranting" at an American comedian who was making jokes about the British. "I thought I was drinking fruit cup," she later claimed, "but it had seven different kinds of rum in it."

Moore told the press that they were separating. At first she said that this must be a joke: "His sense of humour is weird," she told reporters, "sometimes I don't understand it myself."

Moore flew to Italy to begin work on *The Rape of the Sabine Women*, and started an affair with Luisa Mattioli. Miss Squires was appearing at the Talk of the Town and later recalled how she discovered the affair. "Roger was in hospital, and there were some letters for him which I opened." When asked how she knew they were love letters she replied, "Oh come on, *Cara mia, tutti tutti*, of course they were love letters. Anyway I got them translated by the *maître d'* at the Astor Club."

Moore went to live with Luisa Mattioli (who changed her name by deed poll to Moore), but Dorothy Squires refused to divorce him. She served Moore with a writ in 1962, "for the restitution of conjugal rights", in an attempt to force him to come home.

In 1968, Dorothy Squires sued Kenneth More for libel. More had been the *compère* of a charity event and introduced Roger Moore and Luisa as "Mr Roger Moore and his wife". Miss Squires was furious and claimed that "people might think I had never been married to Roger at all".

When asked about the case later, Kenneth More answered: "Well, what could I say? 'Here's Mr Roger Moore and his mistress of eight years'?" Moore was adamant that the marriage was over and they finally divorced in 1969.

Miss Squires found it impossible to accept that Moore no longer loved her. Her behaviour became wilder, and on one occasion she smashed the Moores' French windows. She was arrested several times for driving under the influence of drink. When stopped for a breath test she knelt weeping on the pavement and then attacked her arresting officer, "punching and kicking him".

Dorothy Squires's catalogue of court appearances verged on absurdity. In 1971 she assaulted a taxi driver and was fined £50. In 1972, she was in court again, accused of "kicking a taxi driver in the head". The cab driver (who happened to be the *Carry On* star Bernard Bresslaw's brother) suffered injuries to an ear and had a "huge graze on the side of his face". In court, Miss Squires insisted: "I did not kick that man. I was practically barefoot." The judge told her that if she carried on in this way "some court in the future will have no alternative but to commit you to prison".

In 1970 Dorothy Squires planned a grand comeback with a one-woman show, for which she hired the London Palladium. It was a sell-out, but the coach parties did not all find the Squires magic they had hoped for. She hired the Palladium on three other nights, but there was no comeback. She began singing "My Way" with heavily emotional phrasing. Her career was definitely flagging.

She accused the BBC of carrying on a vendetta. "I intend to do something about it," she said. "I am planning a march on Broadcasting House. Thousands of my fans will demonstrate outside the Houses of Parliament."

The following year she hired Carnegie Hall for $20,000, but the venture made a loss. "I'm prepared to invest money," she said, "to prove that I can still fill a venue as large as this."

Miss Squires was in trouble again in 1973, this time in connection with a BBC "payola" scandal. She was accused of bribing Jack Dabb, the producer of *Family Favourites*, to play her records. She admitted paying Dabb's hotel expenses, but said they were a gift. She was cleared of the charge 18 months later.

After the case her popularity plummeted. She tried to raise interest in a charity show and invited Queen Elizabeth The Queen Mother and other members of the Royal Family to attend. All had "previous engagements".

By the mid-1970s, Dorothy Squires was appearing more often in court than on stage. She continually broke contracts, claiming the fees were too low or conditions were not up to standard.

In 1977 she wrote an autobiography, *Rain, Rain, Go*

Away, in which she wanted to publish several of Roger Moore's love letters, "to prove how much he loved me". Moore took out an injunction to prevent this.

Her publisher arranged for the sale of extracts from her book to Sunday newspapers. Dorothy Squires claimed she did not receive her share of the money. An interminable legal battle followed. Squires brought writ after writ against her publisher, but with no success. At one point she staged a sit-in in his office to publicise the case. "It's not the money," she claimed, "it's the principle." By 1979 it had finally been established in court that she had not been cheated.

Miss Squires's finances were by now in a bad way. She tried to promote a musical, *Old Rowley*, about Charles II, but with no success. She accused "theatreland" of a vendetta to stop the show. In 1981 she was declared bankrupt.

In 1982 she tried to make yet another comeback, at the age of 67, at the Theatre Royal, Drury Lane. Her finances did not improve, and in 1987 she was evicted from her 17-room house at Bray, Berkshire, where she claimed Lillie Langtry had once lived. She eventually accepted the loan of a house at Trebanog in South Wales from a fan who kept a fish-and-chip shop nearby.

By then, she had launched 21 High Court actions in five years. Nine had been dismissed as "vexatious or frivolous". She was prohibited from starting any further actions without High Court consent.

She was declared bankrupt again in 1989 after walking out on a booking in Swansea – her second professional engagement in five years. She had previously been offered £1,500 a week to replace Dolores Grey in

Follies. She turned the part down, claiming: "I'm worth more than that!"

In 1990 the contents of her house were sold by the Trustees in Bankruptcy. In 1997 she sold her jewellery. At the hospital where she died she was registered as Mrs Edna May Moore. She had no children.

April 15 1998

CHARLES HORACE JONES

CHARLES HORACE JONES, the South Wales street-corner poet who has died aged 92, stood beside a lamppost in the High Street at Merthyr Tydfil, Glamorgan, for 45 years with a knuckleduster in his pocket as protection against the Welsh whom his poems had attacked.

Jones, perhaps the only poet to have been thrown bodily out of the National Eisteddfod, also caused trouble by refusing to complete a census form. He appeared in court dressed in black and told the Bench he was attending the funeral of man's freedom. He was fined £2.

In 1950 "Horace the Poet", as he was known, earned as much as £138 a week running a crafts business, but he gave it up to write poetry after waking in the middle of the night and feeling compelled by the Muse to scribble down his first verses on the back of a cigarette packet.

In the years that followed, his wife, Delia, became the breadwinner, taking a part-time job in a baker's shop. Her husband would meanwhile spend the entire day at the lamppost, with only an hour's break for lunch. He denounced with increasing violence the Welsh establishment, such as BBC Wales and the Church in Wales, as well as local politicians.

Jones was short and chubby with bushy, crescent-shaped eyebrows. A pencil-line moustache failed to strap down an upper lip that, even when he smiled, would curl towards hairy nostrils in a sneer. His demeanour was suggestive of a paradise lost, perhaps his own, and implied that a tail might fall unnoticed from behind his Chesterfield overcoat. If Satan had been a spiv he would have looked like Jones.

A passion to discredit the corrupt at first endeared him to passers-by. To these he became a champion of Socratic defiance, standing in the market-place each day exposing the incompetences of all who held office: lawyers, policemen, magistrates, bailiffs, tax commissioners, civil servants, and members of the Labour-controlled council. An assortment of verses, lampoons and aphorisms would be printed by night and circulate throughout the town the next day.

Over the years, even old friends disappeared, repelled by the hatred he generated, for eventually even ordinary people with whom he found disfavour were castigated in his sour poetry. In time all came to tire of Horace the Poet and avoid the lamppost where he stood.

Charles Horace Jones was born on February 6 1906 and educated at Abermorlais School. When he was five his father, a coal miner, was killed in a mining accident, and he left school at 12 to work in the pits, at his mother's insistence.

His mother, without any reason Jones could explain,

gave away his white cat and pet canary. One of his last poems, "The Exorcist", deals with her cruelty. "I used to wake up at night screaming after having nightmares about those experiences," he once said. "It was only after I wrote the poem that the nightmares stopped. That is why I called it 'The Exorcist'."

In adulthood Jones paid the price of his lamppost lampoonery. He was beaten up in the high street, half-strangled in cafes, knocked unconscious and even set on fire. Asked once why he stood next to the lamppost, he said it was because it left one less side from which he could be attacked.

He did, however, leave the lamppost for seven years between 1976 and 1983 when Plaid Cymru, the Welsh Nationalist Party, gained control of Merthyr Tydfil borough council. It was more than he could bear and he spent the seven years exiled in London until the Labour party, which he hated marginally less than the nationalists, regained control.

Despite his hatred for socialism, a collection of his work, *The Challenger*, was published by Merthyr Tydfil council in 1966. It cost them £152 10s. Immediately upon publication Jones criticised the council for wasting ratepayers' money. Even so, *The Challenger* was used by local schools in English literature classes.

"Merthyr is a cosmopolitan town. Generations of Jews, Italians, Irish, Spanish and even Chinese have lived here since the Industrial Revolution," Jones would say. "It is they and not just the Welsh who have shaped this town and to a large extent the South Wales Valleys. The Welsh Arts Council give away thousands of pounds each year to people to make walking sticks or fishing rods. But have you ever heard of any great Welsh writer, poet, or playwright who has made his name with the aid of a Welsh Arts Council grant? And yet they're paying out thousands of pounds for this, too."

Jones first came to attention in 1955 when he was ejected by police from the National Eisteddfod at Cardiff at the request of the Gorsedd of Bards. People had been buying booklets from him for a shilling under the impression they were official programmes. Only upon opening them did they find a collection of satirical verses by Jones entitled *A Dose of Salts*. It contained aphorisms such as: "The Eisteddfod is a cultural circus where everything is Welsh except the money."

A poem of his about Welsh rugby that appeared on the sports pages of a national tabloid before an international game in 1956 did little for his reputation in the Valleys. It read:

> *"Ich Dien! I serve."*
> *The motto of a nation*
> *That has lost its nerve.*
> *Lost its nerve and found it all,*
> *In the blown-up bladder*
> *Of an elongated ball.*

After those verses appeared, a gang of thugs closed in on him outside a butcher's shop. He escaped into the shop and got out through a side door without their knowing. An hour later they were still gathered outside the crowded shop waiting for him to come out. "After that," Jones explained, "I carried a knuckleduster wherever I went."

On another occasion a local businessman whom Jones had mocked invited him to his office above a shop in the town. Inside, he brought a chair down over Jones's head, knocking him unconscious. When he came round Jones was horrified to see that this man had lit a gas ring and was pressing it into his side. He managed to get away down the stairs, beat out the flames, and escaped.

When in 1966 he was refusing to complete the census form, the magistrate told him: "When you are living in a state you have to accept the sovereignty of the state." The theme of freedom and state dominance occupied a number of his poems, chief among them "The Jingle" (1971), a complex work of concise phrases that lie almost beyond the fringe of ordinary meaning. It was published at his own expense.

In Jones's poetry, war, materialism, bureaucracy, pollution, technology, sex and religion are treated with expressions taken from the cradle, the pulpit, the trenches, the town hall, bureaucracy and scientific jargon, The Bible and nursery rhymes.

In 1997 a path named Poet's Walk along the River Taff was opened in his honour. One of his poems, "My River", is displayed there.

In 1928 Jones eloped with Delia Griffin, daughter of an Irish immigrant in a neighbouring valley. They married in a register office in Aberdare. Though an atheist he remarried her six months later, at her parents' insistence, at the Catholic Church of Our Lady of the Rosary, Merthyr Tydfil. He is survived by his wife; they had a daughter.

September 16 1998

BRIGADIER MICHAEL CALVERT

BRIGADIER MICHAEL CALVERT, who has died aged 85, earned the nickname of "Mad Mike" during the Second World War for his exploits in the Burma jungle with the Chindits which effectively destroyed the legend of Japanese invincibility.

The epithet "Mad", however, was never used by his friends, who knew that all he did was carefully calculated, even though the odds against success might be dauntingly high.

In March 1944, when commanding 77th Brigade, Calvert established jungle camps by landing men deep in the Japanese lines of communication, thus completely disrupting Japanese planning and at the same time boosting the morale of British forces in Burma.

Following his exploits in Burma, Calvert played a valuable part in the revival of the SAS, which had been disbanded in 1945. Using his experience of fighting the Japanese, in 1950 Calvert recruited a force in Hong Kong to take on Chinese terrorists in the jungles of Malaya. He named them the Malayan Scouts and they became the nucleus of the regular SAS.

Calvert was an idealist who was chivalrous to the point of folly and would never agree to brutal methods of acquiring information. In training, though, he was ruthlessly efficient: one of his training exercises was to have two men, armed with air guns, stalk each other half-naked through scrub. The impact of a pellet on bare flesh stimulated the recipient's appreciation of skill in fieldcraft.

James Michael Calvert was born on March 6 1913 at Rohtak, India, where his father was a district commissioner. Young Mike was educated at Bradfield, at Woolwich, and at Cambridge University, where he was awarded a half-Blue for swimming and water polo. He also boxed for the university and the Army.

He was commissioned into the Royal Engineers in 1933 and posted to Hong Kong. Having learnt Cantonese, he was allowed to accompany the Chinese Army, then fighting the Japanese near Shanghai. At one point he was taken prisoner by the Japanese, but managed to bluff his way to freedom.

In 1939 Calvert returned to London, but in 1940 resigned his commission to join the Scots Guards Ski Battalion, which had been raised to fight the Russians in Finland. However, before it sailed the Finns had been beaten.

Calvert was now sent to Norway, where he was engaged in demolition work to slow the German advance. At the end of the campaign, in which he once nearly froze to death, he was one of the very last to leave.

His next posting was to Lochailort, in Scotland, as instructor in demolitions to the Commando Training Centre. He was then sent to Australia to train instructors for their future Commando units. Here he himself learnt much about explosives from his pupils, who used them in gold mining.

Next he went to the Bush Warfare School at Maymyo, Burma, and when the Japanese invaded he led a counter-attack. He met Orde Wingate and was soon co-operating with him on plans for guerrilla warfare.

In the closing stages of the retreat from Burma, Calvert was ordered to recruit a force for a last-ditch stand, collecting soldiers from convalescent camps and detention barracks. After a few early desertions, the remainder fought like demons.

Just before the end of the retreat, Calvert was involved in a deception plan, "losing" a briefcase where the Japanese would find it. It contained false information about the strength of the forces available to defend India and undoubtedly dissuaded the Japanese from pressing on. After recovering from the retreat, Calvert was sent to Saugor, central India, to train with 77th Brigade, which he would later command.

The first Chindits expedition went into the jungle on foot in 1943 and wreaked havoc behind the Japanese lines, but suffered badly and lost about a third of its number. Calvert later learnt that the force had upset Japanese strategy, causing them to make fresh plans which proved disastrous.

In May 1943 Calvert was awarded the DSO. The following year, six Chindit brigades (a total of 20,000 men) were sent into Burma, this time by air. Although losses were again high, the achievements were impressive.

Calvert established a blocking position at the "White City" airstrip, where he withstood fierce Japanese attacks from April 6 onwards; his brigade had been virtually decimated by the time it advanced to take Mogaung on June 27.

After 77th Brigade had captured Mogaung, Calvert was astonished to hear the BBC announce that it had been taken by General "Vinegar Joe" Stilwell's Chinese–American forces. Calvert sent a signal to Stilwell: "The Chinese have taken Mogaung. 77th Brigade is proceeding to take umbrage." Stilwell's staff officers spent some time looking for Umbrage on their maps of Burma.

After the second Chindit expedition, and having won a bar to his DSO, Calvert was posted back to Europe in January 1945 to command the Special Air Service Brigade, which took part in the final stages of the campaign in Europe. Then, with 36 men, he flew to Norway, where he had the task of ordering the Germans, numbering many thousands, to lay down their arms.

Calvert ended the war as a temporary brigadier, aged 33, but he was soon brought down to earth. He was sent as a major to a Civil Affairs job in Trieste, a post for which he was entirely unsuited. But Calvert's outspoken support for unorthodox ideas had made him unpopular with his seniors.

After returning from Malaya in 1951 he was posted to Germany. There he rapidly went to seed. He was convicted on three charges of gross indecency and his military career ended.

Subsequently Calvert became a lecturer at Manchester University. He also wrote two books, *Prisoners of Hope* (1952) and *Fighting Mad* (1964).

Mike Calvert was a brave and brilliant guerrilla fighter. He sought nothing more than hand-to-hand combat and personal danger. As well as his two DSOs, Calvert was awarded 12 decorations by other countries.

Major-General James Lunt writes: I first met Michael Calvert when I was in hospital in Maymyo during the retreat from Burma in April 1942. He had just returned from preparing the viaduct across the Goteik Gorge on the Mandalay–Lashio railway line for demolition.

The Army Commander, General Alexander, had expressly forbidden him to blow the viaduct without his personal order, which never came. When Calvert returned he was taken to task for not acting on his own initiative, possibly one of the few occasions in his career when he was blamed for not disobeying orders.

Later in the retreat Calvert was nearly captured when he went up to a jungle hut in the dark, knocked on the door and entered. He found several Japanese officers sitting round a table studying a map. Saying, "Excuse me, gentlemen, good night!" he hastily closed the door and decamped into the jungle.

He said he could hear laughter as he left. He then had to swim the River Chindwin, 600 yards wide, before regaining the British lines. This he did disguised as a closely veiled Indian woman, hoodwinking the Japanese.

It was Calvert's misfortune to come to fame too young, and in operations of a kind unpopular with the more orthodox of his seniors. Like his hero Wingate before him, he aroused opposition by his outspoken views and determination to get his own way.

A veritable tiger in battle, but not always wise out of it, Mike Calvert was one of the finest fighting soldiers produced by the British Army in the Second World War.

November 28 1998

JUDGE MICHAEL ARGYLE

JUDGE MICHAEL ARGYLE, formerly of the Old Bailey, who has died aged 83, was celebrated for his *obiter dicta* from the bench and for imposing sentences that veered between harshness and leniency.

Argyle excited widespread publicity in 1971 when he jailed three young editors for obscenity in the *Oz* magazine "Schoolkids' issue" trial. Two of the convictions were quashed by the Court of Appeal, and although it upheld six-month sentences for sending obscene matter through the post, these were suspended for two years. The Appeal Court found that Argyle had made a "very substantial and serious misdirection" to the jury.

Issue 20 of *Oz* had contained articles on homosexuality and sadism – allegedly written by schoolchildren – and a cartoon depicting Rupert Bear deflowering a character named Gypsy Grannie. Argyle's presence at the trial provoked angry accusations of reactionary bias. "Our case became unrecognisable in your mouth," one of the editors told him. "I don't think you saw the trees for all the naked bears. If you jail us you will damage the already fading optimism of a generation."

Mr John Mortimer, the liberal barrister, acting for the defendants had little difficulty in representing Argyle as absurdly fuddy-duddy. When the trial was later dramatised for television, the *farceur* Leslie Phillips was cast as Judge Argyle.

A succession of defence witnesses made the *Oz* trial irresistibly amusing for many present, though Argyle sought to keep it a sober affair. "Are we going to have *continual* laughter and crosstalk?" he asked. "Are we going to be allowed to smoke and have drinks?" At one stage he even rapped the knuckles of visiting American judges for sniggering. "No doubt these people thought they were in Chicago," he remarked afterwards.

The sentences – ranging from nine to 15 months – were denounced as "disgusting fascism" by John Lennon, who, along with Mick Jagger, offered financial assistance to the convicted men. Effigies of Argyle were burnt, and he was given a police guard at his Nottinghamshire home.

The Daily Telegraph commented that the trial had "brought out all the self-appointed spokesmen of the tear-down-society *demi-monde* which infests our scene."

When Argyle published his memories of the *Oz* trial in *The Spectator* in 1995, 24 years after the event, the magazine was later obliged to print an apology to Mr Felix Dennis, acknowledging that neither he nor his colleagues on *Oz* ever "dealt in drugs or their sale to schoolchildren". Mr Dennis, who went on to become a successful businessman, had not been mollified by Argyle's giving him a lesser sentence on the grounds that he was "very much less intelligent" than his fellow defendants.

But in Argyle's eyes the fight was on a broader issue entirely: a battle for Christian civilisation. During the trial, he recalled, he would fall asleep at night thinking of his war days "fighting the SS alongside the Jewish Brigade in the deep Italian snows, advancing across a valley carpeted with the dead, through the Gothic Line towards the crossroads in a village called Croce, where hung the figure with the sunken head and the helpless outstretched arms of the Redeemer of mankind".

Argyle, who was a Circuit Judge and sat at the Old Bailey as an Additional Judge, felt that he had been mocked as a newcomer. But in other cases he tended to rule his court with an iron rod, whatever eccentric departures he allowed himself.

He once charged a juror who had talked briefly to a witness with contempt of court, put him in the cells for the afternoon and threatened him with a £2,000 fine. He treated drug traffickers harshly and sentenced the mastermind of a cocaine-smuggling ring to a record 24 years.

Despite his toughness, Michael Argyle became known for the help he gave to unemployed defendants. He often gave up his lunch break to find work for young offenders. He told a man from his old regiment who had barricaded himself at home with firearms because he was jobless and desperate: "You are lucky to come before me. I led your regiment across the river Po – they are a good lot." He set the man free and sought him help from the Army.

Unemployed offenders would occasionally let him down. When a man given a suspended sentence for a drunken rampage appeared again before Argyle for a string of burglaries, the judge said: "I should not have trusted him, but one does one's best at the time."

Argyle's apparently whimsical leniency sometimes attracted public criticism, as when he handed a suspended sentence to a barman convicted of attempted rape. "You come from Derby," he said, "which is my part of the world. Off you go and don't come back."

Heathrow ground staff reacted bitterly when the press took up a remark of Argyle's renaming the airport "Thief Row" during a case involving dishonest baggage handlers. Other off-the-cuff remarks that attracted attention included a reference to the politician Denis Healey ("I knew him in the war – of course we were both on the same side then") and his tribute to a woman detective ("You are far too attractive to be a policewoman – you should be a film star").

Argyle grew accustomed to his judgements or comments being criticised by MPs, the press and pressure groups. But in 1987 he was publicly reprimanded by the Lord Chancellor, Lord Havers, after a speech to law students at Trent Polytechnic. Argyle had called for hanging for a wide category of serious crimes; he also hazarded that there were more than 5 million illegal immigrants in Britain. "I don't have the figures, but just go to Bradford," he said. Later that year Argyle told a British-born black defendant convicted of assault: "Get out and go back to Jamaica."

If Argyle's critics were not in short supply, his staff at the Old Bailey – in whom he took a generous personal interest – were fond of him.

He always had a television set in his robing room to keep him abreast of sports, especially those on which money was riding. When a television dispute interrupted coverage of England's 1986 tour of the West Indies, he startled the court with an outburst he was to regret: "Here we are struggling in cold temperatures, while in the Caribbean in glorious sunshine 22 of the best cricketers in the world are playing Test cricket. There is television yet none of us can watch the cricket. It is enough to make an orthodox Jew want to join the Nazi Party."

Michael Victor Argyle was born in Derbyshire on August 31 1915 and educated at Westminster and

Trinity College, Cambridge. He read for the Bar and was called by Lincoln's Inn in 1938.

During the Second World War he was commissioned into the 7th Queen's Own Hussars, serving in India, the Middle East and Italy. It was there, in command of A Squadron, that he won an immediate MC during the final campaign, in which they made opposed crossings of the rivers Po and Adige in amphibious Sherman tanks.

Argyle resumed practice on the Midland Circuit in 1947, took Silk in 1961 and became a Recorder of Northampton in 1962. He had been an unsuccessful Conservative candidate for Belper in 1950 and Lough-borough in 1955. As a QC he defended the train robber Ronald Biggs in 1964.

In Birmingham, where he was a Recorder for five years from 1965, Argyle was renowned not only for his toughness, but also for his courtesy in court. He was careful and fair in his summing up and seldom inter-rupted during cross-examination.

He also became known as the reporters' judge, and was not averse to ensuring that the press box was full before speaking. A typical remark from this era was that "a settlement of Gypsies and tinkers is importing a ready-made criminal community".

Argyle's campaign in 1966 to stamp out burglary through deterrent sentencing was as effective as it was controversial. "If you come, boys, we are waiting for you," said Argyle.

Argyle also claimed to have achieved "more or less a 100 per cent telephone service in the city" through stiffer jail terms for vandals of public telephones. He frequently lambasted the authorities for ineptitude or negligence. He called for legislation to combat the menace of replica firearms, and attacked the early release of violent prisoners, once advising a woman who had been brutally attacked by a paroled killer: "Really go for the Establishment."

He also criticised what he termed the irrelevant introduction of racial prejudice into criminal trials. "Justice in this country is even-handed," he said.

He once told a Rastafarian convicted of possessing cannabis that he knew a number of Rastafarians. "I know them socially," he said. "They are totally honest and hardworking. They have their own religion which is fine."

He advocated legalising prostitution, pointing to the "sensible attitude" of the French. "I worked as a legal clerk in Paris in the Thirties," he explained, "so I got to know something about the city's vice system."

In his short farewell speech from the bench in 1988 Argyle said he felt sure that he had made some mistakes, "for which I apologise", but hoped he had also done some good. He confessed to one "bad thing" – arranging for a copy of the *Sporting Life* to be delivered daily to a barrister and two policemen recovering in hospital after the 1973 IRA bomb atrocity at the Old Bailey. "The result", he said, "was that the whole ward became compulsive gamblers."

A keen family man, Argyle once told a woman who had forged a divorce certificate and married bigamously: "You have caught me on a good day. I became a grandfather this morning again." Instead of jailing her, he put her on probation.

Argyle was a keen boxer – as befitted his square-jawed bulldog looks – and a trustee of the Amateur Boxing Association. He was also a resolute defender of the Rottweiler and a noted whippet breeder, along with his wife, Ann, *née* Newton, whom he married in 1951. They had three daughters. She died in 1994.

January 6 1999

INDEX

Agazarian, Monique
  "Aggie", 227
Allen, Ronald, 144
Allgrove, Nell, 269
Argyle, Judge Michael,
  397

Baker, Tom, 187
Barnett, "Sadie", 156
"Big Daddy", 376
Bland, The Reverend
  Michael, 41
Board, Ian, 277
Booth, Edwina, 141
Bracegirdle, Commander
  Warwick "Braces", 231
Bredin, Brigadier
  "Speedy", 177
Brown Thrush, Princess,
  200
Buckmaster, Colonel
  Maurice, 208
Byng, Douglas, 20

Calvert, Brigadier Michael,
  392
Carter, Billy, 47
Chadwick, Len, 34
Cook, Robin, 279

Cradock, Fanny, 298
Cumming, Anne, 267

Daresbury, Lord, 91
Dash, Jack, 75
Dawson, Les, 246
de la Taste Tickell, Kim,
  98
de Manio, Jack, 53
Divine, 35
Dunderdale, Commander
  "Biffy", 110
Dunlop, Sir Edward
  "Weary", 263

Everett, Kenny, 317

Fairbairn, Sir Nicholas,
  304
Forbes of Craigievar, Sir
  Ewan, Bt, 173
Fountaine, Andrew, 364
Frere, James, 295

Gabor, Jolie, 351
Gainsbourg, Serge, 119
Gamble, Revd Peter,
  368
George, Ann, 85

405

Gingold, Hermione, 13
Gleave, Group Captain
 Tom, 252

Habsburg Windsor, Helle
 Cristina, 104
Hallowes, Odette, GC,
 314
Hawtrey, Charles, 49
Hinds, Alfred, 114
Hinze, Russell "Big Russ",
 148
Hudson, Walter, 189
Hughes, Brigadier Ted, 8
Hyde White, Wilfrid, 129

Isherwood, Lawrence, 80
Ives, George, 243

Jones, Charles Horace, 387
Junor, Sir John, 358

Kite, Sergeant Fred, 257
Knowles, Lieutenant-
 Colonel Geoffrey, 24

Langan, Peter, 56
LaVey, Anton, 373
Liberace, 3
Lindsay, Eldress Bertha,
 106

Maddern, Victor, 260
Marie-la-Jolie, 46
Massereene and Ferrard,
 Viscount, 219
Milford, Lord, 271
Montrose, The Duke of,
 192
Morgan, Colonel Frank
 "Monocle", 204
Moynihan, Lord, 181

Negri, Pola, 16
Newborough, Denisa
 Lady, 6
Nico, 43

Oakeley, Sir Atholl, Bt, 1
Oatts, Lieutenant-Colonel
 "Titus", 223

Parham, Admiral Sir
 Frederick, 124
Parnes, Larry, 83
Pierrepoint, Albert, 215

Rajneesh, Bhagwan Shree,
 87
Rankin, Sir Hugh, Bt,
 37
Rée, Harry, 136
Riding, Laura, 159
Rizzo, Frank "Big
 Bambino", 151

Roger, "Bunny", 354
Rook, Jean, 168
Russell, Earl, 28

Salaman, Peggy, 100
Scott, Ronnie, 348
Skelton, Barbara, 331
Sopwith, Sir Thomas, 60
Speed, Doris, 284
Squires, Dorothy, 380
Stanshall, Vivian, 309
Stevenson, Sir Melford, 31
Stokes, Doris, 11
Swat, The Wali of, 26

Tatham-Warter, Digby, 234
Teresa, Vincent "Big Vinnie", 96
Tiny Tim, 343
Turner, Lana, 322

Watts, James, 289
Whittle, Sir Frank, 336
Winchester, Bapsy Marchioness of, 328

Yates, Jess, 239

Zita, Empress of Austria, 69